The public culture of the
Victorian middle class

D1637929

THE PUBLIC CULTURE OF THE VICTORIAN MIDDLE CLASS

Ritual and authority and the English industrial city

1840–1914

Simon Gunn

MANCHESTER UNIVERSITY PRESS

Manchester and New York

Published by Manchester University Press
Oxford Road, Manchester M13 9NR, UK
and Room 400, 175 Fifth Avenue, New York, NY 10010, USA
www.manchesteruniversitypress.co.uk

Distributed exclusively in the USA by
Palgrave, 175 Fifth Avenue, New York NY 10010, USA

Distributed exclusively in Canada by
UBC Press, University of British Columbia, 2029 West Mall,
Vancouver, BC, Canada V6T 1Z2

British Library Cataloguing-in-Publication Data
A catalogue record for this book is available from the British Library

Library of Congress Cataloging-in-Publication Data
A catalog record for this book is available from the Library of Congress

ISBN 13: 978 0 7190 7546 9

First published in hardcover by Manchester University Press 2000

First digital paperback edition published 2007

Printed by Lightning Source

In memory of Peter Nicholson Gunn (1914–1995)

Contents

Acknowledgements

The debts incurred in writing this book are substantial and numerous. John Walton first proposed its subject many years ago by suggesting that the alleged differences of culture and status implied in the maxim 'Manchester men and Liverpool gentlemen' were worth investigating. Since then I have had many reasons to be grateful for his enthusiasm and support. From John Seed I learned much about the middle class and culture, and his critical advice, always generously given, has been invaluable. My largest debt is to Patrick Joyce, whose commitment to serious and innovative historical writing has consistently stimulated my own thinking. I have been fortunate to benefit not only from his encouragement and insight, but also from his friendship over a long period.

Other historians, too, have given their advice and support at different points in the recent past. In this regard I would especially like to thank Leonore Davidoff, Robbie Gray, Bob Morris and Mike Rose. A number of historians and other specialists provided comments on earlier versions of chapters in this book: Ross Abbinnett, Janet Douglas, John Garrard, Martin Hewitt, Kate Hill, Gordon Johnston, Dave Russell and John Tosh. Their expertise has helped prevent me making more mistakes than I would have done otherwise. The School of Cultural Studies at Leeds Metropolitan University provides an unusually fertile intellectual environment in which to write an inter-disciplinary study of this kind and I wish to thank my colleagues for sharing their knowledge and insights, especially Krista Cowman, Max Farrar, Louise Jackson and Stuart Rawnsley. Pat Cook helped produce the manuscript with her invariable calm professionalism. I would also like to acknowledge the support of the Faculty of Cultural and Education Studies over the years, not least in enabling me to take research leave to finish the book in autumn 1999.

It is customary for historians to acknowledge the various libraries where they have researched their subject. I am pleased to do so, while noting with concern the increasingly precarious position of many local and specialist libraries and the deteriorating conditions of those who work there. I would like to thank the staff of the following: Birmingham Central Library and Archives; the British Library at Euston and Colindale, London; Leeds City Archives, Sheepscar; the Local History Unit, Leeds Central Library; Leeds Metropolitan University Library and the Brotherton Library, University of Leeds; the Local Studies Unit and Archives Department, Manchester Central Library; the John Rylands Library, University of Manchester; the Thoresby Society, Leeds; and Dr Williams' Library, London.

Earlier versions of a number of the chapters in this study have appeared in the following books and journals: A. Kidd and D. Nicholls (eds), *Gender, Civic Culture and Consumerism: Middle-Class Identity in Britain, 1800–1940* (Manchester: Manchester University Press, 1999); R. J. Morris and R. H. Trainor (eds), *Urban Governance in British Towns and Cities Since 1750* (London: Ashgate, 2000); *Journal of Victorian Culture*, 2, 2 (1997).

Finally, I should like to acknowledge the support that has come from closer to home. Gabriele Griffin contributed enormously to the writing of this book and, no less important, demonstrated triumphantly that there is life after 'class'. From my parents, the writers Peter and Diana Gunn, I learned that culture matters in more ways than one might imagine. It is to the memory of my father, who died when I was starting this project, that the book is dedicated.

Introduction

This book is about the public culture of the middle class in the industrial cities of Birmingham, Leeds and Manchester between the early Victorian period and the First World War. It is about the architecture and spatial lay-out of the cities themselves, the principal institutions of bourgeois culture and the characteristic cultural forms of middle-class public life. Since the study is centrally concerned with the wealthiest sections of urban society, it is also about the representation of authority, the ways in which the materiality and exercise of power were given symbolic form. In the later Victorian city, authority was conventionally demonstrated by the regular, formalised and often ceremonial appearance of the rich and powerful in the city centre, at the promenade, on concert nights, and in civic processions. These were the rites – or, for some, the rights – of power, the occasions on which wealth and authority were made visible, displayed to a larger urban audience.

The study is selective in its treatment of culture; it does not attempt to provide a survey of all the diverse cultural forms to be found in the provincial city during the Victorian and Edwardian periods. The focus on the public culture of the city centre means that little is said about other locations, such as the middle-class home, which were also import-ant sites of sociability and cultural activity.[1] Art collections, exhibitions and museums are likewise not dealt with, in part because they have already been the subject of substantial research.[2] Instead, the study concentrates on a set of urban institutions and cultural forms the purpose of which was to display people rather than objects. In Chapter 1 I shall discuss in detail the conceptual framework of this study, and in particular the notions of the industrial city, the middle class, and bourgeois culture. Chapter 2 examines the architectural and spatial reconstruction of the centres of the industrial cities, the meanings of which were bound up with ideas of morality, monumentalism, and spectacle. How the city was perceived and used by middle-class men and women is the subject of

Chapter 3, which considers issues of appearance and status as these were manifested in activities like commuting, shopping and promenading. This is followed in Chapter 4 by an analysis of 'clubland', a private sphere of homosociality in the midst of the public, which, especially in its bohemian forms, gave access to the disreputable, *déclassé* pleasures of the city. From these more vicarious aspects of middle-class life associated with the fluidity and social mixing of the city centre, the study shifts to the respectable heartland of Victorian bourgeois culture. Thus, in Chapter 5, I examine the cult of the Nonconformist minister as the representative of 'spiritual culture', an ideal whose influence was widely registered in the chapel and suburban community. Closely aligned with religion, not least because it took on many of the trappings of a quasi-religious rite, was classical music. Chapter 6 analyses the elevation of the classical concert to the status of most prestigious cultural and social occasion in the industrial cities during the second half of the nineteenth century. Finally, Chapter 7 examines those rites of civic culture like the perennial series of processions, ceremonials and funerals which sought to give physical expression to a hierarchical social order, to align the identity of the cities with their most prominent 'public men', and to lend urban authority the image of stability and permanence.

The book as a whole thus analyses the matrix of institutions and cultural forms that characterised the public culture of the wealthy in the industrial cities between the 1840s and 1914. Despite the increased interest in the nineteenth-century middle classes, this has remained a curiously underdeveloped area of historical research.[3] It is over twenty-five years since the publication of Leonore Davidoff's pioneering study of etiquette and the 'season' in the Victorian and Edwardian period, *The Best Circles*. However, Davidoff's work concentrated primarily on London rather than provincial 'high society'. In contrast, the collection of essays edited by Janet Wolff and John Seed, published in 1988 as *The Culture of Capital*, focused directly on industrial cities such as Leeds, Manchester and Sheffield. But as its editors acknowledged, its principal concern were the fine arts, and painting in particular, rather than any broader conception of a public bourgeois culture.[4] This relative paucity of research contrasts with the profusion of studies of Victorian popular culture, of the music hall, melodrama, the pub, popular religion and the social organisations of the nascent labour movement.[5] Social historians, it would seem, have eschewed the study of high culture, preferring to leave it to their counterparts in architectural, art and music history. Yet this has not prevented social historians from extensively investigating culture and consumption among the 'middle ranks' of eighteenth-century Britain, nor has it inhibited the study of bourgeois culture and society in nineteenth-century Europe.[6] The absence of a critical history of the public culture of the middle class in English industrial cities has been especially noticeable in the long-running debate about 'gentlemanly capitalism', itself predicated on ideas about the relative cultural competence and social prestige of elites based on industry, finance and land.[7] Here representations of the northern industrial elite have rested narrowly on the evidence of literary fiction, patterns of education and the influence of Nonconformity and Liberalism, rather than on any direct analysis of how the culture of the middle class was constituted in cities like Birmingham, Leeds and Manchester. Thus the intentions informing my work are twofold: to fill this gap in the historiography of English culture, and to contribute to a larger historical debate about the formation and identity of the middle class in modern Britain.

The discussion of terms such as 'middle class' and 'bourgeois culture' raises conceptual issues that are complex and contested. These are examined in some detail in Chapter 1. But it also raises the spectre of the 'crisis of class', debates about which have dogged British social history since the mid-1980s.[8] Under the impact of the 'linguistic turn' class has come to be viewed as a discursive construct rather than a social structure, an arbitrary means of organising historical narratives as opposed to an essential concept in accounting for conflict and change in the past. Class and its ally, the 'social', are consequently stripped of any determining agency in historical processes. The classical 'rise' of the middle class between 1780 and 1840, for example, has been construed by Dror Wahrman as a discursive move which did not so much reflect a new social formation as provide a new way of configuring politics; it designated the arrival of a political, not a social, 'middle'. This, in turn, reverses the conventional thrust of social history since the 1960s towards an understanding of high politics as mediated by wider economic and social transformations. Instead, social and economic shifts are now understood as refracted through high politics, which is thus returned to its traditional position as the 'master' narrative of historical studies.[9] Patrick Joyce, on the other hand, has sought to wrest the idea of a popular social imaginary from the hold of a restrictive, teleological class narrative, and to reveal the diverse ways in which nineteenth-century workers represented themselves and the social order outside and beyond class.[10] In many ways the effect of this shift of emphasis has been invigorating, opening up fresh ways of thinking about collective identities, suggesting the multiplicity of sites in which identities can be formed, and pointing to the variety of theoretical perspectives that can fruitfully be deployed in interpreting them.

However, where this shift leaves the study of the middle class (or, indeed, the landed class) is by no means clear. With the exception of Wahrman's account, the middle class has been a bystander in the debate about class, which has been overwhelmingly concerned with the identity and outlook of manual workers. How employers, the propertied and the rich saw their relationships with other groups, envisaged the social order, and ordered their social and cultural world in the period between 1850 and 1914, are questions which have been broached for the most part only in an indirect or sketchy manner.[11] More fundamentally, studies that concentrate on class as a discursive or rhetorical construct tend to neglect the issues of power and inequality that are central to any effective understanding of the concept. Class becomes a matter of social description and the social imaginary, rather than of repeated, patterned social inequalities over time or of division and conflict. In effect, class has ceased to hurt in the manner which Richard Sennett and Jonathan Cobb indicated when they spoke of the 'hidden injuries of class'.[12] Furthermore, despite the sound and fury generated by the debate about class within social history, it has had remarkably little impact outside the subject. In areas such as sociology and cultural studies, as in much of history, the understanding of class has broadened from a concentration on relations of production to encompass issues of identity, sexuality and consumption, but the issue of class has not disappeared.[13] In this book I argue that culture itself was a crucial domain for the articulation of class in the nineteenth-century industrial city, through a series of oppositions between 'high' and 'low', the cultured and the culture-less, mental and manual labour.

The work of two theorists in particular has helped to shape these ideas as well as the general approaches to culture adopted in the book. One is Pierre Bourdieu whose work on culture and its relationship to the social order suggests that cultural hierarchies reproduce and reinforce social divisions and inequalities. Attributes such as 'taste' and 'distinction' act as markers in delineating and maintaining social boundaries between status groups and, more fundamentally, between classes. These attributes endow ordered inequalities with a patina of naturalness by converting what are in practice artificial and acquired differences, learned through upbringing and education, into seemingly innate and natural qualities of the individual and the group. Art and culture do not, then, constitute an autonomous sphere as educated men and women liked to believe in the later nineteenth century but instead represent a field of power. Although, for Bourdieu, the cultural field operates according to a distinct logic which is not simply reducible to the economic or the social, embodying a form of 'capital' in its own right, it is permeated by wider sets of power relations. Culture therefore occupies a central place in the reproduction and legitimisation of categories of class and status.[14]

The ideas of Richard Sennett have likewise informed my interpretation of the city and of the historical meanings of urban bourgeois culture. In a series of works, Sennett has suggested how cultural forms and institutions helped to make sense of the increasingly anonymous experience of social life in cities like Manchester, London and Paris during the nineteenth century. Modes of self-presentation and conduct in the street, the theatre, and the concert hall were instrumental in forging new social identities and new ways of managing social relationships in the city. Above all, Sennett is sensitive to the manner in which architecture and the disposition of urban space served as more than simply the backdrop to historical events. They actively worked to shape individual and collective behaviour in specific and identifiable ways at different historical moments. For Sennett the city is always as much a symbolic as a physical space, a place where social and cultural differences consistently intrude in significant and unexpected ways, in the past as in the present.[15]

The most important primary source used in this study is the provincial periodical press, and in particular the satirical journals produced from the early 1860s onwards such as the *Dart*, the *Owl* and the *Town Crier* in Birmingham, the *Yorkshire Busy Bee* and *Toby*, the *Yorkshire Tyke* in Leeds, the *Freelance*, the *Sphinx* and the *City Lantern* in Manchester. These weekly journals covered a wide range of subjects, as suggested by the subtitle of the Manchester *Freelance*, 'a journal of humour and criticism, political, municipal, social, literary and artistic'. Their subject matter was eclectic, including commentaries on fashion, street life, and social 'types', and on institutions such as the music hall and the concert hall, in which as much attention was often paid to the character of audiences as to the events themselves. The satirical weeklies were intended to provide an entertaining account of city life, especially of those aspects considered of interest to the educated and well-to-do. They clearly differentiated themselves in this respect from the more august daily papers, such as the *Birmingham Daily Post*, the *Leeds Mercury* and the *Manchester Guardian*. In the satirical journals there was no commercial information and limited direct reportage of political events. The focus of the majority of articles was local, assuming an intimate knowledge of the city, its social geography, institutions, and leading personalities. In some cases, journals had a specific political affiliation, as with the Birmingham-based *Town Crier*, established in 1861 by a group of journalists and businessmen associated with an emergent municipal Liberalism, including J. T. Bunce and Samuel Timmins.[16] More commonly, though, they were produced by journalists and writers associated with the cities' 'bohemian' milieu, which was celebrated in their columns. In Manchester, for example, J. H. Nodal was editor of the *Sphinx* and the *Freelance* from the late 1860s. Significantly, he was also a member of the Manchester Literary Club as well as the city's premier bohemian establishment, the Brasenose Club.[17] The journals therefore tended to eschew formal association with any particular party, and to treat politics as a generalised source of satire.

Detailed evidence of the readership of the periodical press is limited. In many cases the satirical journals were short-lived, lasting a few years or even months, though the most successful, such as the *Birmingham Dart* and the *Manchester Freelance*, survived for a decade and more. They were generally priced cheaply at 1*d.*, and were sold in shops and at railway stations throughout the region as well as in the city itself. In January 1883 the Leeds-based *Yorkshire Busy Bee* claimed to have sold 31,000 copies in the previous week, though this was probably an exaggeration given that within six months the journal had closed down.[18] But it is clear that the journals targeted a specific, local audience of educated men and women, interested in the arts and assumed to possess a familiarity with the literary, artistic and musical products of European culture. While the periodical press described, often in graphic detail, the institutions of low and popular culture, this was invariably in a tone that mixed the prurient with the censorious. Representations of particular groups, such as Jews, prostitutes and crowds of workers, were explicitly hostile, revealing a visceral antipathy to those perceived to be alien and threatening. In these ways the periodical press was positioned and positioning, identifying both the journal and its readership with the sources of moral and cultural authority in the city located in the cultivated and civic-minded classes, against those forces which appeared to be hostile or indifferent to them.

Recent critics have argued that the periodical press should be understood 'not as a mirror reflecting Victorian culture', but as a 'constitutive medium' of that culture.[19] However, the categories through which urban society was presented are significant in understanding how prosperous, educated contemporaries perceived the social order, the predominant cultural assumptions and characteristic modes of behaviour. Evidence of attitudes is likely to be most reliable where it was concerned with the better-off sections of local society with which writers were most familiar and which formed the mainstay of their readership. In this sense, the periodical press of Birmingham, Leeds and Manchester provides important insights into the behaviour and identities that served to constitute the bourgeois culture of the period. Here, as perhaps nowhere else, it is possible to eavesdrop on members of the provincial middle class talking candidly and ironically among themselves.

This book, then, is about the creation of a distinct bourgeois culture and its institutional forms. It is a culture associated with the rise and the fall of Birmingham, Leeds and Manchester as centres of industrial modernity, sandwiched between the periods before 1800 and after 1914 when London represented the undisputed centre of national cultural life, as of much else. According to John Brewer, in the eighteenth century London acted as a 'cultural magnet'; its institutions 'had the power to shape culture in Britain as a whole'.[20] After the First World War, as I shall argue in the conclusion to the study, the provincial bourgeois culture of the industrial cities went into a decline, concomitant with the break-up of an older, locally based middle class with which it was closely identified. But in the intervening period Birmingham, Leeds and Manchester were centres of considerable cultural dynamism and innovation in their own right, independent and in some respects in advance of London. How this cultural transformation occurred, and what forms it took, are the subjects of the chapters that follow.

Notes

1 L. Davidoff, *The Best Circles* (London: Hutchinson, 1973); J. Tosh, *A Man's Place: Masculinity and the Middle-Class Home in Victorian England* (New Haven: Yale University Press, 1999).

2 T. Bennett, *The Birth of the Museum* (London: Routledge, 1995); K. Hill, 'Municipal museums in the north-west 1850–1914: social reproduction and cultural activity in Liverpool and Preston' (Ph.D. thesis, Lancaster University, 1997); D. S. Macleod, *Art and the Victorian Middle Class: Money and the Making of Cultural Identity* (Cambridge: Cambridge University Press, 1996); J. Wolff and J. Seed (eds), *The Culture of Capital: Art, Power and the Nineteenth-Century Middle Class* (Manchester: Manchester University Press, 1988).

3 For recent studies of the middle classes see A. J. Kidd and D. Nicholls (eds), *The Making of the British Middle Class?: Studies of Regional and Cultural Diversity Since the Eighteenth Century* (Stroud: Sutton, 1998); Kidd and Nicholls (eds), *Gender, Civic Culture and Consumerism: Middle-Class Identity in Britain 1800–1940* (Manchester: Manchester University Press, 1999). Both these collections derive from a conference, 'Aspects of the

history of the British middle classes since 1750', held at Manchester Metropolitan University in September 1996.

4 For full references to these works see notes 1 and 2 above.

5 A brief sample might include P. Bailey, *Leisure and Class in Victorian England* (London: Routledge, 1978); A. Davies, *Leisure, Gender and Poverty: Working-Class Culture in Salford and Manchester, 1900–1939* (Buckingham: Open University Press, 1992); B. Harrison, *Drink and the Victorians* (London: Faber, 1971); E. J. Hobsbawm, 'The formation of British working-class culture' in *Worlds of Labour* (London: Weidenfeld and Nicholson, 1984); P. Joyce, *Visions of the People: Industrial England and the Question of Class, 1840–1914* (Cambridge: Cambridge University Press, 1991); C. Waters, *British Socialists and the Politics of Popular Culture* (Manchester: Manchester University Press, 1992).

6 For studies of the eighteenth century see, for example, J. Barry and C. Brooks (eds), *The Middling Sort of People: Culture, Society and Politics in England, 1550–1800* (Basingstoke: Macmillan, 1994); A. Bermingham and J. Brewer (eds), *The Consumption of Culture, 1600–1800: Image, Object, Text* (London: Routledge, 1992); J. Brewer, *The Pleasures of the Imagination: English Culture in the Eighteenth Century* (London: Harper Collins, 1997); P. Borsay, *The English Urban Renaissance: Culture and Society in the Provincial Town, 1660–1770* (Oxford: Clarendon Press, 1991); P. Langford, *Public Life and the Propertied Englishman, 1689–1798* (Oxford: Oxford University Press, 1991). For bourgeois culture in nineteenth-century Europe see the current five-volume study by Peter Gay published under the generic title *The Bourgeois Experience: Victoria to Freud* (London: Harper Collins, 1984–1999); J. Kocka and A. Mitchell (eds), *Bourgeois Society in Nineteenth-Century Europe* (Oxford: Berg, 1993).

7 M. J. Daunton, ' "Gentlemanly capitalism" and British industry, 1820–1914', *Past and Present*, 122 (1989); H. L. Malchow, *Gentlemen Capitalists: The Social and Political World of the Victorian Businessman* (Basingstoke: Macmillan, 1991); W. D. Rubinstein, *Capitalism, Culture and Decline in Britain* (London: Routledge, 1993); M. J. Wiener, *English Culture and the Decline of the Industrial Spirit, 1850–1980* (Cambridge: Cambridge University Press, 1981).

8 The literature on this subject is by now voluminous. However, many of the more important contributions can be found in two recent collections: K. Jenkins (ed.), *The Postmodern History Reader* (London: Routledge, 1997), part 4 and P. Joyce (ed.), *Class* (Oxford: Oxford University Press, 1995).

9 D. Wahrman, *Imagining the Middle Class: The Political Representation of Class in Britain, c. 1780–1840* (Cambridge: Cambridge University Press, 1995).

10 Joyce, *Visions of the People* and *Democratic Subjects: The Self and the Social in Nineteenth-Century England* (Cambridge: Cambridge University Press, 1994).

11 For some pointers see G. Crossick, 'From gentlemen to the residuum;

languages of social description in Victorian Britain' in P. J. Corfield (ed.), *Language, Class and History* (Cambridge: Cambridge University Press, 1991); S. Gunn, 'The ministry, the middle class and the "civilising mission" in Manchester, *c.* 1850–80', *Social History,* 21, 1 (1996); P. Joyce, *Work, Society and Politics: The Culture of the Factory in Later Victorian England* (Brighton: Harvester, 1980).

12 R. Sennett and J. Cobb, *The Hidden Injuries of Class* (New York: Basic Books, 1972).

13 See, for example, R. Jenkins, *Social Identity* (London: Routledge, 1998); D. Morley and K.-H. Chen (eds), *Stuart Hall: Critical Dialogues in Cultural Studies* (London: Routledge, 1996). In history see, for example, P. Bailey, 'Conspiracies of meaning: music hall and the knowingness of popular culture', *Past and Present,* 144 (1994); 'Parasexuality and glamour: the Victorian barmaid as cultural prototype', *Gender and History,* 2 (1990); J. Walkowitz, *City of Dreadful Delight: Narratives of Sexual Danger in Late Victorian London* (London: Virago, 1992).

14 Key works by Pierre Bourdieu which develop these ideas are *Distinction: A Social Critique of the Judgement of Taste* (London: Routledge, 1992); *The Field of Cultural Production* (Cambridge: Polity, 1993); *The Logic of Practice* (Cambridge: Polity, 1990).

15 For the present study the most significant work by Richard Sennett is *The Fall of Public Man* (London: Faber and Faber, [1977] 1992). Also valuable are *The Conscience of the Eye: The Design and Social Life of Cities* (London: Faber and Faber, 1993); *Flesh and Stone: The Body and the City in Western Civilisation* (London: Faber and Faber, 1994).

16 For comments see E. P. Hennock, *Fit and Proper Persons: Ideal and Reality in Nineteenth-Century Urban Government* (London: Edward Arnold, 1973), p. 77.

17 M. Beetham, ' "Healthy reading": the periodical press in late Victorian Manchester' in A. Kidd and K. W. Roberts (eds), *City, Class and Culture: Studies of Cultural Production and Social Policy in Victorian Manchester* (Manchester: Manchester University Press, 1985), p. 190; A. Darbyshire, *A Chronicle of the Brasenose Club, Manchester,* vol. 1 (Manchester, 1892). More generally, see F. Leary, 'History of the Manchester periodical press' (1903), unpublished manuscript, Manchester Central Reference Library Archives Department.

18 *Yorkshire Busy Bee,* 13 January 1883. It reappeared shortly afterwards under a different name.

19 L. Pykett, 'Reading the periodical press: text and context' in L. Brake, A. Jones and L. Madden (eds), *Investigating Victorian Journalism* (Basingstoke: Macmillan, 1990), p. 7. For a useful discussion of this type of journalism in Liverpool see J. K. Walton and A. Wilcox (eds), *Low Life and Moral Improvement in Mid-Victorian England: Liverpool Through the Journalism of Hugh Shimmin* (Leicester: Leicester University Press, 1991), introduction.

20 Brewer, *Pleasures of the Imagination,* pp. xxv and 55.

1

The industrial city, the middle class and bourgeois culture

For almost two hundred years Birmingham, Leeds and Manchester have been synonymous with nineteenth-century industrial civilisation. 'Grim, fortress-like' creations, the cities formed an integral component of the 'nineteenth-century England' which, according to J. B. Priestley, still characterised much of the Midlands and the north in the 1930s: 'the industrial England of coal, iron, steel, cotton, wool, railways; of thousands of little houses all alike, sham Gothic churches, square-faced chapels, Towns Halls, Mechanics Institutes, mills, foundries, warehouses'.[1] As part of this picture, the cities were seen as the birthplace and home of a new breed of self-made industrialists who came to form the core of an authentic British 'middle class' during the course of the nineteenth century. The public culture of this middle class was often presented as narrow and utilitarian, extending little beyond the building of town halls as monuments to new-found wealth and civic pride. Estimates of the significance of the industrial middle class within the larger political nation varied, but its social and economic importance was largely unquestioned. The manufacturers and merchants of cities like Manchester, Birmingham and Leeds were the motive-force behind the emergence of Britain as the world's leading economic power and a major reason why Britain could be termed a 'middle-class' society by 1850.

This portrait of the industrial cities and of the middle class has been remarkably enduring. Its outlines are to be found in social and economic histories from the early twentieth century, and were reproduced, scarcely altered, in the new social history that developed from the 1960s. Over the last two decades, however, the picture has all but dissolved. Just as the cities themselves have sought to shake free of their industrial inheritance and to reshape their economy and public image since the early 1980s, so an established history identified with them has been dismantled piece by piece. The impulse for historical revision has come not so much from studies of the middle class as from a variety of debates about the pace and extent of industrialisation, the nature of British economic decline, the role of gender in social formation, and the salience of class itself as a form of identity and agency. As a result, historiography now operates in a radically changed landscape and old questions have to be asked anew. In what senses were cities like Birmingham, Leeds and Manchester 'industrial'? In what ways can the wealthy population of these cities be considered to have formed a 'middle class'? What is meant, in this context, by 'bourgeois culture'? The purpose of this chapter is to provide some answers to these questions in the light of recent historiography and to lay the groundwork for the arguments about city, class and culture that inform the study as a whole.

The industrial city

The emergence of Birmingham, Leeds and Manchester as industrial centres occurred in the second half of the eighteenth century. The concentration of manufacturing trades of particular types – metalwares in what was to become known as the Black Country, textiles in the West Riding and Lancashire – was observed by a stream of visitors from Daniel Defoe to Arthur Young. Birmingham, Leeds and Manchester grew as finishing and marketing centres for these regional trades as well as centres of manufacturing in their own right. By 1801 the three towns had become among the most populous in England, each with over fifty thousand inhabitants.[2] The transition from manufacturing town to industrial city, however, was a feature of the nineteenth century. It is well-known that between 1801 and 1851 the towns experienced a population explosion: Manchester's population increased from 75,000 to 303,000, Birmingham's from 75,000 to 247,000, that of Leeds from 53,000 to 172,000, with the most rapid growth rates occurring in the 1820s and 1830s. Of equal significance, however, was the less dramatic but cumulatively weightier expansion of the second half of the nineteenth century. Between 1851 and 1901 the populations of Manchester and Birmingham doubled to 645,000 and 522,000 respectively, while that of Leeds increased two and a half times to 429,000.[3] Boundary changes, suburbanisation and unregulated growth all meant that it became increasingly difficult to define what the city was by the later nineteenth century. A Manchester Corporation report in the early 1880s noted that 'the merchants, manufacturers and general population of Manchester, and those connected with industries closely allied to the city, are to be found in an area extending beyond the limits of the city, [and] the district known to the world as "Manchester" is much more populous than it appears in any printed returns'.[4] After 1850, in effect, Manchester, Birmingham and Leeds began to take on the character of provincial metropolises, the largest urban centres in Britain outside London with the exception of Glasgow and Liverpool.

The identity of the cities was bound up with the major manufacturing trades carried on within them and in the surrounding districts. Birmingham was termed the 'Hardware Village', associated with an array of metal trades, Leeds was the 'principal seat of the woollen manufacture in England', while Manchester was simply and grandly 'Cottonopolis'. Recent research has tended to emphasise their role as organisational rather than production centres, specialising in marketing, distribution and services such as banking and insurance. But the industrial profile of each of the cities remained significant throughout the nineteenth century. In 1861 over half the active population of Manchester, Birmingham and Leeds was defined as engaged in manufacturing; building, transport, retail, wholesale, commerce and the professions employed between a quarter and a fifth.[5] In the last decades of the century larger manufacturing firms tended to relocate to sites on the urban fringe or in nearby towns, and the old-established trades began to decline as sources of employment. In both Leeds and Manchester textile manufacture was increasingly rivalled and surpassed by engineering and the clothing trades.[6] Yet this did not efface the industrial identity of the cities concerned. In the early twentieth century they remained the home of some of the largest manufacturing firms in the country, whether judged by capital or by employment: Cadbury and Guest, Keen and Nettlefold at Birmingham, Fairbairn at Leeds, Rylands, Mather and Platt, and the great textile combines such as the Spinners and Doublers Association at Manchester.[7]

The cities developed as regional as well as industrial capitals. This role was symbolised by the exchanges and cloth halls that formed the meeting place and hub for the industries that colonised the larger manufacturing districts. In Lancashire, manufacturers were divided between 'town' and 'country', the latter designating the outlying cotton towns. Manchester was 'an axis, a metropolis; it had provinces'. Birmingham was 'the Mecca of surrounding populous districts'. Leeds, according to Angus Bethune Reach in 1849, was 'the manufacturing capital of Yorkshire, surrounded by a group of satellites'.[8] Reach's estimation of Leeds' importance was exaggerated, given the growth of industrial Sheffield to the south. By the time of his writing, moreover, the city's claim to pre-eminence even within the woollen districts of the West Riding was challenged by the rapid rise of Bradford, a mere nine miles to the west, as 'Worstedopolis', the capital of the worsted textile region.[9] Nevertheless, during the second half of the century all the cities possessed a regional importance, not simply in economic or industrial terms but also as centres of culture and consumption. By the 1880s the combination of theatres, arcades and department stores made the industrial cities a major attraction for shoppers and pleasure-seekers from the suburbs, the outlying towns and further afield.[10] As Thomas Wemyss Reid, editor of the *Leeds Mercury* in the 1870s, put it with characteristic provincial pride, the time had arrived when Manchester, Birmingham and Leeds were 'ceasing to be mere humble dependants upon the capital of the nation', and were becoming instead 'the capitals of the districts in which they were situated'.[11]

The industrial and metropolitan character of the cities was the foundation of their perceived modernity in the nineteenth century, on which other features were superimposed. In a long tradition, the industrial city has been viewed as the progenitor of class relations, defined by the stark opposition of capital and labour and social conflict. According to Friedrich Engels in 1845, Manchester, Birmingham and Leeds were united by a single factor: they were all in a state of class warfare. For the historian Mark Girouard the Victorian industrial cities represented a 'battlefield'; they were characterised by an intense struggle between social classes, political parties and architectural styles in contrast to the Georgian town whose organising principle was consensus.[12] Increased residential segregation under the impact of suburban development, which occurred earliest in cities like Manchester and Birmingham, was taken to be both cause and consequence of social conflict, and to prefigure the spatial arrangements characteristic of the modern city.[13] All these features have been widely debated, but other aspects of the industrial cities were also significant in denoting their modernity. For contemporaries, a defining characteristic of the expanding industrial metropolises was their anonymity. In his description of Birmingham following a visit in 1840 Dickens commented on the sense of solitude of the individual caught up in a vast crowd of strangers. In Leeds and Manchester a frequently stated aim of social and cultural institutions was to bring together individuals of similar status, taste and interests from what was acknowledged to be an 'unconnected population'.[14] Even more than London, before the 1880s, the industrial cities were represented as depersonalised, anonymous places where individuals pursued their business in silent isolation. By extension, the crowds of workers, the mills and warehouses were viewed by visitors as a passive spectacle, which, in accordance with the dictates of the sublime, inspired a mixture of awe and exhilaration, but also cast the observer in the role of detached spectator.[15] The industrial city therefore offered a new experience of city life and new ways of perceiving the relationship between the individual and the urban environment.

It is misleading, of course, to treat Birmingham, Leeds and Manchester as identical creations. There were significant differences of economic and social structure between the cities which historians have systematically explored since Asa Briggs' pioneering work in this field.[16] Birmingham has conventionally been depicted as a centre of workshop-based manufacturing, Manchester as a site of large-scale factory production, and there was truth in this picture even if recent research has shown the differences to be overdrawn.[17] Equally, the predominance of the textile and clothing trades in Manchester and Leeds meant that there was a far higher proportion of women in the manufacturing workforce than in the Birmingham metal trades.[18] More generally, Leeds, and arguably even Birmingham, could not match the metropolitan credentials of Manchester. As Robert Gray has noted, in the early and mid-Victorian years 'Manchester stood for the whole cotton region, or even for modern industrialism'.[19] Yet for all their differences the industrial cities were marked off, on the one hand, from London, which for its scale, size of population and role as an imperial and national capital was unique even by international standards, and, on the other, from industrial towns, like Blackburn, Keighley and Wolverhampton, often dominated by a small number of employers and still subject in the later Victorian period to modes of paternalist influence based on a highly localised web of dependent personal relationships.[20] By the mid-nineteenth century cities like Manchester, Birmingham and Leeds were differentiated from other kinds of urban centre. They represented a new and recognisable urban type as provincial, industrial metropolises.

The middle class

In historical writing the English middle class has been closely linked to the growth of the industrial cities, though definitions of the group have been broad and inclusive. The middle class in England has been defined as comprising property-owning groups which engaged in active occupations, usually connected with manufacturing, trade and the professions. The middle class was differentiated from the aristocracy and gentry by active participation in the productive economy and from the working class by ownership of property and abstention from manual wage labour.[21] Traditional interpretations of the emergence of the middle class focused on the late eighteenth and early nineteenth centuries and depicted class formation as the spontaneous outcome of economic and political change. On one side, the class was given social form by the industrial revolution between 1780 and 1830 which brought into being a new group of manufacturers and merchants, concentrated in the burgeoning towns of the Midlands and north. On the other side, the middle class established a political presence by means of a series of national campaigns concerned with taxation, parliamentary and municipal reform, and repeal of the Corn Laws.[22] Subsequent detailed studies of the 'making' of the middle class in the same period, however, have pointed to other sources of social cohesion. In their study of Colchester and Birmingham, Leonore Davidoff and Catherine Hall argued that the 'rise' of the middle class between 1780 and 1850 was characterised by the development of a 'domestic ideology' and a sharp division between a public world of work and politics associated with men, and a private world of home and family to which women were confined. Articulated with evangelical religion, these discourses represented the basis of a moral order that differentiated the middle class from the dissolute and irresponsible aristocracy and the urban poor deemed feckless and atheistic. The English middle class was 'made' through a fundamental reworking of gender relations.[23] A different, though not irreconcilable, account is provided by R. J. Morris in his study of Leeds in the first half of the nineteenth century. Morris's analysis of propertied groups revealed a population significantly divided by economic status, denominational allegiance and political rivalry. What enabled these groups to come together as a class was the wide-ranging network of voluntary societies that allowed a diversity of opinions and interests to be accommodated, the security of property to be upheld and social action to be undertaken. Yet according to Morris, this was not achieved on an equal basis. The middle class in Leeds was an 'elite-led class'. The principal role in forging a public class-based culture was undertaken by an influential group of merchant and professional families who were able to assert authority over the amorphous, divided ranks of urban property and to enable them to engage in action as a class.[24]

However, all these accounts, which rest explicitly or implicitly on a concept of the middle class as a social formation centred on urban industrialism, have been brought into question by recent re-interpretations. In the first place, a revisionist historiography has depicted the English middle class as divided between a commercial and financial elite, based on London, and a northern manufacturing interest. In terms of wealth, economic and political power, and cultural influence, it was the former that predominated over the latter between the eighteenth and the twentieth centuries. Despite the challenge of the northern manufacturing interest which culminated in the repeal of the Corn Laws in 1846, it was an older 'gentlemanly capitalism' associated with the City, and with strong connections to the landed order, that prevailed. In this perspective northern merchants and manufacturers were the 'poor relations' of the British capitalist class.[25] More critically still, Dror Wahrman has argued that the idea of the 'making' of the middle class is fundamentally misconceived. The 'middle ranks' already constituted a substantial and growing element in eighteenth-century England; merchants and manufacturers did not therefore emerge as a new social presence after 1780. What changed was the rhetoric not the reality; the 'middle class' was deployed in political discourse from the 1790s to designate moderate or 'middle opinion' between Burkean conservatism and Paineite radicalism. After 1815 the concept of the 'middle class' was construed primarily in moral terms and seized upon by the Whig party, in particular, as a means of preserving the political and social order. The concept did not denote, therefore, a new or specific social constituency; rather, it was a rhetorical construct whose meanings were political and moral, not social.[26]

The idea that industrial interests were subordinate to those of finance, commerce and land in the nineteenth century has been extensively contested. It is the interconnection of these various forms of capital that has been emphasised by critics such as Martin Daunton, rather than their opposition, dominance or subordination.[27] Wahrman's more recent arguments have also been influential and are important.[28] It is clear, for example, that in the first half of the nineteenth the term 'middle class' was politically and morally loaded. As Geoffrey Crossick observes, 'middle class' was a 'term of pride in oppositional politics, whether against aristocratic government or working-class excesses, and referred less to a social group than to the right-thinking, morally upright core of British society'.[29] Yet as Crossick acknowledges, there was a 'social content' to the speeches of James Mill, Cobden and other propagandists, however ambiguous. Contemporary references identified the middle class with public opinion and moral worth, but these were usually linked to other criteria – industry, commerce, property, wealth, education – not least in the discourses of urban Nonconformity; as Briggs noted, 'the term "middle class" was first popularised in dissenting journals'.[30] In short, while 'middle class' did not denote a clear-cut sociological constituency (no social category in the nineteenth-century did), it is only with some contextual wrenching that the political and moral attributes of the term can be divorced from the social and the economic.

The meanings of 'middle class' after 1850 are still less clear. David Cannadine argues that it possessed a stronger social referent, but denies the validity of the term in the singular because it encompassed a heterogeneous population: 'There was no such thing as *the* late Victorian and Edwardian middle class: it was far too protean, varied and amorphous for that'.[31] In the industrial areas the term was used promiscuously. It was more likely to be applied in a national context and from outside the town than from within it. Thus the London-based *Times* attacked a speech by John Bright at Birmingham in 1866, attempting to rally trades and friendly societies, by claiming that the main reason for the delay in political reform was 'the tacit fear of the middle class of this very organisation of the artisans'. In the 1850s the Earl of Dartmouth condemned the Wolverhampton vestry as a 'noisy, fidgety busybody of the middle class'.[32] In the industrial cities the description tended to be reserved for lower status groups, such as clerks, shopkeepers, and even 'superior' artisans. Large employers, merchants and professionals were more likely to be identified as the 'middle and upper classes', or by epithets such as the 'opulent and influential', the 'wealthy and educated' and 'our leading families'.[33] Indeed, after the inclusion of skilled male workers in the franchise in 1867, 'class' became invested with negative connotations, a synonym for collective political self-interest.[34] If the notion of the 'middle class' was urged for moral and political reasons in the first half of the nineteenth century, it was no less frequently denied during the second.

The absence of an explicit class-based language among the propertied is unsurprising, and serves as a warning against attaching excessive importance to a particular vocabulary in analysing the social order. As Roland Barthes has put it, with reference to the history of the French bourgeoisie:

> As an economic fact, the bourgeoisie is named without any difficulty; capitalism is openly professed. As a political fact, the bourgeoisie has some difficulty in acknowledging itself: there are no 'bourgeois' parties in the Chamber. As an ideological fact, it completely disappears: the bourgeoisie has obliterated its name in passing from reality to representation, from economic man to mental man ... The bourgeoisie is defined as the social class which does not want to be named.[35]

In the English case the problem is compounded by the vagueness of the concept of the middle class itself. Whereas in Germany terms such as *Bürgertum* and *Mittelstand* denoted relatively precise socio-occupational groups, 'middle class' could either refer to a narrow group of merchants and manufacturers or to a much broader grouping incorporating small employers and white-collar workers. Similarly, there was no equivalent in English for the French term *notables*, which effected a bridge in the nineteenth century between older aristocratic, land-owning families and the wealthiest urban property-owners.[36] Indeed, ideas of 'old Corruption' or Cobbett's 'the Thing', as well as the enduring usage of an aristocratic terminology to describe the urban wealthy, suggests the difficulties in identifying or naming the powerful in nineteenth-century England by contrast with the persistent, detailed classifications of workers and the poor.[37] Power was marked by a linguistic hiatus or by a process of loose terminological association. For these reasons it is necessary to move away from social description to examine aspects of the formation of the propertied in the industrial cities in the Victorian period.

The various estimates of the propertied or non-manual population in the industrial cities during the early and mid-Victorian period range between a tenth and a fifth of the urban population. In occupational terms, based on the census, this group represented 17 per cent of the population of Birmingham in 1851 and 18 per cent of that of Manchester in 1861; on the more generous basis of the trade directories for Leeds in the 1830s, Morris came to a figure of 13 per cent.[38] The sources, of course, are inherently problematic, compounded after 1850 by the effects of the out-migration of the wealthy to suburbs outside the city boundaries. Nevertheless, some insight into the comparative proportions of the better-off can be gauged from the percentage of male taxpayers in the three cities in 1861; the threshold for income tax was £100 p.a., a figure considered to represent the minimum necessary to maintain any semblance of gentility. Here Manchester led the way with 15 per cent, followed by Birmingham with 14 per cent and Leeds with 10 per cent.[39] In none of the cities did manufacturers represent a majority of the propertied; they were flanked by substantial commercial, professional and rentier groups. Equally important, all of the recent studies of the middle class in Birmingham, Leeds and Manchester have noted a significant distinction between the wealthiest and most politically influential group within the propertied, estimated at between 3 per cent and 5 per cent of the urban population, and the bulk of the non-manual population. Beyond the former, which comprised the major industrial, commercial and professional families, there lay a long social tail of small entrepreneurs, shopkeepers, tradespeople and, increasingly, clerical workers.[40]

It is worth examining the characteristics of this wealthy segment of the propertied in more detail. In terms of background, there is little systematic evidence of the social origins of mid-Victorian employers and professionals born in the decades around 1800, outside the best-known industrial families. But what evidence there is suggests geographical, social and occupational diversity. A sample of 'middle-class' households in Manchester in 1861 revealed that almost 80 per cent of heads of household and their spouses had been born outside the city, a substantial proportion (41 per cent) having undergone long-distance migration.[41] By mid-century there remained an important group of older manufacturing, commercial and professional families – Kenricks, Cadburys and Galtons at Birmingham, Nusseys, Luptons and Atkinsons in Leeds – as well as branches of wealthy European families, such as the Behrens, Schunks and Souchays in Manchester. But backgrounds in the retail and wholesale trades, tenant farming, and the putting-out system were common among major mid-Victorian employers.[42] In many ways, therefore, this was a new social formation, mobile and disparate. Furthermore, there was no common pattern of education in the early nineteenth century. While the wealthiest Nonconformist families sent their sons to academies and to university at Edinburgh, Glasgow or on the Continent, and Anglicans patronised the local grammar schools, the education of those from modest backgrounds usually extended little beyond the three 'R's, together with religious instruction. However, this was to change significantly from the 1830s. The grammar schools in Manchester, Leeds and Birmingham were reformed; girls' schools were established in suburbs such as Edgbaston; the opening of Owen's College, Manchester and University College, London provided non-denominational higher education; and public schools such as Rugby, Winchester and Shrewsbury were increasingly favoured for the sons of employer families, Nonconformist as well as Anglican.[43] In effect, a framework was created between 1840 and 1870 that largely overrode earlier social and sectarian divisions in the education of the well-to-do and ensured that children from wealthy provincial families were educated separately from the rest of the urban population.

While education helped to bring a greater unity by the mid-Victorian decades, the upper reaches of urban society were also increasingly affluent. The provincial industrial centres could not match the City of London or the aristocracy for numbers of millionaires before 1914, according to W. D. Rubinstein, but they still bore witness to formidable accretions of wealth, above all in Manchester. An analysis of the recorded wealth of over two hundred of the city's major bankers, cotton and engineering employers who died between 1858 and 1914 revealed that almost half left over £100,000 and a quarter over £200,000.[44] Estimates of average tax paid per capita under Schedule D (business and professional profits) for 1862–63 shows the leading provincial centres of Manchester and Liverpool well behind the City of London. Yet the average sum paid in Manchester and Leeds was higher than that in Westminster, while Birmingham similarly outstripped Finsbury and Marylebone.[45] Indeed, the tax returns almost certainly underestimated the scale of wealth in the industrial cities since out-migration meant that many of the richest urban families were resident outside their boundaries. Statistics for 1878–79 show that the parliamentary divisions which produced the largest overall tax returns were those bordering northern industrial and port cities: South East and South West Lancashire and the three divisions of the West Riding of Yorkshire.[46] However, as critics have pointed out, there are technical problems with measuring industrial wealth by probate and tax returns.[47] The evaluation of individual wealth at death, in particular, tends to under-estimate the effects of life-cycle and inheritance patterns. R. J. Morris's analysis of the accounts of the Leeds woolstapler, Robert Jowitt, between 1806 and 1862 shows marked fluctuations in profit and income, stabilised by diversification of capital into shares following Jowitt's withdrawal from the family firm in the 1840s. Rather than an unceasing drive to maximise profits the main priority was to achieve financial security in a volatile capitalist economy.[48] More generally, lack of attachment to the principle of primogeniture meant that capital resources would normally be dispersed across familial networks. What was important was not so much the scale of individual wealth as a sufficiency and stability of income to maintain a style of life characterised by substantial mansions, servants, handsome equipage and Continental holidays.

The diversification both of capital and of kinship networks were indices of the growing stability of the well-to-do in the provincial cities, and helped to foster the idea of a dynastic order in the later Victorian period.[49] Economic diversification was less a matter of the purchase of country estates, as is often assumed, than investment in a wide range of productive sources, including banking, urban property, railways and manufacturing industry. A Manchester syndicate established in the 1860s organised the take-over of family firms in iron, steel and engineering and their conversion into limited companies. They included John

Brown, Cammells and Bolckow Vaughan, all listed among the fifty-two largest British industrial firms in 1905, and provided Manchester businessmen with investments and directorships nationwide. By the 1880s it was common for successful employers in the industrial cities to hold directorships, internationally as well as at home.[50] The second half of the nineteenth century also saw the burgeoning of extended kinship networks across the region and the nation. Clyde Binfield has described the wealthy Leeds Congregational families like Baines, Nussey, Morley and Willans as the 'core of Nonconformist cousinhoods, widespreading beyond Yorkshire and often beyond Congregationalism'.[51] But the movement outward was not confined to Nonconformity as the example of the Manchester banking family, the Heywoods, indicates. In the first half of the century the family was linked by marriage to Unitarian cotton families in Manchester and Liverpool, such as Kennedy and Robinson. The family's shift to Anglicanism in the 1840s was followed by alliances further afield in the second half of the century, with the higher reaches of the law, the Anglican church and the army, through marriage into the Foster, Sumner and Lemprieve families, and with the Yorkshire gentry, in the form of the Bartons and Ramsdens.[52] By means of complex networks of kinship, wealthy urban families enhanced both their economic and social capital; economic capital was diversified, no longer dependent on a single economic sector, while intermarriage widened the sphere of connections with significant others. The extension of these networks did not inevitably presage removal from the city or some insidious process of 'gentrification'; the Heywoods, for example, retained their base in Manchester into the twentieth century.[53] The decentralised nature of the Victorian state, among other factors, underpinned the primacy of the local for most of the nineteenth century. Looking back from the 1920s W. H. Mills found it 'astonishing to reflect how in the late eighties the State had left us high and dry. And knowing so little of the central State, we had built little States of our own, thinking to abide in them for ever'.[54] Before 1900 at least the lives of the wealthy were lived out principally on the stage of the urban and the local. The city was the bourgeois estate.

It is against this backdrop that the dividing forces of politics and religion need to be assessed. Historians have depicted urban politics between 1820 and 1850 as marked by intense rivalry between local elites, Tory Anglican against Nonconformist Whig/Liberal, with other groups in the urban population mobilised differentially behind them.[55] This struggle encompassed the whole range of institutions of local authority, from the vestry to the council, and was fierce partly because politico-religious divisions within the propertied were finely balanced. In Leeds, for example, the 1834 election was won by the Whig, Edward Baines, by a mere nine votes over his Tory rival, the Leeds banker Sir John Beckett. In religious terms, the 1851 census showed Anglicanism to have a slight lead over Nonconformity in Manchester and Leeds, and a more substantial one in Birmingham, in the urban population as a whole. But among major employer and professional groups this situation was reversed in all three cities, Nonconformists predominating marginally over Anglicans.[56] After mid-century, however, the rivalry between urban elites waned, even if that between political parties did not. In Leeds and Manchester there was a gradual withdrawal of larger manufacturers, merchants and professionals from the city councils; in Birmingham, conversely, the municipal revival of the 1870s and 1880s was predicated on the re-entry of these groups into the municipal arena under the banner of a revitalised Liberalism.[57] The picture of mid- and later Victorian local politics as a contest between an economy-minded petty bourgeoisie and a more established, expansionist-minded group of large employers and professionals may be overdrawn. Yet it does indicate that municipal politics was no longer the source of rivalry between elites of equivalent power and status. Equally, the inter-denominational competition which characterised the 'civilising mission' after 1851 needs to be set against its underlying commonality of purpose, to enable wealthy congregations, Anglican and Nonconformist, to engage in social action in the name of reclaiming workers and the urban poor for 'civilised' Christian society. More important than the movement's alleged success or failure in these aims was its capacity to involve large sections of the propertied in a sustained cultural offensive against the perceived deficiencies of an alien, atheistic other.[58] Thus if politico-religious allegiances remained an important part of the identities of wealthy families in the industrial cities before 1914, they were underpinned by still more fundamental imperatives: by the need to undertake positions of leadership in local institutions, to assert authority over others whether servants, workers or the 'deserving' poor, and, above all, to externalise the connection between wealth and power. In this sense, the content of politics and religion was less significant than the modes in which they were enacted.

From these aspects it is possible to discern the configuration of the middle class in the industrial cities between 1850 and 1914. Occupationally, the core of the middle class was composed of large manufacturing, commercial and professional families. There were substantial differences of wealth between these groups – clerics and lawyers, for instance, rarely matched the incomes of industrialists and bankers – but they were increasingly integrated through education, intermarriage, and leading roles in urban institutions, as well as by participation in a common style of life in city and suburb. Within the urban context, the middle class was seldom named as such, but was identified rather by its chief characteristics: wealth (connoting substantial property ownership), leadership (designated by terms such as 'influence' or 'standing'), and education (often defined as 'intelligence' or 'cultivation'). These characteristics distinguished the middle class from the larger 'middle classes' identified with retailers and wholesalers, white-collar workers and the newer professions, groups which from the 1870s began to be defined as a 'lower middle class' differentiated from manual workers.[59] The larger notion of the middle classes not only allowed for the notion of upward (and downward) mobility which was important to the ideology of the self-made man, but also gave endorsement to a concept of class resting on the distinction between mental and manual labour. In a speech to his workforce in 1857, for example, the cotton master Samuel Greg argued that wealth brought with it 'avenues of pain and sorrow' arising from the 'sufferings of the inward life' of which they, his workers, were happily ignorant. Similarly, in rejecting the wage-claims of striking builders in 1871 the Manchester Society of Architects earnestly hoped that 'the working classes may be disabused of the idea that full pecuniary results should follow on mere muscular, unaccompanied by intellectual, exertion'.[60] On the other side, what distinguished the middle class from the regional gentry and aristocracy were not simply links to trade and manufacturing, but a strong identification with the urban. Landed families such as the Calthorpes, Egertons and Ripons owned land in or close to Birmingham, Manchester and Leeds respectively, and inter-class relationships were eased from the 1870s by common participation in public schools, Oxbridge, social clubs and hunting. But urban institutions themselves were sacrosanct; landed involvement in urban life was limited to honorific roles and any suspicion of undue political influence met with fierce resistance. While the Duke of Norfolk and Earl Fitz-william served as mayors of Sheffield in the 1890s and 1900s, such deference was unthinkable in Birmingham, Leeds and Manchester.[61]

The concept of the middle class outlined here corresponds closely to that of the German *Bürgertum* in the nineteenth century; it included rentier and professional groups alongside business, and excluded the nobility and the military, as well as the lesser propertied groups that in Germany were identified separately as the *Mittelstand*. Like the *Bürgertum* the middle class represented more than an elite, by virtue of

its size and relative openness to new wealth, and rather less than a
bourgeoisie in the classic Marxian sense of a class of industrial owners
whose interests were reflected in political domination of the state
apparatus.[62] The power of the middle class as a group was focused on,
and to some extent circumscribed by, the urban and the local, at least
before 1900. Whereas the notion of the middle class was deployed most
prominently in political discourse in the first half of the century, by the
1870s the term represented, rather, a particular social formation defined
broadly by scale of ownership, leadership and way of life. When a
contemporary described Manchester in 1870 as a 'middle-class paradise',
it was to these characteristics he was referring.[63] By the later nineteenth
century, in effect, the middle class denoted less a political agency than
a specific social order, a mode of existence rather than an instrument
of collective action. If paradise had been realised, why should it be
otherwise?

Bourgeois culture

Nevertheless, even in these terms the middle class was a fragile formation, marked by distinctions of wealth, religious identity and political
affiliation and subject to the constant pressures of economic competition.
The precarious unity of the propertied was always prone to splintering
along one or more of these axes. Beyond the fact of property ownership,
what served to unify the middle class, above all, was culture, conceived
from the early nineteenth century as a sphere of consensus and recon-
ciliation. At the art exhibition, the concert hall and the social club, men
– and, in some cases, women – could engage in activities that were
deemed to transcend the divisions of sect and party. 'No religion, no
politics' was an explicit or implicit rule of such gatherings.[64] Yet culture
was not simply an attribute of class; it was also the terrain on which
class was reproduced. This was apparent in the manner in which
education, identified with intellectual breadth and moral self-discipline,
informed a conception of class based on the mental/manual division
during the second half of the nineteenth century. Urban society was
regularly represented as divided between the 'cultivated' classes on the
one hand, identified with the educated and well-to-do, and the lower
classes on the other, which lacked culture and were defined in terms of
a physical, or even 'animal', nature. As Pierre Bourdieu has put it, 'by
symbolically shifting the essence of what sets them apart from other
classes from the economic field to that of culture ... the privileged
members of bourgeois society replace the difference between two

cultures, historic products of social conditions, by the essential difference between two natures, a naturally cultivated nature and a naturally natural nature'.[65] If culture was increasingly defined as a sphere distinct from the political and the economic, its meanings in the mid-Victorian period were broad. For Matthew Arnold the possession of culture, associated with the capacity for disinterested reflection, was a necessary precondition both of the state and of citizenship. Culture also retained many of its earlier associations with spiritual and intellectual self-development.[66] Yet by encompassing moral, ethical and aesthetic attributes, culture pointed outwards more broadly still, from the individual and the institutions of urban self-improvement to the family as the fount of moral education, to church, chapel and suburbia itself, conceived as representing a distinct civilisation.[67] In this sense the meanings of culture already extended from art and knowledge to way of life by the mid-Victorian period.

To be sure, the culture of the urban middle class has not conventionally been viewed in such inclusive or positive terms. For Perry Anderson, the sole ideology produced by the English bourgeoisie was utilitarianism, itself a form of 'cultural nihilism'; the concept of a 'middle-class culture' in nineteenth-century England was to all intents and purposes an oxymoron.[68] Where Anderson led, others have followed, albeit in less polemical vein. In Martin Wiener's influential account, for example, the economic and political drive of the industrial middle class was dissipated after 1850 by a process of 'gentrification' in which a radical entrepreneurialism was supplanted by more conservative values of duty and service identified with the aristocracy, the gentry and sections of the literary intelligentsia. Again, it is the absence of a distinctive middle-class culture that is emphasised, especially in the industrial centres, together with the singularity of England in this respect.[69] Yet in order to consider the composition and significance of this culture it is important to place it in European perspective, especially in relation to Germany where similar issues have been analysed and debated. What this suggests is less the singularity of the English case, than the strong degree of correspondence in the character of nineteenth-century bourgeois culture in different national contexts.[70]

Culture was of central importance to notions of middle-class or bourgeois identity in nineteenth-century Europe. It represented an essential source of unity for propertied groups and a means of distinction from other social classes. Terms such as *bourgeois* and *Bürgerlichkeit* in relation to culture denoted not merely a certain attachment to art and education, important as these were, but also a style of life identified with etiquette and appearance. As Jürgen Kocka has observed: 'If one considers the cohesion and specificity of the *Bürgertum* to be defined by its culture and its *sociabilité*, one appreciates the importance of symbolic forms in middle-class life, of bourgeois table manners and conventions, of quotations from classical literature, titles, customs, and dress'.[71] Two other features were significant in this conception of bourgeois culture. The first was the family household, the prime site in which the cultural habitus of the next generation was transmitted and which also represented the focus for important elements of bourgeois sociability including dinners, parties, dancing and reading.[72] The second feature was the creation of an urban public sphere. In Germany, and to a lesser extent France, the development of civil society from the late eighteenth century in opposition to a society of legally-defined estates was closely associated with the middle class, signalled in terms such as *bürgerliche Gesellschaft*. Crucial here was the development of a network of voluntary associations in individual towns and cities, including choral and learned societies, social clubs and sporting associations, which formed the basis of a local, public bourgeois culture. Such associations were bourgeois in the sense not only that they were dominated by propertied urban groups but also that they stood in contradistinction to the traditional corporate society of legal privileges and distinctions. More generally, unlike older aristocratic and artisan cultures, bourgeois culture was not wholly congruent with the bourgeoisie or middle class as a social formation. In line with its post-Enlightenment inheritance, bourgeois culture in the nineteenth century was marked by universalist aspirations, even if in practice these were always at odds with tendencies to social exclusivity.[73]

This bourgeois culture was not confined to the Continent; culture, as a recent historian has expressed it, was a 'convertible coinage' in the nineteenth century, a national and international 'bourgeois currency'.[74] Just as wealthy Germans travelled to Paris, London and Manchester from the 1820s as part of a new 'journey of modernity', so their English counterparts travelled abroad for education and inspiration. In the 1830s the sons of Manchester employers, like Thomas Ashton and William Langton, attended German universities, and holidays on the Continent were a cultural rite of all sections of the well-to-do in the industrial cities after 1850.[75] Architecturally, too, Continental examples were influential. Joseph Chamberlain was not alone in looking to the Low Countries, Germany and Italy as inspiration for the renaissance of civic building in the 1870s, while Haussman's reconstruction of Paris from the 1850s provided a model of urban redevelopment for corporations in both Leeds and Birmingham.[76] The cultural impress of German and

Jewish merchant communities in cities like Manchester and Bradford was similarly registered, especially in fields such as music.[77] In effect, the middle class of the industrial cities did not stand outside the mainstream of European bourgeois culture; it had close connections with that culture and shared many of its social and organisational forms. In this sense, the culture of the English middle class should be viewed as part of a larger, international bourgeois culture by the mid-nineteenth century. At the same time, bourgeois culture was not synonymous with the middle class even if urban propertied groups played a leading role in its construction and reproduction. In the words of Wolfgang Kaschuba, 'as a style of life and a code of conduct, bourgeois culture claimed universal social validity for itself. It saw itself as the point of reference for all other social groups. It developed not on the basis of its own inner continuity and exclusivity, but exhibited its greatest vitality in its dialogue with other group cultures and in the constant change and exchange that this involved'.[78] In this context, the term 'bourgeois' had less to do with social origins than with the development of a specific cultural praxis at least partly independent of any single group or class. For these various reasons, therefore, it is more appropriate to speak of a 'bourgeois' rather than a 'middle-class' culture in the nineteenth century.

What, then, were the key characteristics of a bourgeois culture as this took shape in English provincial cities in the first half of the nineteenth century? In many ways they were very similar to those evident on the Continent, especially Germany. On the one side there was the cult of the home, indulged by both men and women. 'Practised first and most intensively by the bourgeoisie, domesticity became the talisman of bourgeois culture', John Tosh has argued in a recent study of masculinity and the middle-class home.[79] On the other side, there was the construction of a burgeoning network of voluntary associations, fostering sociability and cultural improvement. These two facets were not contradictory but linked. As Jurgen Habermas observed, the public sphere of the late eighteenth and early nineteenth century developed out of the forms of sociability and interiority nurtured in the bourgeois home.[80] The voluntary societies formed the 'theatrical scaffolding for the nineteenth-century bourgeois drama'. They provided both a distinct urban milieu for middle-class men (and, on limited occasions, for women), and a platform from which a succession of cultural projects were launched, aimed variously at improving, disciplining and reforming what were viewed as subordinate elements in the town's social hierarchy: clerical and factory workers, the improvident and immoral poor.[81] The

Enlightenment belief in the steady, inter-connected advance of morality, culture and technology was projected especially strongly through provincial associations such as the Literary and Philosophical societies. Yet the urban bourgeois culture of the early nineteenth century was also confined and exclusive. It was small-scale, directed by self-selecting urban elites, based on the home or on clubs and societies, membership of which was bounded by high annual subscriptions. It was in such terms that Richard Cobden described Manchester in 1838:

> The tone which has so long prevailed in the government of the town has naturally enough pervaded all our public institutions, and even entered into the private arrangements of social life. It is well understood, for example, that if the shopkeeper's family be not formally interdicted from entering our public assemblies, they will not be consulting their own interest or enjoyment by attending them, and the retailer would find it, probably, almost as difficult to gain admission to our clubs and our concerts, as he might to obtain the privilege of 'entré' to the Queen's court.[82]

From the 1840s, however, significant elements of this culture were to change. In provincial cities like Birmingham, Leeds and Manchester the highpoint of a public bourgeois culture occurred in the decades between 1870 and 1900. This has been identified in conventional historiography with the rise of the civic, associated with grandiose town halls and programmes of urban improvement carried out under municipal auspices.[83] But while the middle class had a heavy investment in civic pride and institutions, they were not the sole or even the main constituents of mid- and late Victorian bourgeois culture. In part, change represented an intensification of processes already apparent in the early nineteenth century. Suburbanisation after mid-century, for example, enhanced the seclusion and intimacy of the middle-class home. An analysis of Manchester's northern suburbs in 1861 revealed that over three-quarters of substantial merchant, manufacturer and professional households were nuclear, defined as lacking boarders and non-nuclear kin, whereas the proportion for small employer and white-collar households was less than two-thirds, that for skilled workers well under half.[84] This sense of privacy was reinforced by the growth of a distinct suburban social life in the later nineteenth century, centred primarily on church and chapel and the multifarious societies and agencies which they spawned. But the most significant changes occurred in the city itself from the 1840s, signalled by the extensive reconstruction of the central area on monumental lines and the creation of an expanded public sphere based on culture, sociability and consumption. By the 1870s a new world

of bourgeois leisure had opened up, encompassing public exhibitions and concerts, gentlemen's clubs, restaurants and department stores. In the process it largely displaced an older culture mixing 'polite learning and utility' with select conviviality. After 1850 the formerly prestigious Manchester Literary and Philosophical Society was dominated by a narrow group of professional scientists, while in Leeds the Phil. and Lit. declined steadily from the 1870s.[85]

The public bourgeois culture of the later nineteenth century was distinguished by a number of characteristics. Firstly, it was increasingly based on cash payment rather than on subscription, as had earlier been the case, reflecting a shift from a culture predicated on relatively small elites and personal acquaintance to the more anonymous public world and social relationships of the mid-Victorian city. This applied less in institutions such as the prestigious gentlemen's clubs, where membership continued to depend on personal recommendation and ballot, but the proliferation of clubs by the 1880s with a range of entrance fees meant that opportunities for male participation in 'clubland' were plentiful. The institutions of bourgeois culture retained a certain social exclusivity not only by the levels of payment, which in most cases put them beyond the reach of manual workers, but also by the need to demonstrate social competence. To visit the concert hall, art gallery or restaurant it was not sufficient merely to be able to afford the experience, but to know the etiquette or 'form' which dictated behaviour in those settings. Nevertheless, the bourgeois culture of the second half of the nineteenth century was open to wider sections of the educated and prosperous than had been the case in the first. In this sense, Cobden's criticisms were answered.

The second key feature of mid- and later Victorian bourgeois culture was an emphasis on public visibility and display. Whereas in the early nineteenth century much of the culture of the well-to-do was lived out in interiors – the home, the society or club, themselves often based in taverns and hotels – after 1850 it was more often conducted outdoors, as in the case of promenades and civic processions, or in settings, like the concert hall or the giant exhibitions of art and industry, where the events could be presented as spectacle. Thirdly, and by extension, much of public bourgeois culture was distinguished by its ritualistic and performative character. This applied to formal events such as promenades, processions and attendance at the concert hall as well as to less formal activities such as the daily journey to work and the conduct of business itself. Middle-class appearance in public, I shall argue, was strongly ritualised and formalistic, whether this concerned individual self-presentation or collective display. Linking divergent activities, from civic ceremonial to promenading in the shopping streets, therefore, was the impulse to convert appearance in public into images of authority, to make social difference and the assertion of power over others visible by symbolic means.

All these features, however, were contingent on the physical development of the cities themselves. Just as the building of Haussman's boulevards in Paris and the *Ringstrasse* in Vienna were intended to transform those cities into spectacles of motion and monumentality, so the architectural reconstruction of Birmingham, Leeds and Manchester rendered their city centres both an object of awe and a backdrop for bourgeois display.[86] The architecture and the spatial lay-out of the city centres was an integral part of the bourgeois culture of the mid- and later nineteenth century as well as providing the context in which many of the rituals of middle-class life were played out. For these reasons it is to the recreation of the industrial cities in the decades after 1840 that we shall first turn.

Notes

1 J. B. Priestley, *English Journey* (London, 1934), p. 400.
2 The literature on this is voluminous, but for overviews see M. Berg, *The Age of Manufactures, 1700–1820* (London: Fontana, 1985); P. J. Corfield, *The Impact of the English Towns* (Oxford: Oxford University Press, 1982).
3 B. R. Mitchell and P. Deane, *Abstract of British Historical Statistics* (Cambridge: Cambridge University Press, 1962).
4 Cited in A. Redford, *A History of Local Government in Manchester*, vol. 2 (Manchester, 1940), ch. 24.
5 S. Gunn, 'The Manchester middle class, 1850–80' (Ph.D. thesis, Manchester University, 1992), p. 55; E. J. Connell and M. Ward, 'Industrial development, 1780–1914' in D. Fraser (ed.), *History of Modern Leeds* (Manchester: Manchester University Press, 1980), pp. 156–7. While the figures for Manchester and Birmingham were collated on the same basis, those for Leeds were not. The proportions are therefore treated as approximate.
6 Gunn, 'Manchester middle class', pp. 52–83; Connell and Ward, 'Industrial development', pp. 156–7.
7 F. L. Payne, 'The emergence of the large-scale company in Great Britain, 1870–1914', *Economic History Review*, 20 (December 1967), pp. 539–40; C. Shaw, 'The large manufacturing employers of 1907', *Business History*, 25 (1983), pp. 42–59.
8 W. H. Mills, *Sir Charles Macara, Bart.: A Study of Modern Lancashire* (Manhester, 1917), p. 22; T. Anderton, *A Tale of One City: The New Birmingham*

(Birmingham, 1900); A. Bethune Reach, *The Yorkshire Textile Districts in 1849*, ed. C. Aspin (Helmshore Local History Society, 1974), p. 24.

9   D. G. Wright and J. A. Jowitt (eds), *Victorian Bradford* (Bradford: City of Bradford Libraries Division, 1981).

10 These developments are discussed more extensively in ch. 2.

11 T. Wemyss Reid, *A Memoir of John Deakin Heaton* (London, 1883), p. 143.

12 Engels cited in B. I. Coleman, *The Idea of the City in Nineteenth-Century Britain* (London: Routledge, 1973), p. 109; M. Girouard, *The English Town* (New Haven: Yale University Press, 1990), pp. 190–2.

13 R. Fishman, *Bourgeois Utopias: The Rise and Fall of Suburbia* (New York: Basic Books, 1987); D. Cannadine, 'Victorian cities: how different', *Social History*, 2 (1977), pp. 457–87.

14 Coleman, *Idea of the City*, p. 75; J. Seed, ' "Commerce and the liberal arts": the political economy of art in Manchester, 1775–1860' in Wolff and Seed, *The Culture of Capital*; Wemyss Reid, *Memoir*, p. 157.

15 For further discussion of these points from an art historical perspective see C. Arscott, G. Pollock and J. Wolff, 'The partial view: the visual representation of the early nineteenth-century city' in Wolff and Seed, *Culture of Capital*.

16 A. Briggs, 'The background of the parliamentary reform movement in three English cities', *Cambridge Historical Journal*, 10 (1950–52), pp. 293–317; Briggs, *Victorian Cities* (Harmondsworth: Penguin, 1968).

17 C. Behagg, 'Custom, class and change: the trade societies of Birmingham', *Social History*, 4, 3 (October 1979); V. A. C. Gatrell, 'Labour, power and the size of firms in Lancashire cotton in the second quarter of the nineteenth century', *Economic History Review*, 30 (1977); R. Lloyd-Jones and M. J. Lewis, *Manchester and the Age of the Factory* (London: Routledge, 1988).

18 Gunn, 'Manchester middle class', pp. 61–4; R. J. Morris, *Class, Sect and Party. The Making of the British Middle Class: Leeds, 1820–50* (Manchester: Manchester University Press, 1990), pp. 94–101.

19 R. Gray, *The Factory Question and Industrial England 1830–60* (Cambridge: Cambridge University Press, 1996), p. 135.

20 G. Stedman Jones, *Outcast London* (Oxford: Oxford University Press, 1971); P. Joyce, *Work, Society and Politics: The Culture of the Factory in Later Victorian England* (Brighton: Harvester, 1980); R. H. Trainor, *Black Country Elites: The Experience of Authority in an Industrial Area 1830–1900* (Oxford: Oxford University Press, 1993).

21 E. J. Hobsbawm, 'The example of the English middle class' in J. Kocka and A. Mitchell (eds), *Bourgeois Society in Nineteenth-Century Europe* (Oxford: Berg, 1993), p. 133; J. Seed, 'From "middling sort" to middle class in late eighteenth- and early nineteenth-century England' in M. L. Bush (ed.), *Social Orders and Social Classes in Europe Since 1500* (Harlow: Longman, 1993), p. 115.

22 Classic accounts include A. Briggs, *The Age of Improvement* (Harlow:

Longman, 1959); S. G. Checkland, *The Rise of Industrial Society in England 1815–1885* (Harlow: Longman, 1971).

23 L. Davidoff and C. Hall, *Family Fortunes* (London: Hutchinson, 1987).

24 Morris, *Class, Sect and Party*.

25 Key works here include P. J Cain and A. G. Hopkins, *British Imperialism: Innovation and Expansion, 1688–1914* (Harlow: Longman, 1993); W. D. Rubinstein, *Men of Property* (London: Routledge, 1981); M. J. Wiener, *English Culture and the Decline of the Industrial Spirit, 1850–1980* (Cambridge: Cambridge University Press, 1981).

26 D. Wahrman, *Imagining the Middle Class: The Political Representation of Class in Britain c. 1780–1840* (Cambridge: Cambridge University Press, 1995).

27 M. J. Daunton, ' "Gentlemanly capitalism" and British industry, 1820–1914', *Past and Present*, 122 (1989). See also S. Gunn, 'The "failure" of the Victorian middle class: a critique' in Wolff and Seed, *Culture of Capital*, pp. 17–43.

28 They are drawn on extensively, for example by D. Cannadine, *Class in Britain* (New Haven: Yale University Press, 1998), pp. 69–84, and by P. Joyce, *Democratic Subjects: The Self and the Social in Nineteenth-Century England* (Cambridge: Cambridge University Press, 1994), pp. 161–3.

29 G. Crossick, 'From gentlemen to the residuum: languages of social description in Victorian Britain' in P. J. Corfield (ed.), *Language, Class and History* (Cambridge: Cambridge University Press, 1991), p. 158.

30 A. Briggs, 'The language of "class" in early nineteenth-century England' in A. Briggs and J. Saville (eds), *Essays in Labour History* (London: Macmillan, 1960), pp. 52–60; Briggs, *Age of Improvement*, p. 170.

31 Cannadine, *Class in Britain*, p. 121.

32 *The Times*, 5 December 1866; R. Trainor, 'Peers on an industrial frontier' in D. Cannadine (ed.), *Patricians, Power and Politics in Nineteenth-Century Towns* (Leicester: Leicester University Press, 1982), p. 94.

33 Gunn, 'Manchester middle class', p. 23; Joyce, *Democratic Subjects*, p. 166; Morris, *Class, Sect and Party*, p. 12.

34 P. Joyce, *Visions of the People: Industrial England and the Question of Class, 1840–1914* (Cambridge: Cambridge University Press, 1991), ch. 3.

35 R. Barthes, *Mythologies* (London: Paladin, 1973), p. 150.

36 J. Kocka, 'The European pattern and the German case' in Kocka and Mitchell, *Bourgeois Society*, pp. 3–4; Crossick, 'From gentlemen to the residuum', p. 164.

37 J. Garrard, 'Urban elites, 1850–1914: the rule and decline of a new squirearchy?', *Albion*, 27, 3 (1995), p. 586.

38 Davidoff and Hall, *Family Fortunes*, pp. 23–4; Gunn, 'Manchester middle class', p. 93; Morris, *Class, Sect and Party*, pp. 22 and 58.

39 *Parliamentary Papers*, 1861, 1, p. 785.

40 Davidoff and Hall, *Family Fortunes*, pp. 24 and 229–71; Gunn, 'Manchester middle class', pp. 92–4; Morris, *Class, Sect and Party*, pp. 318–31.

41 Gunn, 'Manchester middle class', p. 206.

42 Gunn, 'Manchester middle class', ch. 2; A. Howe, *The Lancashire Textile Masters, 1830–60* (Oxford: Oxford University Press, 1984), ch. 2; Joyce, *Work, Society and Politics*, ch. 1; J. Smail, *The Origins of Middle-Class Culture: Halifax Yorkshire, 1660–1780* (London: Cornell University Press, 1994).

43 Davidoff and Hall, *Family Fortunes*, pp. 234–40 and 289–99; Gunn, 'Manchester middle class', pp. 111–25; G. Kitson Clarke, 'The Leeds elite', *University of Leeds Review*, 17 (1974–75), pp. 235, 242; Trainor, *Black Country Elites*.

44 Gunn, 'Manchester middle class', p. 148; Rubinstein, *Men of Property*, ch. 3.

45 *Parliamentary Papers*, 1863, lvii, p. 593 and 1861, l, p. 785.

46 *Parliamentary Papers*, 1878–79, xlii, p. 255.

47 See, for example, Daunton, '"Gentlemanly" capitalism'; Gunn, ' "Failure" of the middle class'.

48 R. J. Morris, 'The middle class and the property cycle during the industrial revolution' in T. C. Smout (ed.), *The Search for Wealth and Stability* (London: Macmillan, 1979). See also Morris's recent essay, 'Reading the will: cash economy capitalists and urban peasants in the 1830s' in A. J. Kidd and D. Nicholls (eds), *The Making of the British Middle Class? Studies of Regional and Cultural Diversity Since the Eighteenth Century* (Stroud: Sutton, 1998).

49 Joyce, *Work, Society and Politics*, pp. 23–5; Mills, *Sir Charles Macara*, pp. 38–41.

50 P. L. Cottrell, *Industrial Finance 1830–1914* (London: Methuen, 1983), pp. 113–41; *Directory of Directors* (London, 1881).

51 C. Binfield, *So Down to Prayers: Studies in English Nonconformity, 1780–1820* (London: Dent, 1977), p. 73.

52 Gunn, 'Manchester middle class', pp. 241–2.

53 Gunn, ' "Failure" of the middle class'; R. H. Trainor, 'The gentrification of Victorian and Edwardian industrialists' in A. Beier, D. Cannadine and L. Rosenheim (eds), *The First Modern Society* (Cambridge: Cambridge University Press, 1989).

54 W. H. Mills, *Grey Pastures* (London: Chatto and Windus, 1924), p. 95.

55 D. Fraser, *Urban Politics in Victorian England* (Leicester: Leicester University Press, 1976), p. 115; Fraser (ed.), *Municipal Reform and the Industrial City* (Leicester: Leicester University Press, 1982).

56 Davidoff and Hall, *Family Fortunes*, p. 82; Gunn, 'Manchester middle class', p. 259; E. P. Hennock, *Fit and Proper Persons: Ideal and Reality in Nineteenth-Century Urban Government* (London: Edward Arnold, 1973), p. 357.

57 Hennock, *Fit and Proper Persons*, pp. 61–80, 179–230; A. J. Kidd, 'Introduction' in Kidd and K. W. Roberts (eds), *City, Class and Culture: Studies of Social Policy and Cultural Production in Later Victorian Manchester* (Manchester: Manchester University Press, 1985), pp. 13–14.

58 S. Gunn, 'The ministry, the middle class and the "civilising" mission in Manchester, 1850–80', *Social History*, 21, 1 (1996).

59 Crossick, 'From gentlemen to the residuum', pp. 173–4.

60 S. Greg, *A Lecture on the Condition of the Working Classes in the Manufacturing Districts* (Macclesfield, 1857), p. 12; *Report of the Manchester Society of Architects* (Manchester, 1871), p. 6.

61 Cannadine (ed.), *Patricians, Power and Politics*, p. 6; Gunn, 'Manchester middle class', p. 202–9; E. D. Steele, 'Leeds and Victorian politics', *University of Leeds Review*, 17 (1974–75), p. 263.

62 Kocka, 'European pattern', p. 4.

63 W. H. Mills, *The Manchester Reform Club, 1871–1921* (Manchester, 1921), p. 30.

64 C. Arscott, 'Without distinction of party: the Polytechnic Exhibitions in Leeds, 1839–45' in Wolff and Seed, *Culture of Capital*; Morris, *Class, Sect and Party*, ch. 11.

65 P. Bourdieu, *The Field of Cultural Production* (Cambridge: Polity Press, 1993), p. 236.

66 Joyce, *Democratic Subjects*, p. 167; D. Lloyd and P. Thomas, *Culture and the State* (London: Routledge, 1998), pp. 14–15.

67 Binfield, *So Down to Prayers*, ch. 8.

68 P. Anderson, 'Origins of the present crisis', *New Left Review*, 23 (1964), pp. 26–54.

69 Wiener, *English Culture*, chs 2–3. For the wider influence of Wiener's arguments see Cain and Hopkins, *British Imperialism*, ch. 3.

70 For important overviews see the series of works written by Peter Gay under the generic title, *The Bourgeois Experience: Victoria to Freud* (London: Harper Collins, 1984–1998); E. J. Hobsbawm, *The Age of Capital 1848–1875* (London: Weidenfeld and Nicholson, 1975), ch. 13.

71 D. Blackbourn, 'The German bourgeoisie: an introduction' in D. Blackbourn and R. J. Evans (eds), *The German Bourgeoisie* (London: Routledge, 1991), pp. 8–11; J. Kocka, 'The middle classes in Europe', *Journal of Modern History*, 67 (1995), p. 787.

72 R. J. Evans, 'Family and class in the Hamburg grand bourgeoisie, 1815–1914' in Blackbourn and Evans, *German Bourgeoisie*; P. Gay, *The Education of the Senses* (London: Collins, 1984); Hobsbawm, *Age of Capital*, pp. 278–83.

73 Blackbourn, 'German bourgeoisie', pp. 11–12; D. Blackbourn, 'The discreet charm of the bourgeoisie' in D. Blackbourn and G. Eley, *The Peculiarities of German History* (Oxford: Oxford University Press, 1984), pp. 190–205; W. Kaschuba, 'German *Bürgerlichkeit* after 1800: culture as symbolic practice' in Kocka and Mitchell, *Bourgeois Society*, pp. 397–8.

74 Kaschuba, 'German *Bürgerlichkeit*', p. 418.

75 Gunn, 'Manchester middle class', p. 114; Kitson Clarke, 'Leeds elite', p. 243.

76 Girouard, *The English Town*, p. 205; K. Hill, ' "Thoroughly embued with the spirit of ancient Greece": symbolism and space in Victorian civic

culture' in A. J. Kidd and D. Nicholls (eds), *Gender, Civic Culture and Consumerism: Middle-Class Identity in Britain 1800–1940* (Manchester: Manchester University Press, 1999), p. 102.

77 For comments see P. Gay, *Pleasure Wars* (London: Harper Collins, 1998), pp. 75–89.

78 Kaschuba, 'German *Bürgerlichkeit*', p. 398.

79 J. Tosh, *A Man's Place: Masculinity and the Middle-Class Home in Victorian England* (New Haven: Yale University Press, 1999), p. 4.

80 J. Habermas, *The Structural Transformation of the Public Sphere* (Cambridge: Polity Press, 1994), p. 28.

81 G. Eley, 'Nations, publics and political cultures: placing Habermas in the nineteenth century' in C. Calhoun (ed.), *Habermas and the Public Sphere* (Cambridge, Mass.: MIT Press, 1992), p. 298; Joyce, *Democratic Subjects*, pp. 161–76; Morris, *Class, Sect and Party*, chs 7–8.

82 Cited in V. A. C. Gatrell, 'Incorporation and the pursuit of liberal hegemony in Manchester 1790–1830' in Fraser, *Municipal Reform*, p. 48.

83 Briggs, *Victorian Cities*; J. Garrard, *Leadership and Power in Victorian Industrial Towns 1830–1880* (Manchester: Manchester University Press, 1983); Joyce, *Visions of the People*, pp. 182–5; H. E. Meller, *Leisure and the Changing City, 1870–1914* (London: Routledge, 1976).

84 Gunn, 'Manchester middle class', p. 197.

85 R. H. Kargon, *Science in Victorian Manchester* (Manchester: Manchester University Press, 1977), ch. 2; R. J. Morris, 'Middle-class culture, 1700–1914' in Fraser, *History of Modern Leeds*, pp. 219–20.

86 D. J. Olsen, *The City as a Work of Art: London, Paris, Vienna* (New Haven: Yale University Press, 1986); C. Schorske, *Fin de Siècle Vienna* (London: Weidenfeld and Nicholson, 1980).

2

Building the city

Between the 1820s and the 1840s the emerging industrial centres of Birmingham, Manchester and Leeds became the objects of a novel kind of urban tourism. Politicians, writers and well-to-do travellers from Britain, Europe and the United States came to gaze at the awesome prospect of the industrial metropolis as the sign of a new civilisation. Following the dictates of the sublime, it was a prospect which simultaneously excited and disturbed observers. The cities were viewed pre-eminently as the embodiment of the 'factory system', with all its technological marvels and possibilities of wealth. At the same time, they were marked by concentrations of filth and squalor, as well as by degrees of anonymity and social division, which filled sensitive observers with alarm. As Alexis de Tocqueville reflected on Manchester: 'From this foul drain the greatest stream of human industry flows out to fertilise the world; here civilisation works its miracles and civilised man is turned almost back into a savage'.[1] The effort to encapsulate the significance of industrial cities such as Manchester strained the language of contemporaries to its limits. While at one extreme, writers like Carlyle and Disraeli relied on romantic hyperbole, at the other, critics like Engels developed a style of grimly detailed reportage in order to extract meaning from the profusion of sense impressions. As Steven Marcus noted, the industrial metropolis appeared to defy comprehension and expression – it was, literally, 'unspeakable'.[2]

The 1840s are usually taken as the high watermark of contemporary fascination with the industrial city. In his classic study, *Victorian Cities*, Asa Briggs argued that after 1850 attention turned to London as the exemplar of urban modernity. According to D. G. Olsen, 'London offered possibilities of conspicuous self-indulgence and significant display which would have been out of place in an industrial city'.[3] While London clearly occupied centre-stage in debates about urban poverty by the 1880s, such generalisations can obscure as much as illuminate. Firstly, commentators did not cease to visit and observe the industrial cities as the published travelogues of Henry Adams, Nathaniel Hawthorne and Hippolyte Taine in the 1860s and 1870s indicate. But what these commentators observed was significantly different from earlier accounts. The general focus had shifted; the industrial city was no longer seen predominantly as the site of production, but of distribution, exchange and consumption. Writing in 1861, the American Henry Adams described Manchester as 'a collection of enormous warehouses, banks and shops', while the factories had receded to a 'distance varying from one mile to fifty thereabouts'.[4] Secondly, the periodisation adopted from Briggs's account has had the effect of directing historical attention away from the industrial cities at a crucial point in their development. For it was from the 1840s that Birmingham, Leeds and Manchester underwent a radical transformation in urban form and design whose consequences were only recognised in the last decades of the nineteenth century. As a guide to Birmingham put it in 1900:

> If Thomas Attwood or George Frederick Muntz could now revisit the town they once represented in Parliament they would probably stare with amazement at the changes that have taken place in Birmingham, and would require a guide to show them about the town – now a city – they once knew so well. It is no longer 'Brummagem' or the 'Hardware Village', it is now recognised as the centre of activity and influence in Mid-England; it is the Mecca of surrounding populous districts, that attracts an increasing number of pilgrims who love life, pleasure and shopping.[5]

In effect, the full consequences of urban modernity were only registered in English industrial cities in the second half of the nineteenth century. The transformation was at once architectural, spatial, and representational; it involved nothing less than the remaking and reimagining of the city as a whole. As such, it was both an important element of provincial bourgeois culture in its own right and the precondition of many of the activities that served to define this culture in the Victorian period.

Suburbs and centre

In an important tradition of urban studies the outflow of population from the old town centre to suburbs on the fringe has been seen as a principal index of urban 'modernisation'. Key features of this development include the separation of workplace from home and the growing residential and social segregation of different urban groups. The significance of English industrial cities lies in the fact that they were among the first to undergo this process in the early nineteenth century.[6] In London, outflow from the City to the West End was under way in the eighteenth century and the advent of the railways in the 1840s led to the development of suburbs further afield, such as Sydenham and Dulwich. However, large numbers of the wealthy eschewed the suburbs, preferring to remain resident in the West End through the nineteenth century. In Continental metropolises such as Paris and Vienna, high social status was identified with the city centre and seen to decline outwards.[7] Suburbanisation in English industrial cities was therefore a precocious development. It is generally held to have been precipitated from the 1830s by a series of forces: increasing social and industrial conflict, environmental pollution, and escalating property values in the central areas combined with the availability of cheap building land on the rural fringes. The result was the urban configuration classically described by E. W. Burgess and the Chicago School from the 1920s: a central business district surrounded by a zone of factories and worker's housing, with bourgeois suburbs providing an expanding outer ring.[8]

This model of urban form was already apparent in Manchester in the 1840s, as Engels observed, and has subsequently been taken to be typical of most if not all nineteenth-century industrial cities. Thus, a recent historian has described mid-Victorian Leeds as composed of a 'central business district with few permanent inhabitants surrounded by a ring of factories and working-class cottages', with 'burgeoning suburbs' beyond.[9] During the 1970s and 1980s, however, a body of research appeared which questioned the pace and extent of suburbanisation as well as some of the teleological assumptions on which the Chicago School model was premised. In Birmingham, Leeds and Manchester the movement of population from centre to suburbs was protracted and uneven. It was already evident in the 1790s as the wealthiest merchants built or leased mansions in rural locations close to the city. Yet it only appeared as a continuous, inexorable process after 1870, with the expansion of distinct suburban communities such as Headingley and Potternewton in Leeds, and Edgbaston and Moseley in Birmingham.[10] Before the 1870s city centres continued to be socially mixed, only the very richest families possessing the means to move to suburban retreats. Indeed, in a seminal study of Leeds David Ward argued that, with the exception of the very wealthy, the central township became more, not less, socially mixed in the mid-Victorian decades.[11] When suburbanisation did occur it tended to be a stepwise movement, middle-class families progressively shifting to increasingly distant residential locations. In the

process, formerly exclusive suburbs were transformed into socially
variegated neighbourhoods. As the *Manchester City News* observed in
1871: 'The district known as Greenheys will be found to contain as
complete a combination of wealth and poverty, respectability and vice,
as could well be got together in a single suburb'. Insofar as social
segregation existed, it was not solely residential but also temporal, a
product, for instance, of different working hours among manual, white-
collar and employer groups.[12]

Recent studies, therefore, have shown suburbanisation to be a
lengthy and complex process. Yet by continuing to direct critical attention to the impact of suburbanisation they have distracted from the
simultaneous transformation of the city centre, and from the ways in
which it came to represent much of what was distinctively modern in
the industrial city during the mid- and later Victorian period. For the
most part this transformation occurred within the boundaries of the old
central area. In Manchester the commercial district which Engels described in 1840s was almost identical with that defined in guidebooks
fifty years later. The same applied to Birmingham and Leeds; rather
than fragmenting a pre-existing centre, the advent of the railways
consolidated it by concentrating commercial, municipal and retail activities within an area delineated by railway lines, viaducts and stations.[13]
The transformation was therefore one of style and function rather than
of extent. Already by the 1840s more perceptive observers were noting
the novel organisation of the central area. Describing Manchester in
1844, Leon Faucher observed how, despite its 'indifferent combination',
the business district was laid out according to the circulation of capital
and commodities, creating 'an economy of both time and wealth in
production'.[14] The idea of the centre as providentially designed and
self-regulating lent substance to the conception of the modern city as a
system, based on unseen but definite laws akin to those regulating the
economy, the social order and the body.[15] Furthermore, the city centre
became the locus of technical and aesthetic innovation, the place where
new types of building, architectural styles, street lighting and shops
were first open to public view. Increasingly the city was identified with
its major monuments, squares and architectural landmarks, symbolically
representing the new forms of urban modernity. From this perspective,
it was not so much the slow, uneven development of the suburbs that
marked out the industrial city as modern in the second half of the
nineteenth century, as its obverse, the transformation of the central core.

Architecture: monumentalism and morality

Whatever their sources of fascination, England's industrial cities were not distinguished for their architectural appearance in the early Victorian period. For Faucher, Manchester in 1844 was 'devoid of picturesque relief', while a year later Cobden called it the 'shabbiest city in Europe for its wealth'. In 1852 the *Leeds Mercury* admitted that 'as to arrangement', Leeds 'might have had an earthquake for an architect'. Likewise, Pugin described Birmingham as 'the most hateful of all hateful places, a town of Greek buildings, smoky chimneys, low radicalism and dissent'.[16] Yet within a generation such views had dramatically altered. 'Manchester is a more interesting city to walk over than London', the *Building News* commented in 1861. 'One can scarcely walk about Manchester without coming across frequent examples of the *grand* in architecture. There has been nothing to equal it since the building of Venice'. By the 1880s Birmingham was attracting praise nationally for its innovative civic building, making it, according to the London-based *Magazine of Art*, 'perhaps the most artistic town in England'. Leeds, too, drew admiration for the use of brick, tiles and terracotta, creating, in the words of one architectural observer, 'whole streets vibrating with colour'.[17] In each case, the aesthetic remodelling of the city was largely the product of locally-based architects such as Salomons and Worthington in Manchester, Brodrick and Corson in Leeds, Chamberlain and Martin in Birmingham. During the second half of the nineteenth century the provincial cities became major centres of architectural practice. The numbers of architects in Manchester increased from 9 in 1825 to 164 by 1900, and from 23 in 1853 to 59 by 1891 in Leeds.[18]

To contemporary observers the most striking architectural feature of industrial cities was the monumentality of their buildings. As Mark Girouard has noted, throughout the nineteenth century the manufacturing districts evoked images of the sublime, identified with the towering chimneys and massive walls of the mills.[19] But from the 1860s similar ideas were applied to the new buildings of the city centre, warehouses, banks and town halls. In Manchester it was the *palazzo* warehouses, built from the mid-1840s, which gained national attention for their scale and decoration. Lining the major streets of the commercial district the warehouses were represented as 'Babylonian monuments' or palaces, with façades equivalent to 'ornamental and fantastic advertisements'.[20] Their interiors provoked similar images of gigantism and superabundance: the ground floor of the Watts warehouse was 'one vast apartment', the Philips warehouse 'like ten thousand shops rolled into one'.[21] Manchester's warehouses were unique for their size and ambition. But they were matched for architectural fantasy by the Hispano-Moorish Barran's warehouse built in Park Square, Leeds in 1878, and for scale by New Street Station, Birmingham, opened in 1854, whose immense roof was considered one of the 'latter-day wonders of the world'.[22] In all three cities the creation of new public buildings from the 1850s contributed significantly to the monumental effect. Rotundas, used for Brodrick's Corn Exchange at Leeds and the Manchester Royal Exchange, created an effect of 'womb-like immensity', while assize courts built at Manchester and Birmingham used Venetian Gothic to evoke the awful majesty of the law. Above all, there were the town halls whose scale was intended to dwarf other buildings, to enable them to be visible from every direction and thus to dominate the cityscape and skyline.[23]

The rebuilding of the centre was characterised not only by its architectural scale but also by the adoption of novel (or 'neo') styles. While public buildings remained predominantly neo-classical up to the 1860s in Birmingham and Leeds, albeit with ever more elaborate variations, Italian Renaissance epitomised the modern in commercial architecture from the 1840s, most notably evinced in Manchester's warehouses. In each city the turn to Gothic was inaugurated or confirmed by the design of a major public building: Waterhouse's Assize Courts in Manchester in 1859; George Gilbert Scott's General Infirmary at Leeds in 1867; and Edward Holmes's Exchange, opened in 1865, responding to the 'rage' for Italian Gothic which the *Builder* noted in Birmingham in the early 1860s.[24] Under Ruskin's influence, Venetian Gothic flourished over the next two decades, especially in Birmingham where the city's leading architect, J. H. Chamberlain, established it as the official style of the municipal revival. Yet no one style predominated. By the late nineteenth century, city centres were seen, happily or unhappily, as an architectural medley. As a local satirist noted of Birmingham's Corporation Street in 1883: 'Choice, chaste, classic, rustic, gothic, noble, nondescript, confectionery Italian, sublime stucco are here exhibited in well-mixed profusion'.[25]

The appropriation of older architectural styles did not denote nostalgia for the past or a retreat from the modern. On the contrary, Chamberlain's Board Schools and Waterhouse's Manchester Town Hall, like the *palazzo* warehouses, were understood as fundamentally modern in their design, in their use of materials and the incorporation of the latest technical facilities.[26] Nor did the 'battle of the styles' in the provincial industrial context carry with it specific party political overtones.[27] Rather than a conflict between particular architectural styles –

classical, Gothic or Renaissance – the central opposition in the industrial city was between larger representational categories, as Nicholas Taylor has suggested. In the mid- and later Victorian period the city centre came to represent the sublime in its eighteenth century sense, designating vastness, awe and astonishment. This stood in direct contrast to suburban villadom as the embodiment of the picturesque with its intimations of a domesticated rusticity.[28] Thus the central area was defined not simply by its spatial or functional dimensions, but by its identification with monumentalism, modernity and power.

The sublime architecture of the city centre was, in Taylor's phrase, the 'architecture of rhetoric', expressly designed to evoke certain ideas and sentiments in the beholder. An essential part of this rhetoric was moral. For Ruskin, the most influential critic of the mid-Victorian period, architecture in its highest forms was pure morality, and his ideal was widely shared.[29] Public buildings in particular were viewed as a form of moral address. According to Wemyss Reid, editor of the *Leeds Mercury*, the new town hall represented a 'practical admonition to the populace' of the values of art and civic responsibility. For Joseph Chamberlain, the new civic architecture of Birmingham expressed the 'great principles' of a tradition of urban liberty descending from the European Middle Ages.[30] This type of evocation was not restricted to the civic, but extended generally to the architecture of the centre. Thus in Manchester the local press represented the warehouses as 'huge stone guardians watching over the morals and health of the city', and stressed 'the humanising, educating influence of stately edifices on the plastic minds of early youth'.[31] The plethora of symbols and inscriptions on buildings, exalting public and private virtues, made the moral message explicit and visible. Indeed, their frequency in banks, warehouses and exchanges attracted the ire of some architectural critics. Viewing the maxim 'a good name is rather to be chosen than great riches, and loving favour rather than silver and gold', painted on the interior dome of the new Manchester Royal Exchange, the correspondent of *The Builder* was moved to complain in 1874: 'One gets rather tired of this cant of painting up such texts in places of business. Everyone on the floor of the room will be occupied in the pursuit of riches, so what is the point of denying it on the ceiling?'.[32]

Between the 1840s and the 1880s, therefore, the centres of provincial cities were rebuilt on the symbolic principles of monumentalism and morality. Reconstruction was based on a massive investment of capital and labour. Manchester's most spectacular warehouse, that of S. and J. Watts in Portland Street, was financed by profits from the family's drapery firm; the land was purchased for £29,000 in 1855 and the building cost a further £71,000.[33] However, the construction and owner-ship of buildings by individuals or single families appears to have become increasingly rare, given the scale of capital required. The arcades of the later nineteenth century were developed by speculators, backed by the capital of private shareholders. As a Birmingham periodical commented in 1883, 'Those who have money to invest are naturally anxious to place their "all" in such sound stock as local arcades shares must be'.[34] Similarly, 'public' buildings such as Manchester's Free Trade Hall and Royal Exchange were paid for by small groups of wealthy proprietors and run as private companies.[35] By the 1870s municipal authorities, acting on behalf of ratepayers, had become investors in the urban infrastructure on an unprecedented scale. While the Manchester Town Hall cost £859,000, Birmingham's Council House and Art Gallery totalled over £200,000. Between 1869 and 1884 Birmingham's munici-pal debt increased from £588,000 to £7,400,000 as a result of the Corporation's multiple improvement schemes in which urban rebuilding was an important part.[36]

Further evidence of the scale of the building project can be gauged from the rise of rateable values in the industrial cities. Between 1847 and 1882 the rateable value of property in Birmingham increased by 198 per cent, in Leeds by 273 per cent and in Manchester and Salford by 324 per cent. By this latter date the combined boroughs of Man-chester and Salford had the highest gross valuation of any urban area outside London. Land in the centre of Manchester was held to double in value in each generation between the 1830s and the First World War.[37] Where capital led, labour followed. In 1861 building was second only to cotton and silk as a source of male employment in Manchester and Salford, and to toolmaking and tin manufacture in Birmingham; by 1881 it was the largest single category of male employment in Manchester. Similarly, in Leeds the numbers of building workers trebled in the second half of the century, peaking in 1901.[38] In effect, the reconstruction of the industrial city in the mid- and later Victorian period was an enterprise of extraordinary magnitude, whether judged in terms of capital, labour or design. It was not simply a by-product of industrialisation, but a major economic project in its own right.

Cleansing the city

However, there was always another dimension to this project. The creation of the 'moral city' implied not only architectural renovation and improvement, but also the effort to cleanse the city of elements considered impure, contagious or dangerous. Moral, sanitary and social prescriptions were conflated in the drive to render the city centre an uninhabited, sanitised space, enabling the visual power of buildings and monuments, squares and widened streets to achieve its full effect.

A significant aspect of the spatial reorganisation of industrial cities between the 1840s and the 1860s was the displacement of disciplinary and remedial institutions from the centre to the urban fringe. As ever, Manchester was to the forefront in such developments. Between 1836 and 1866, new buildings were provided for the workhouse, asylums, courts and gaols, outside the old township in nearby districts such as Crumpsall, Strangeways and Old Trafford. Elsewhere the same tendencies were apparent from the later 1840s. In Birmingham, the borough gaol and lunatic asylum were relocated at Birmingham Heath in 1849–50; in Leeds, Armley gaol was built in 1847, while the workhouse and moral and industrial training school were established on a single site at Burmantofts between 1848 and 1861.[39]

Rising land values in the centre were an important reason behind this shift. As J. W. R. Whitehand has emphasised, during building booms those uses in which land was a relatively small proportion of the total cost, such as warehouses, commanded the most valuable sites in the central district. Where land was a significant proportion of the total cost, as in the case of hospitals or prisons, the tendency was for such institutions to be relocated to cheaper sites on the urban periphery.[40] In the mid-nineteenth century the forces of the building boom conjoined with moral imperatives. By the 1860s reforming institutions came to represent a sanitary cordon around the city centre and workers' districts, isolating the inmates from the mass of the urban population while simultaneously standing as a warning of the dangers of behavioural transgression. The size and architectural design of such institutions, and their frequent high degree of visibility, made them important symbols of moral authority. From its location on a hill above Leeds township, R. J. Morris has noted, Armley gaol 'used the image of the medieval castle for an aggressive statement to terrify the captive and assure the strong of their safety'. Nor did the symbolic connection between the improving institutions of the centre – libraries, museums and mechanics' institutes – and the disciplinary institutions on the periphery escape the notice of contemporary observers. As a visitor to Manchester's public library in King Street speculated in 1872: 'The kind friend who accompanied me [to the library] subsequently drove me to the Assize Courts – from a building calculated to prevent crime to a palace devoted to its punishment. What is the bearing of the former on the latter?'. In the nineteenth-century city, Tony Bennett has observed, the museum and the penitentiary represented the 'Janus face of power', an opposition underlined by the distinct spatial locations of improving and disciplinary institutions.[41]

The removal of the sick and the criminal paved the way for a thoroughgoing cleansing of the central areas. Again, moral and sanitary priorities were in harmony. The filth of streets in the industrial cities was widely noted in the 1840s and 1850s. At the visit of Prince Albert to Birmingham in 1855, the *Builder* observed that 'every place on that occasion was positively flooded with liquid slimy mud'.[42] The incidence of cholera in 1832 and 1848–49, and the investigations into public health that ensued, prompted the introduction of sewerage and the cleaning and drainage of streets that became a central feature of the various improvements acts passed in Birmingham, Leeds and Manchester from the 1840s.[43] The sanitary concerns that stimulated interventionist measures were part of a larger conception of the city as a social 'body', promoted by medical and social investigators, especially in Manchester and Leeds. In this anatomical perspective, 'deformations' in the life of the city necessitated identification and treatment in much the same way as diseases of the human body required diagnosis and cure.[44] The anatomical view also promoted the idea that the sources of disease and deformation lay hidden in the courts, cellars and slums of the city centre. A principal aim of sanitary and social investigation, therefore, was to make these secret places visible, open to public and official view. Thus the Leeds reformer James Hole described the cholera reports of Robert Baker as 'revelations', and linked the state of working-class housing directly to the health and morals of the town.[45]

This conflation of moral and sanitary priorities enabled the rhetoric of improvement to become a flexible instrument of urban policy. It was possible to extend medical analogies to the level of urban design, to move from the cleansing of dirt and disease to the dispersal of the populations most associated with these problems, the urban poor who remained clustered in the slums of the city centre. Complaints of the presence of the 'Jew element', 'street arabs' and musicians in public places were persistent in the columns of the local press. 'There is no excuse for allowing organ and piano beggars to take their instruments of torture into the busiest thoroughfares of the town, nor is there any excuse for allowing them to dodge the police as they do', a Birmingham journal protested in 1884. Consequently, police activity from the 1860s was increasingly directed to clearing the main streets of undesirable elements associated with poverty and the poor.[46]

But the most radical aspect of the cleansing of the city centre were the programmes of demolition and slum clearance carried out under the name of improvement from the 1850s. In Manchester it was estimated that thirteen thousand people had been displaced from Market Street, London Road and Deansgate by street widening and rebuilding in the 1860s. In Birmingham, some forty acres of slums were demolished under the improvement scheme of 1875, forcing out an estimated nine thousand people; in Leeds the building of Kirkgate Market in the 1870s rendered almost two thousand people homeless.[47] These were only stark instances of a sustained process by which the urban poor were driven from the city centre. Given the very limited efforts at constructing municipal housing in any of the three cities before 1914 – Leeds council provided housing for only 906 people displaced before 1900, for instance, while in Birmingham the new housing promised under the 1875 Act remained unbuilt – the short-term result was merely to exacerbate the situation.[48] A Manchester journal commented in 1870: 'As the tide of street improvement advances, we are apt to congratulate ourselves upon the annihilation of this or that rookery of crime, without troubling ourselves to consider what must become of the unhoused tenants. They, on their part, from sheer necessity huddle closer and closer together in the only hovels available, and thus over-crowded districts become gorged with a redundant and uncleanly population'.[49]

Nevertheless, the outflow of population from the city centre was a marked feature of the later nineteenth century. The central wards of Birmingham declined steadily from the 1860s. Some areas of central Manchester had been losing population from as early as the 1820s, but after the mid-century it became a torrent; between 1861 and 1881 the numbers resident in Market Street and Deansgate halved. In Leeds the effect was registered later, the population of the township declining only from 1891. But thereafter it was dramatic, a recent historian calculating an out-migration of forty thousand people between 1891 and 1911.[50] Such figures tend to underestimate the pace and scale of the exodus, since the township was normally more extensive than the central business district, as in Leeds, incorporating substantial areas of worker's housing on the central fringe. But in all cases, the movement was outwards, enabling the creation of a monumental, depopulated centre, an empty space at the heart of the city by night.

While the language of moral and sanitary reform was invoked as justification for the cleansing of the city from the 1830s, commercial development in the form of railways, warehouses and retail shops exerted its own continuous pressure. 'The exigencies of commerce have done more to sweep away the old fever dens of Manchester than could have been accomplished by any of the requirements of sanitary legislation', the city's Medical Officer of Health sardonically remarked in 1876.[51] Together with the imperative to cleanse and sanitise the city went the drive to create new and widened streets. Following the improvement acts of the 1840s, the Manchester Statistical Society estimated in 1862 that sixty miles of the city's streets had been paved and drained.[52] The widening of Deansgate, like the creation of Corporation Street in Birmingham and the renovation of Boar Lane in Leeds, were major municipal projects of the later nineteenth century, in the first two cases taking more than two decades to complete. Such streets became emblematic of civic pride as well as a source of satire: 'New York's a fine city, but it don't come up to Birmingham. Broadway is elegant, but it don't level up to Corporation Street. This latter may be slightly crooked, somewhat hump-backed, and kind o' expensive, but it's a fine boulevard'.[53]

As this implies, street-building and widening had several purposes. It was seen as 'ventilating' the city by providing open spaces in the densely built environment, and by facilitating the circulation of traffic. Straight, wide boulevards gave a pattern of regularity to the central area and a sense of grandeur, enabling buildings and monuments to be visible from a distance. With the railways, they served to define the boundaries of the city centre and, as Engels noted, to contain the workers' and slum districts which bordered it. Frequently combined with slum clearance, new and renovated streets became synonymous with urban improvement by the 1870s. Birmingham's municipal 'revolution' of the 1870s and 1880s was measured in terms of the 'care and attention [paid] to our streets, miles of which have been paved'.[54] The possession of one or more 'grand boulevards' became an essential part of the claim to metropolitan status. In 1866 the *Leeds Mercury* argued that the widening of Boar Lane would make a 'wide and handsome and imposing street, worthy of the wealth of the inhabitants, [and] of the metropolitan character of the borough'; in the 1890s Park Row was styled the 'Pall Mall of Leeds'. By 1900 Birmingham's Corporation Street was seen to 'compare favourably with any thoroughfare in any other British city', and to confirm the city's status as the 'Metropolis of the Midlands'. Similarly, the progressive rebuilding of Manchester's Market Street enabled it to be viewed as rivalling London's West End for the 'living panorama' it presented.[55] New and widened streets lent glamour to the industrial city; they covered over and completed the cleansing of the city that was the other face of urban improvement.

Consumption and specialisation

An important consequence of renovation was to recreate streets as sites of consumption and display. For Richard Sennett, the construction of London's Regent Street as a prime shopping location in the 1820s was 'an epochal event in urban design', privileging motion over assembly, the individual moving body over the organised crowd.[56] The building of streets with wide pavements and regular frontages facilitated the emergence of the shopper, the promenader and the 'street philosopher' as distinct urban types. 'The streets are to me one vast museum', a Leeds observer attested in the 1880s, 'a museum far more interesting than any collection'.[57] By the 1870s distinct 'shopping districts' had emerged in the provincial cities, based on new and rebuilt streets, and acting as a consumerist cynosure for the region. A Birmingham guide commented in 1900:

> At one time residents in the adjoining counties looked down upon Birmingham shopkeepers, and would say rather contemptuously that they never 'shopped' in this city, but went to Leamington, Cheltenham, or London to make their purchases. But we do not hear so much of this now. On the contrary, I have heard of people – even aristocratic people – who actually say that they now, for many reasons, prefer to 'shop' in Birmingham rather than go to London.

In similar vein, a guide to Leeds proudly asserted in 1909:

> No city in England can boast a more wonderful transformation than that witnessed in Leeds during the past two or three decades. The centre of Leeds has been practically re-carved and polished. Nearly the whole of the ramshackle property that skirted the east side of Briggate has been demolished, and on the site has been erected a class of shop property that would do credit to any city in the country. For some time past there seems to have been a wholesome rivalry among the owners of shop property in Commercial Street to remodel their premises on the most up-to-date and withal artistic lines.[58]

A major attraction was the new types of shopping environment. The department stores were pioneered in English provincial cities from the 1830s; Kendal Milnes, for example, was established in Manchester in

1836, before the development of the Paris or London stores. By the 1880s other department stores included Lewis's in Manchester and Birmingham, and Marshall and Snelgrove in Leeds.[59] The last quarter of the nineteenth century also saw the spread of arcades, offering the shopper a 'lofty, elegant, well-lighted promenade', enclosed from the 'out-door nuisances' of the street. Such was the vogue for arcades in Birmingham in the 1880s that a local periodical ironically proposed roofing the entire central area and re-naming the city 'Arcadia'.[60]

Stores and arcades made for a wholly new and quintessentially modern experience of shopping. In their studies of London, Judith Walkowitz and Mica Nava have emphasised the particular importance of department stores for women, creating a public space in the centre of the city where women could meet and browse without the social pressures of the street or the obligation to buy.[61] The sense of liberation and excitement of the department store is evoked in the description of visiting Lewis's in Margaret Penn's autobiographical novel, *Manchester Fourteen Miles*: 'It was so big and, no matter what time she went there, always full of people moving up and down the aisles or buying at the many counters. Being in Lewis's was nearly as exciting as being in Market Street itself. There were almost as many people in the shop as in the street'.[62] With its elaborate interiors and carefully staged lighting, the department store epitomised modernity in forms that were accessible to all sections of the well-to-do and respectable classes. The new sense of democratised luxury was satirised in an account of a Brummagem man, recently returned from the United States, confronted with the lavish interior of a Birmingham store. '"How good on yer", I continued, 'to have all these gorgeous dickorations and these superb electrick lights, and to charge yer customers nothink for 'em, but pay for 'em all out of your private puss. It's nobil, it's sublime", I said, and I wep'.[63]

The installation of single-pane windows in larger stores by the 1870s and of electric lighting in the 1880s, did much to enhance the allure of shops and to promote the activity of window-shopping. The 'chief delight' of Leeds, a local reporter asserted, was the 'study of shop windows': 'I stand and gaze and speculate, weaving all kinds of strange romances out of the often remarkably prosaic articles of food and wearing apparel which are displayed before me'.[64] As an activity, shopping was constituted as a form of entertainment, an idea given physical form in the layout of the new spaces of consumption. In Leeds, for example, the Grand Theatre, opened in 1878, was combined with shops and an assembly room, while the Empire Palace music hall formed part of the County Arcade complex designed by the theatre architect, Frank

Matcham, in the 1890s.[65] Within the shopping district, restaurants, coffee houses and hotels proliferated, replacing the tavern or inn, a trend lamented by an older generation of habitués. 'We have clubs now and restaurants, also hotels. The present generation of prosperous well-to-do men, too, are of a different stamp from their predecessors. They do not take their ease at the inns of their fathers. They have been educated differently, and take their pleasures in a more refined way, as is the fashion of the time'.[66]

Consumption itself formed part of the 'radical discrimination of function' which Steven Marcus has viewed as integral to the modernity of the Victorian industrial city.[67] In Birmingham, Leeds and Manchester the 'shopping district' was located in streets close to the railway station. Within this district, shops of particular types were clustered together. 'One thing that engaged our attention in Market Street was the multiplicity of people in the same business', a Manchester reporter commented in 1877; 'there is scarcely one tradesman that has not a number of rivals'.[68] This principle was seen to operate more widely. Noting the large number of churches and chapels in All Saints, Manchester, in the 1860s an 'urban rambler' was led to wonder: 'Does the spirit of opposition, emulation and competition enter into the elements of religious worship and animate the various denominational bodies, as it does the professions of the law or medicine, or trades or theatres, and even taverns, most of which are generally to be found congregating in the same district?'.[69] Thus by the 1860s it was becoming common to see the city centre as composed of a series of functionally distinct zones: the warehouse district, the shopping district, streets defined by particular occupations and professional activities. A disaggregated view of the city centre was developing based on the idea of a multiplicity of different functional and social spaces.

Dignifying and romancing the city

The attempt from the 1860s to create new civic spaces was both a part of, and a response to, the perception of the city centre as increasingly fragmented. On the one hand, civic spaces created a further distinct area, the 'official city', defined by squares, monuments and statues, separate and aloof from the commercial bustle. On the other, such spaces represented the attempt to impose a symbolic identity that would stand for the city as a whole and unify its disparate parts. Given contemporary reliance on anatomical metaphors for the city, linking it to the human body, the construction of squares was seen as necessary to urban health, as 'lungs' ventilating an increasingly congested centre. But of equal importance after the mid-century were the calls for the construction of dignified central places that would compliment the monumental architecture and create the requisite impression of metropolitan grandeur. In Leeds, Victoria Square in front of the Town Hall was regarded as little more than a pavement and there were persistent demands to enlarge it to create an open space with fountains and monuments. The same complaint was widely voiced in Manchester in the 1870s: 'Practically, we have no single square or open space worthy of the name'.[70]

Efforts had been made to develop such spaces in the first half of the nineteenth century in all three cities. William Fairbairn's grandiose vision for the redesign of Manchester's Piccadilly in 1836 was especially notable, combining widened streets, imposing statuary and a miniature lake in front of the colonnaded façade of the Infirmary. However, little significant was achieved in Birmingham, Leeds or Manchester before the 1870s. Despite improvements to Piccadilly in the 1850s, including an esplanade and statues of Peel, Wellington, Dalton and Watt, it remained a 'wilderness', the haunt of beggars and 'loungers of the poorer class'.[71] Instead, from the 1860s Manchester's civic centre was developed away from traffic and the commercial area in Albert Square. Here in the shadow of the new Town Hall it was possible to construct what the *Builder* termed a dignified 'architectural centre', complete with the Albert Memorial and statues of other departed Liberal heroes such as Gladstone, Bright, and Oliver Heywood.[72] The major civic square of Birmingham, Chamberlain Place, was likewise constructed around the Council House and municipal buildings in the 1880s. With shrines to Joseph Chamberlain, George Dawson and Josiah Mason, the whole site was a monument to the city's municipal revival, simultaneously celebrating and memorialising it in stone.[73] In Leeds the creation of an appropriate civic space was not initiated till 1896 and was developed away from the Town Hall, close to Wellington Station. Civic pretensions were underlined, however, by its designation as City Square, and by the placing of a massive statue of the Black Prince at its centre. According to the chief proponent of the scheme, Colonel Harding, 'so large a space seemed to require a monument of heroic proportions to lend dignity to the Square', while the Black Prince was acclaimed, altogether dubiously, as a representative symbol of Leeds, of popular democracy, commerce and the woollen trade.[74]

The construction of civic spaces contributed to the development of the 'official city' in the later nineteenth century, identified with municipal authority and an ebullient politico-historical iconography. Memorials,

statues, public clocks and older public buildings were all appropriated
to the cause, taking their place in the symbolic repertoire of civic pride.
In Manchester it was proposed in the 1870s that the Infirmary in
Piccadilly should be emptied of its patients and turned into a civic
monument: 'with its cupola and quartet of clock dials, [the Infirmary]
would stand as of old, the patriarchal dignity intact, a permanent
memorial to the benevolence of our forefathers'.[75] Most important in
carving out a dignified official zone was the creation of a specific
civic–cultural complex in the city centre. The classic example of this
mixture of municipal, cultural and educational institutions was Birmingham's Chamberlain Square, incorporating the classical Town Hall,
Council House, Art Gallery, Museum, School of Art and Free Library,
together with the massive Gothic façade of Mason College. This clus-
tering of public institutions was viewed as a special source of civic
distinction as a local guide emphasised in 1902:

> One feature of interest distinguishes Birmingham from most other cities,
> and that is the fact that nearly all the important public buildings are
> situated close to one another in the centre of the city. The Council House,
> the Town Hall, the University, the Free Library, are all within a stone's
> throw of one another, and this part of the city certainly has a stately and
> imposing appearance.[76]

Birmingham, however, was not unique. A similar complex, albeit on
more modest lines, was established in Leeds from the 1880s, the
Municipal Buildings, housing the Central Library and Art Gallery,
standing next to the Town Hall, with Corson's new School Board
building alongside. Civic squares and complexes were rapidly established
as the symbolic centre of the city, a consequence less of their spatial
location than of their identification with municipal authority and civic
power. As such, they became the natural focus of all types of civic
occasion and political demonstration in the late nineteenth and early
twentieth centuries.[77]

The creation of civic spaces was significant in the recasting of the
industrial city as a spectacle in the later Victorian period. In the early
nineteenth century, industry, epitomised by the landscape of factory
chimneys, was the focus of romantic representations of cities like Manchester, Leeds and Birmingham.[78] From the 1860s onwards, however, it
was the city centre, effectively stripped of industrial connotations, which
was viewed as romantic, especially at night. While dusk and night-time
were regarded anxiously in the 1840s as times of physical and moral
danger in the city, by the 1870s nocturnal Manchester was frequently

represented in more benign and quixotic terms. On 'calm, clear, moonlit nights the busy Lancashire capital becomes wondrously transfigured and beautified', an observer noted in 1876; the shadows cast by the Town Hall and major public buildings evoked 'grand old Venice itself', while the warehouses suggested 'the deserted temples of a forgotten hierarchy'.[79] The newly created civic buildings and squares, in particular, were integral to representations of the night-time city, allowing the familiar to be made strange and mysterious. The local literary and satirical press specialised in stories with a large element of gothic fantasy, in which civic statuary was imagined to come alive against the backdrop of the town hall, 'like some unquiet spirit flitting guiltily in the dead of night through the former haunts of its mortality'.[80]

The extension of street and shop lighting after the mid-century contributed to the romantic image of the city centre, as well as making it safer for night-time walking. Civic buildings were illuminated on special occasions, and routinely from the 1890s. The central streets, too, were transformed after dusk by the exotic effect of different types of lighting: 'To see Boar Lane, wait until dusk, until the street glows with a blaze of myriad lights, amethyst, ruby, emerald and gold. If we can divest ourselves of the idea that this is Leeds, that the jewels are tram-lamps and gaslights, and that the palaces are only shops, we might easily imagine ourselves – well, elsewhere'.[81] By gaslight even poverty could be construed as 'picaresque' to the well-to-do nightwalker seeking vicarious amusement.[82] This emphasis on the fantasy and theatricality of the city centre was conveyed primarily through the local press, but also in paintings such as those of Atkinson Grimshaw and Adolphe Vallette which showed an equal concern with the city at dusk or at night. The cumulative effect of such representations was to project the cityscape as a giant stage-set, with a force and vitality of its own. Emptied of population save the lone walker, and a residual urban poor viewed alternately as vicious or quaint, the nocturnal city became mythological, both the object of speculation and a spectacle in its own right.[83]

Between 1840 and 1900, therefore, the industrial cities underwent a series of multiple, interlocking changes which radically affected their architectural and spatial forms, and the ways in which they were discursively represented. This did not happen at the same pace in Birmingham, Leeds and Manchester, but the trends were nevertheless in the same direction. The city centre was progressively emptied of population and recreated as a monumental, moral and aesthetic space and a site of consumption and spectacle. All these aspects contributed to the idea of the city centre as the locus of a new kind of urban modernity, defined by the types of experience it offered and by its spatial and representational distinctness from suburbia.

The transformation of Birmingham, Leeds and Manchester was the product of the most powerful agencies in the mid- and later nineteenth-century city, both 'private' in the form of major industrial, commercial and financial firms, and 'public' in the form of the municipal authorities, acting on behalf of the propertied ratepayers. It was these agencies that made the substantial capital investment on which the transformation of the city centre was predicated. Moreover, that transformation was enacted upon the poorest and least organised sections of the city's population. In the industrial cities the twin faces of reconstruction, cleansing and improvement, were phrased in terms of moral categories which were also ineluctably social.

Reflecting on the history of urban form, Richard Sennett has remarked that 'the space of authority, in Western culture, is a space of precision'. In modern cities, 'the secular space of authority is empty'. Emptiness within the city is identified with authority and with safety: 'Safe because empty; safe because clearly marked'.[84] The cleansing and emptying of the industrial city in the second half of the nineteenth century, together with the construction of monumental buildings and distinct functional spaces, represented the attempt to order the modern city in ways that sought to embody and envision the concepts of precision, authority and security. It recreated the city centre as a stage-set, a place where authority and identities of class and gender could be performed and tested.

The description of the architectural and spatial layout of the city centres, however, only provides an approximate and abstract guide to how the new spaces were understood by contemporaries. In the next chapter, therefore, I shall examine in greater detail how the centre was perceived and used, how identities of class and gender were fashioned and classified, and the means by which middle-class identity, in particular, was asserted in the fluid conditions of the city streets.

Notes

1   A. de Tocqueville, *Journeys to England and Ireland*, ed. J. P. Mayer (New York: Anchor Books, [1835] 1968), p. 96.

2   S. Marcus, *Engels, Manchester and the Working Class* (London: Weidenfeld and Nicholson, 1974), p. 181.

3   A. Briggs, *Victorian Cities* (Harmondsworth: Penguin, 1968), ch. 8; D. G. Olsen, *The City as Work of Art: London, Paris, Vienna* (New Haven: Yale University Press, 1986), p. 6.

4   H. Adams cited in H. Silver, *Manchester Men and Indian Cotton 1842–72* (Manchester: Manchester University Press, 1966), p. 5. See also N. Hawthorne, *Passages from the English Notebooks of Nathaniel Hawthorne* (London, 1870); H. Taine, *Notes on England* (London, 1872).

5   T. Anderton, *A Tale of One City: The New Birmingham* (Birmingham, 1900), pp. 1–2.

6   D. Cannadine, 'Victorian cities: how different?', *Social History*, 2 (1977), pp. 457–87; R.Fishman, *Bourgeois Utopias: The Rise and Fall of Suburbia* (New York: Basic Books, 1987); F. M. L. Thompson (ed.), *The Rise of Suburbia* (Leicester: Leicester University Press, 1982).

7   M. D. George, *London Life in the Eighteenth Century* (Harmondsworth: Penguin, 1966), p. 104; D. G. Olsen, *The Growth of Victorian London* (London: Batsford, 1976), pp. 120, 239–40; C. Schorske, *Fin-de-Siècle Vienna* (London: Weidenfeld and Nicholson, 1980), ch. 2.

8   Fishman, *Bourgeois Utopias*, ch. 3; E. W. Burgess, 'The growth of the city' in R. Park *et al.* (eds), *The City* (Chicago: Chicago University Press, 1967).

9   C. Morgan, 'Demographic change, 1771–1911' in D. Fraser (ed.), *A History of Modern Leeds* (Manchester: Manchester University Press, 1980), p. 61. For Birmingham see D. Cannadine, *Lords and Landlords: The Aristocracy and the Towns, 1774–1967* (Leicester: Leicester University Press, 1980).

10 For comment and statistics on the development of these suburbs see C. Treen, 'The process of suburban development in north Leeds, 1870–1914' in Thompson, *Rise of Suburbia*; A. Briggs, *The History of Birmingham: Borough and City, 1865–1938* (London: Oxford University Press, 1952).

11 D. Ward, 'Environs and neighbours in the "two nations": residential differentiation in mid-nineteenth century Leeds', *Journal of Historical Geography*, 6, 2 (1980), pp. 133–62.

12 S. Gunn, 'The Manchester middle class, 1850–80' (Ph.D. thesis, Manchester University, 1992), ch. 4; 'Round about Manchester', *Manchester City News*, 18 November 1871; R. Dennis, *English Industrial Cities in the Nineteenth Century* (Cambridge: Cambridge University Press, 1984), p. 77.

13 F. Engels, *The Condition of the Working Class in England in 1844* (London: Granada, [1844] 1969), p. 46; J. Mortimer, *Mercantile Manchester Past and Present* (Manchester, 1896), p. 78; J. Kellett, *The Impact of Railways on Victorian Cities* (London: Routledge, 1969); R. Unwin, 'Leeds becomes a transport centre' in Fraser, *History of Leeds*, pp. 133–5.

14 L. Faucher, *Manchester in 1844* (London, 1844), pp. 17–18.

15 G. Davison, 'The city as a natural system: theories of urban society in early nineteenth-century Britain' in D. Fraser and A. Sutcliffe (eds), *The Pursuit of Urban History* (London: Edward Arnold, 1983).

16 Faucher, *Manchester in 1844*, p. 16; Mortimer, *Mercantile Manchester*, p. 73; *Leeds Mercury*, 25 September 1852; M. Brooks, *John Ruskin and Victorian Architecture* (London: Thames and Hudson, 1989), p. 235.

17 C. Stewart, *The Stones of Manchester* (London: Edward Arnold, 1956), p. 13;

     A. St Johnston, 'The progress of art in Birmingham', *The Magazine of Art* (1887); *The Builder*, vol. xx (1862), p. 623; *Royal Institute of British Architects Journal*, 3 (1896), p. 365.

18 J. Archer, 'Introduction' in Archer (ed.), *Art and Architecture in Victorian Manchester* (Manchester: Manchester University Press, 1985), pp. 6, 8; D. Linstrum, *West Yorkshire Architects and Architecture* (London: Lund Humphries, 1978), pp. 35, 42.

19 M. Girouard, *The English Town* (New Haven: Yale University Press, 1990), p. 251.

20 'Adrift in Manchester', *Manchester City News*, 3 February 1872; *The Builder*, vol. xviii (1860), p. 643.

21 'In a Manchester warehouse', *Freelance*, 15 April 1867; 'Adrift in Manchester'.

22 Linstrum, *West Yorkshire Architects*, p. 306; *Allday's Gossiping Guide to Birmingham* (Birmingham, 1893), p. 36.

23 N. Taylor, 'The awful sublimity of the Victorian city' in H. Dyos and M. Wolff, *The Victorian City*, vol. 2 (London: Routledge, 1973), pp. 437, 442–3; Girouard, *The English Town*, pp. 210–11.

24 Archer, 'Introduction', pp. 18–20; S. T. Anning, *The General Infirmary at Leeds* (London: E. and S. Livingstone, 1963), p. 23; *Birmingham Daily Post*, 3 January 1865; Brooks, *John Ruskin*, p. 238.

25 R. Hartnell, *Pre-Raphaelite Birmingham* (Studley: Brewin Books, 1996), pp. 57–60; 'Our architects', *Town Crier*, August 1883.

26 Brooks, *John Ruskin*, pp. 246–8; J. Archer, 'A classic of its age' in Archer, *Art and Architecture*, p. 147.

27 K. Hill, '"Thoroughly embued with the spirit of ancient Greece": symbolism and space in Victorian civic culture' in A. J. Kidd and D. Nicholls (eds), *Gender, Civic Culture and Consumerism: Middle-Class Identity in Britain 1800–1940* (Manchester: Manchester University Press, 1999).

28 Taylor, 'The awful sublimity', pp. 431–47.

29 Taylor, 'The awful sublimity', p. 444. Ruskin's views on architecture and morality were expressed in his lecture in Bradford in 1863, reprinted as 'Traffic' in *The Crown of Wild Olives* (London, 1866).

30 T. Wemyss Reid, *A Memoir of John Deakin Heaton* (London, 1883), p. 142; C. W. Boyd, *Mr Chamberlain's Speeches* (London, 1914), pp. 41–2.

31 'Adrift in Manchester'; 'Manchester in its transition state', *Freelance*, 19 September 1873.

32 *The Builder*, vol. xxxii (1874), p. 889.

33 'S. and J. Watts and Co.', *Manchester City News*, 4 and 11 March 1865.

34 'Happy "Arcadia"', *Town Crier*, November 1883.

35 *The Builder*, vol. xiv (1856), p. 526; D. Farnie, 'An index of commercial activity: the membership of the Manchester Royal Exchange, 1809–1948', *Business History*, 21 (1979), p. 100.

36 Archer, 'A classic of its age', p. 145; J. T. Bunce, *History of the Corporation of Birmingham*, vol. 2 (Birmingham, 1885), pp. xxxvii and 548–50.

37 *Parliamentary Papers*, vol. lvi (1886), pp. 377–8.; F. Moss, *Pilgrimages*, vol. 6 (Manchester, 1913), p. 210.

38 Gunn, 'The Manchester middle class', pp. 56–7; E. J. Connell and M. Ward, 'Industrial development, 1780–1914' in Fraser, *History of Modern Leeds*, pp. 156–7.

39 The movement of these institutions can be charted using contemporary ordnance survey maps and guide books to the respective cities.

40 J. W. R. Whitehand, *The Changing Face of Cities: A Study of Development Cycles and Urban Form* (Oxford: Oxford University Press, 1987), chs 2–3.

41 R. J. Morris, 'Middle-class culture, 1700–1914' in Fraser, *History*; 'Adrift in Manchester'; T. Bennett, 'The disciplinary complex' in N. Dirks, G. Eley and S. Ortner (eds), *Culture/Power/History* (Princeton: Princeton University Press, 1995), p. 151.

42 'Birmingham and its progress', *The Builder*, vol. xxi (1855), p. 587.

43 For details see Bunce, *History of the Corporation of Birmingham*, vol. 2, p. xxx; S. Burt and K. Grady, *The Illustrated History of Leeds* (Derby: Breedon Books, 1994), pp. 162–4; A. Redford, *A History of Local Government in Manchester*, vol. 2 (Manchester, 1940), ch. 17.

44 M. Poovey, *Making a Social Body: British Cultural Formation, 1830–1864* (Chicago: Chicago University Press, 1995), chs 3 and 4.

45 J. Hole, *The Homes of the Working Classes* (Leeds, 1866), p. 123.

46 'A "row"-dy place', *Town Crier*, December 1884. For similar comments in Leeds see 'In Commercial Street', *Yorkshire Busy Bee*, 27 August 1881.

47 H. Baker, 'On the growth of the commercial centre of Manchester', *Transactions of the Manchester Statistical Society* (1872), pp. 87–101; G. Cherry, *Birmingham: A Study in Geography, History and Planning* (Chichester: John Wiley, 1994), p. 72; B. J. Barber, 'Aspects of municipal government, 1835–1914' in Fraser, *History of Modern Leeds*, p. 309.

48 Barber, 'Municipal government', p. 315; Briggs, *Victorian Cities*, p. 228. On municipal housing in Manchester see M. Harrison, 'Housing and town planning in Manchester before 1914' in A. Sutcliffe, *British Town Planning: The Formative Years* (Leicester: Leicester University Press, 1981).

49 'Manchester slums', *Freelance*, 12 March 1870.

50 Cherry, *Birmingham*, p. 67; Dennis, *English Industrial Cities*, pp. 69 and 87; Morgan, 'Demographic Change', in Fraser, *History*, pp. 52 and 56.

51 Cited in Stewart, *Stones of Manchester*, p. 115.

52 T. S. Ashton, *Economic and Social Investigations in Manchester, 1833–1933* (London, 1934), ch. 4.

53 'Alderman Chamberlain across the "pond"', *Town Crier*, June 1883.

54 'A general epistle to the Brums', *Town Crier*, January 1883.

55 *Leeds Mercury*, 16 October 1866; *The Builder*, vol. liv (1896), p. 510; Anderton, *Tale of One City*, p. 121; *Cornish's Strangers Guide Through Birmingham* (Birmingham, 1902), pp. 4 and 18; 'A walk down Market Street', *Comus*, 13 December 1877.

56 R. Sennett, *Flesh and Stone: The Body and the City in Western Civilisation* (London: Faber, 1994), p. 328.

57 'Leeds shop windows', *Yorkshire Busy Bee*, 10 December 1881.

58 Anderton, *Tale of One City*, p. 29; Anon., *Shopping In Leeds* (Leeds, 1909), p. 27.

59 A. Adburgham, *Shops and Shopping, 1800–1914* (London: Allen and Unwin, 1981), p. 138. See also W. Lancaster, *The Department Store: A Social History* (London: Pinter, 1995).

60 'Deansgate and other improvements', *Freelance*, 29 May 1874; 'Happy "Arcadia"'.

61 J. R. Walkowitz, *City of Dreadful Delight: Narratives of Sexual Danger in Late Victorian London* (London: Virago, 1992), p. 47; M. Nava, 'Modernity's disavowal: women, the city and the department store' in M. Nava and A. O'Shea (eds), *Modern Times: Reflections on a Century of English Modernity* (London: Routledge, 1996), p. 47.

62 Cited in Adburgham, *Shops and Shopping*, p. 281.

63 'Birmingham as she is', *Town Crier*, February 1886.

64 'Leeds shop windows'.

65 Linstrum, *West Yorkshire Architects*, pp. 273–80.

66 Anderton, *Tale of One City*, p. 105. For observations on the growth of restaurants in Manchester see the series 'The dining rooms of Manchester', *Freelance*, February 1867–May 1868.

67 Marcus, *Engels, Manchester and the Working Class*, p. 172.

68 'A walk down Market Street'.

69 'Urban rambles II', *Freelance*, 2 November 1867.

70 M. Beresford, 'The face of Leeds, 1780–1914' in Fraser, *History of Modern Leeds*, p. 110; 'On improvements', *Yorkshire Busy Bee*, 17 September 1881; 'The lungs of Manchester', *Freelance*, 1 September 1876.

71 W. Fairbairn, *Observations of the Improvements of the Town of Manchester* (Manchester, 1836); A. J. Pass, *Thomas Worthington* (Manchester: Manchester Literary and Philosophical Publications, 1988), pp. 28–9; L. Grindon, *The Infirmary Sites Question* (Manchester, 1876), p. 16; *Manchester Faces and Places*, vol. 1 (1889–90), p. 14.

72 *The Builder*, vol. xxxii (1874), p. 859.

73 *Allday's Gossiping Guide*, pp. 27–44; Hartnell, *Pre-Raphaelite Birmingham*, pp. 59–60.

74 *Leeds Mercury*, 17 September 1903, p. 8.

75 Grindon, *Infirmary Sites Question*, p. 17.

76 *Cornish's Strangers Guide*, p. 17.

77 R. J. Morris and R. Rodger, 'Introduction' in Morris and Rodger, *The Victorian City 1820–1914* (London: Longman, 1993), p. 9. See also ch. 7 of this book.

78 C. Arscott, G. Pollock and J. Wolff, 'The partial view: the visual representation of the early nineteenth-century industrial city' in J. Wolff and

J. Seed (eds), *The Culture of Capital: Art, Power and the Nineteenth-Century Middle Class* (Manchester: Manchester University Press, 1988).

79 Faucher, *Manchester in 1844*, p. 26; 'Manchester by night', *Freelance*, 11 August 1876.

80 'A fearful night', *Yorkshire Busy Bee*, 3 September 1881. For similar stories in Birmingham see 'Another meeting of the statues', *Town Crier*, August 1882.

81 'Busy Boar Lane by lamplight', *Yorkshire Busy Bee*, 26 November 1881.

82 'Through Deansgate', *City Lantern*, 4 April 1879.

83 For an extended discussion of the nocturnal city between 1840 and 1930 see J. Schlör, *Nights in the Big City* (London: Reaktion Books, 1998).

84 R. Sennett, *The Conscience of the Eye: The Design and Social Life of Cities* (London: Faber, 1993), pp. 36–7.

3

The social uses of public space

The rebuilding of the city centre in Birmingham, Leeds and Manchester had significant consequences for the spatial organisation of urban populations and for their representation. One effect of emptying the centre of its inhabitants and recreating it as a monumental space was to throw into relief the identities of the different social groups that entered it. Who people were and how they were socially positioned became an issue of vital interest. In London as well as in the industrial cities, the decades between the 1840s and the 1880s saw an extraordinary attention to the minute detailing of matters such as appearance, dress and behaviour on the street.[1] This social phenomenology was not neutral. Implicit in it was the consistent, if indefinite, idea of a threat posed by certain groups to the social order in the double sense of the term, both hierarchical and regulatory. In London the fault-line of concern took spatial form in the division between a proletarian East End and a fashionable West End. In the industrial cities, however, attention was directed to the central zone itself, together with the slums and workers' districts immediately bordering it. Between the 1840s and the 1880s these areas of the industrial cities became a highly sensitised testing-ground, not only for new efforts at policing and moral regulation, but also for new forms of social identity and ways of representing authority.

The reconstruction of the industrial cities therefore raised a series of questions in sharp and immediate ways. Who was to have access to the centre and on what terms? How were social identities and relationships to be handled in the newly created environment of the city? The idea of the city centre as a space designed to represent morality and power indicates some of the ways middle-class commentators envisioned the new urban 'design'. But it does not specify with any precision how the centre was used by different sections of the population: men, women, workers, employers, the urban poor. In practice as well as at the level of representation the idea of the 'moral city' was inseparable from its designation as a space of physical and moral danger. For groups such as middle-class women, appearance in the city centre raised in acute form issues of security and identity. Recent critics have followed contemporaries like Engels in viewing the nineteenth-century metropolis as a whirlpool or vortex in which the individual was caught in a bewildering spiral of sense impressions. In this context, the experience of the centre betokened not so much a recovery of moral order as disorientation and even temporary loss of identity.[2]

For these reasons, how the city centre was to be regulated and how appearance and social interaction were to be managed were perceived by mid-Victorian observers to be important issues. This chapter will specify these concerns as they were articulated in Birmingham, Leeds and Manchester from the 1840s onwards. The vicissitudes of the streets and the threat to social identity that they posed to contemporaries can be exaggerated. Historians have rightly pointed to the varied strategies by which migrants and workers handled the pressured conditions of city life, and the resilient vitality of urban popular cultures.[3] The wealthier, suburbanised sections of local society equally devised their own strategies for negotiating the city centre and for representing status and hierarchy on the streets. Principal among these were the description and classification of social 'types' and the regular enactment of what I shall term 'ritualised performances' at the heart of the city. Both of these strategies operated with the idea of the city centre as a stage for the display of social identity and difference, and worked to stabilise and limit the democratic flux of city life.

The perils of the streets

The perception of the city as physically and morally dangerous was not new in the mid-nineteenth century. It was a significant theme in Henry Fielding's descriptions of eighteenth-century London as the home of the idle, profligate and debauched, as also in William Cobbett's well-known denunciation of the capital and the new industrial centres as 'wens'.[4] But the residential withdrawal of the wealthy from the industrial city to suburbs like Victoria Park, Edgbaston and Woodhouse in the 1830s and 1840s intensified the idea of a collapse of moral authority at its centre at times when a middle class was absent, at night and weekends. Leon Faucher articulated the idea powerfully in his description of Manchester in 1844: 'At the very moment when the engines are stopped, and the counting-houses closed, everything which was the thought – the authority – the impulsive force – the moral order of this immense industrial

combination, flies from the town and disappears in an instant'.[5] The idea
that the centre became, at certain times, a moral vacuum was a staple
and more or less constant observation in all the provincial cities between
the 1840s and the 1880s. 'We must not measure the civilisation of Leeds
by what we see in Park Row, Bond Street, Commercial Street, Briggate
and Boar Lane during the day time', a local journalist warned in 1883;
'our streets in the dark and lonesome hours of midnight and early
morning also bear witness to the social cancers which may be covered
up, but never healed'.[6] From the last decades of the nineteenth century
many commentators looked back nostalgically to a golden age of urban
community, located vaguely in the early 1800s, when different classes
were seen to have harmoniously inhabited adjacent streets in the old
centre.[7] Yet the representations of the industrial city as dangerous and
as romantic were not antithetical or contradictory; in the mid-Victorian
decades the idea of the centre as a space of danger became part of its
romance.

In Birmingham, Leeds and Manchester the dangers of the city had
a specific socio-spatial location in the slums and workers districts that
bordered on the central area. The city centre was portrayed as an island
surrounded by a sea of crime and immorality. 'The town is encircled by
a huge cordon of beastliness and filth, enough to strike fear into the
heart of every civilised inhabitant', a Manchester journal proclaimed in
1870. In similar vein, visitors to Birmingham were advised that if they
stepped 'outside the magic circle' of the central area they would immediately encounter squalor, stench and the 'rookeries of vice'.[8] Streets on
the fringes of the commercial district were identified as especially
dangerous for respectable passers-by; they included parts of Deansgate
and Oldham Road in Manchester, Thomas Street in Birmingham and
York Street in Leeds. As late as 1892, when fears of violent crime were
subsiding in many cities, the Chief Constable of Leeds warned of the
dangers of entering the Dark Arches, Swinegate and Whitehall Road,
in which prostitution, assault and larceny were seen as rife.[9] Where the
new police led, journalists followed. The reports of Angus Bethune
Reach on the slums of Angel Meadow, Manchester in the 1850s, were
succeeded by a stream of accounts in the press of the industrial cities,
describing drunkenness, violence and immoral behaviour in a style which
mixed the frankly censorious with the slyly picaresque.[10] In this way,
not only was suburban respectability alerted to the dangers lurking at
the edges of the city centre, but the city itself was subjected to a detailed
moral mapping, from the level of districts down to that of specific streets,
markets and pubs.

Particular concern was voiced at moments when social and spatial boundaries appeared to break and the population of the slums and worker's districts spilled on to the main city streets, principally at night and weekends. In the 1870s and early 1880s the Birmingham press complained vociferously at the 'drink-delirium' which overtook the working population on Saturday nights, creating 'disgraceful scenes at the very heart of the town'. Similarly, the *Leeds Mercury* bemoaned the 'crowds of men and women drunk, surging up and down the streets' on Saturday nights, and 'the disgusting immorality, the ribald jesting, the cursing and profanity' which accompanied these occasions. In Manchester, considerable attention was given to the popular promenade in Oldham Street on Sunday evenings, a 'surging mass of human beings overflowing from the broad pavement into the roadway', from Ancoats into Market Street and Piccadilly.[11] What was at issue here was not simply the perception of immorality on show. It was also the perceived transgression of the social and spatial boundaries of the mid-Victorian city, the outflow from the slums into the symbolic centre of bourgeois authority. Such occasions were seen as incarnating the idea of disorder on the 'principal thoroughfares' and of the dangers of the streets.

Fears about the permeability of the boundaries between slums and centre led to concerns about crime and violence on the city streets. In the 1840s and 1850s much attention was given to crimes against property. Following Engels, commentators noted the elaborate use of iron plates and shutters to protect shops and warehouses in Manchester; theft from workshops in the metal trades was viewed as a serious social problem in mid nineteenth-century Birmingham.[12] But from the 1860s there was a discernible shift in all three cities to a focus on crimes against the person carried out in the central streets. There were fears of a crime epidemic in Manchester, set off by the Deansgate 'garotting panic' of 1862–63 and evidence of rising numbers of arrests. In Leeds there was similar anxiety about the rising crime rate, perpetuated by a number of well-publicised attacks on notable local figures; in 1882, for example, the painter Atkinson Grimshaw was reported to have been assaulted in a 'moonlight outrage' in Kirkgate.[13] However, statistical evidence does not suggest an increase in crime in the central areas of the city, even allowing for the problems of interpreting police statistics. The police returns for Manchester, for example, show an absolute decline in the number of arrests in the central wards of Exchange and St Ann's between 1847 and 1865. Arrests for crimes committed in each ward were most numerous, and increased most rapidly, in working-class areas such as Ancoats, Angel Meadow and Deansgate.[14] But neither this evidence,

nor the efforts to distinguish the 'dangerous' and 'criminal' classes from
'upright' workers, appeared to reassure propertied opinion before the
1890s. The high-profile reporting of murder, assault and theft meant
that the centre, and areas immediately bordering it, continued to be
represented as the site of criminality and random violence, especially
'out of hours'.

More insidious, however, and in many ways more alarming to
respectable opinion since it was pervasive and hard to regulate, was
prostitution, 'the great sin of great cities' as a Birmingham periodical
termed it.[15] In Leeds, police reports indicated that there were one
hundred and fifty prostitutes in 1852, mainly gathered in brothels off
Kirkgate. The figures for Manchester were between five hundred and a
thousand at any time between the 1840s and the 1880s.[16] These numbers
were relatively small by comparison with port cities like Liverpool, but
they underestimated the scale of the phenomenon since they failed to
take into account the numbers of women using prostitution as a form
of casual work to supplement wages.[17] Official attitudes were ambiguous,
the police in Leeds, for example, tolerating prostitution where it was
restricted in fixed brothels. But the concern of the police and the press
escalated when prostitutes were seen to enter the central streets and
squares. In 1844 Faucher estimated that there were over five hundred
prostitutes in the vicinity of the Manchester Exchange at dusk, and the
opening up of the city at night with improved lighting and commercialised entertainment enhanced public awareness of prostitution. In
1882 a woman contributor to a Leeds journal commented that 'it is
impossible to walk along [Boar Lane] after nightfall without observing
the large number of very young girls', while in 1877 a Birmingham
periodical cryptically noted the 'stream of gaily-dressed women' who
gathered outside the Midland Hotel 'as soon as the theatres closed'.[18]

The presence of prostitutes on the streets of the city centre, rather
than in enclosed brothels on its fringes, was seen as destabilising for a
number of reasons. Firstly, it brought into the open the association
between prostitution and middle-class youths and businessmen who
made up an important part of the clientele, thus exposing men's 'double
standard'. Secondly, prostitutes were seen not only to flout codes of
femininity and public morality, but also to permeate 'society' occasions
such as concerts, balls and soirées. At the Annual Ball of the Lancashire
Artillery Volunteers, a Manchester journalist professed shock at the
number of prostitutes present who, in the quadrilles, 'would have to take
the hands of the wives, sisters and sweethearts of the members of the
gallant L.A.V!'.[19] Thirdly, as this suggests, the presence of prostitutes

was seen to compromise the respectability of middle-class women in public places. 'Nearly every respectable woman who may be out after dusk', a Leeds correspondent complained, 'knows that if she is compelled to stand or loiter for a single moment she is addressed by some man or other'.[20] The issue of prostitution therefore displaced on to women as a whole responsibility for men's sexual behaviour. At the same time, the prostitute was cast as the transgressive figure *par excellence*, capable of moving across established boundaries of space and class in ways which disrupted bourgeois notions of respectability and social order.

The idea of the city centre as a moral space, then, coexisted with its representation as a space of danger. From the later 1850s there is evidence that police strategy turned to moral regulation of street behaviour in the forms of drunkenness, prostitution and begging. It was these offences which largely accounted for the increase in arrests between the 1860s and the 1880s in cities such as Manchester and Leeds.[21] Yet from their formation in the 1830s until at least the 1880s, the new police were consistently perceived by propertied opinion as ineffective. In the 1830s and 1840s opposition could be put down to urban Tory hostility to Liberal reforms, but from the 1850s it was general. 'The fact must be confessed that during the still hours of every night and day our streets are insufficiently protected' a Birmingham journal lamented in the 1880s, while in Leeds the police were depicted as incompetent as they were autocratic.[22] Consequently, there was little middle-class confidence in the police's ability to protect either person or property before the late 1880s, when crime rates began to decline and observers perceived cities like Manchester to be safer than at an earlier period.[23] Means other than policing were necessary to bring a sense of order and stability to the city streets.

Within the ranks of the middle classes, the city centre was used and experienced differentially. Age was one factor here, the centre being strongly identified in reportage with the 'gilded youth' of both sexes as a focus for courtship, consumption and fashionable display. Equally, there were specific problems for middle-class women in entering the central area. The volume of traffic, mud on the streets and the unwanted attentions of male 'pests' were among the difficulties which had to be negotiated. While men might benefit from the opening up of the city at night and find in its streets a new freedom, the spatial and temporal liberties of women were restricted by the sense of danger lurking at the city's edge and the heightened visibility of prostitution.[24] Yet if women faced in particularly acute form the 'perils of the streets', the experience of the city raised problems of status and authority for middle-class populations as a whole, men as well as women. Centrally important here was the issue of appearance on the street, of how a sense of hierarchy and social order were to be upheld in an urban society characterised by fluidity, democratic mixing and a weakening of the traditional markers of social distinction.

Appearance, street philosophy and social 'types'

Appearance on the street, and how one appeared to others, was of vital importance to the mid-Victorian middle class. It had to signal distinction, respectability and authority in an anonymous social context where personal or social recognition was far from automatic, and where an aristocratic display of conspicuous wealth was likely to be frowned upon, to be seen as out of place. Changes in fashion from the 1860s, notably the production of cheap crinolines and ready-made suits, meant that dress itself no longer served as a reliable index of a person's class or status.[25] Yet, paradoxically, dress and appearance became more important as a guide to who someone was. For the critic Thomas Carlyle, clothes might be 'despicable' but they were also 'unspeakably significant' since they provided clues to a person's identity at a period when a conventional sign-system of appearance was disintegrating. As Elizabeth Wilson suggests, 'it became essential to read character and proclivity from details that were immediately perceived, for in the metropolis everyone was in disguise, incognito, and yet at the same time an individual more and more *was* what he [or she] wore'.[26]

These concerns about appearance and status, of course, were not novel. The comedy of manners attendant upon social pretension and mobility was a staple subject of eighteenth-century depictions of Bath and London. However, the transformation of the industrial towns into provincial metropolises, and the recreation of the city centre as a form of monumental stage-set, meant that concerns about appearance intensified. Indeed, evidence from the provincial cities reveals something akin to a crisis of representation in this respect between the 1860s and the 1880s. The crisis was characterised by a series of oppositions in bourgeois representations of the public self, between concealment and disclosure, between conformity and individualism, and, above all, between authenticity and pretence. In Manchester, it was asserted in 1871, wealthy men and women out in public 'have determined to convert themselves into clothes-screens'. Changing male fashions since the 1830s were perceived to conceal men's figures in loose-fitting suits and their faces behind beards. Black frock coats and trousers were adopted as a uniform, giving mid-Victorian men an aspect of funereal conformity at a point when 'individualism' was assumed to be on the ascendant in other domains of social and economic life.[27] The provincial satirical press, meanwhile, provided a running critique of social pretension, contrasted with an always elusive ideal of authenticity: 'We too constantly sail under false colours, travel under false pretences amongst our fellow men; in short, perpetually perpetrate upon them a contemptible programme of social humbug'.[28]

Respectable appearance was therefore crucially important and problematic for those assuming middle-class status. This duality related to a basic contradiction in social perception. On the one hand, it was desired that class or status should be immediately recognisable, to spring automatically from an authentically 'classed' self; on the other, respectable appearance was seen to be contrived, something that required mastery of complex social codes. Difficulties were compounded by the reconstruction of the city centre itself. Whereas in the suburbs, roles and identities were clearly defined, and it was generally known who individuals were, in the centre the lines of identity were prone to dissolve. The city centre was characterised not only by anonymity in social relationships, but also by its conceptualisation as a social stage. It was here, as Judith Walkowitz has noted, that 'new social actors' first made their appearance, the 'new woman' and the 'swell', in the 1880s.[29]

These issues took shape in specific, and often gendered, ways. Respectable 'ladies' were confronted by the difficult task of conforming to the dictates of femininity and fashion while establishing a clear visual demarcation from increasingly public, well-dressed prostitutes. Significantly, in Leeds during the 1880s a Rational Dress Society worked to dispense advice to women on appropriate dress in public.[30] But the problems of appearance affected all sections of the middle class, men as well as women. The figure of the 'gentleman' was seen as continuously threatened by counterfeits, the 'mashers' and 'counter-jumpers' whose true identity the satirical press delighted in exposing. Thus a Birmingham journal rejoiced in the tale of a tram passenger 'who had the appearance of a gentleman, but soon showed himself that contemptible creature, a masher'.[31] Respectable appearance was especially important for those on the fringes of gentility, such as clerks. Ironically, however, it was precisely these occupational groups which were most often identified by the local press as dressing 'above their station'.[32]

A central concern for those with a claim to middle-class status, therefore, was to establish recognisable lines between different social groups and to sustain an idea of hierarchy in appearance on the street. At a general level, novelists like Dickens, George Eliot and Charlotte Brontë, were useful guides to these issues. In their works such novelists paid detailed attention to dress and appearance. Their particular skill, as John Harvey has noted, was to interpret the 'inner meaning of externals'.[33] But of more specific importance at the local level was the periodical press, which provided a running commentary on social life in provincial cities like Birmingham, Leeds and Manchester. A key figure in these accounts was the 'street philosopher' whose pleasure, as one such put it, was 'to watch the passers by, to speculate on character from a chance expression, and an occupation from the cut of a coat or the shape of a pair of boots'.[34] For the street philosopher, the city appeared as a 'living panorama', a 'vast museum', from which general truths could be deduced about human character: 'What a world of speculation lies open to the man who, himself placid and unmoved in the strife, attentively regards his fellow man, and what golden lessons are to be derived by one who indulges in such contemplation'. The new industrial cities were regarded as especially favourable terrain for such speculation compared to older urban centres, as one commentator explained: 'In a large manufacturing town, [there] is more room for the display of the ever shifting chances and changes of life'.[35]

This 'gastronomy of the eye', Richard Sennett has suggested, was a feature of urban bourgeois perception in the mid- and later nineteenth century, in France as well as in England.[36] But if the city was seen as a spectacle, it was not an undifferentiated one. Through the figure of the street philosopher the periodical press engaged in a systematic process of categorising and classifying individuals as 'social types', providing a sociological guide to the streets and restoring order to the confusion of sense impressions.

Much of this social description was concerned with specifying occupational and status differences within a propertied population. W. H. Mills recalled the 'type' of the Manchester man of the 1870s, generally a large employer, identified by the panoply of horses, carriages and grooms.[37] In the early 1880s a Leeds journal noted the increasing 'grandeur and sublimity of the word professional', identified with the law, medicine and the clergy, but now aspired to by accountants and architects. Here, as in other literary genres, the gentleman represented the apogee of masculine status. The same Leeds journal dwelt lovingly on the details of old-fashioned gentlemanly appearance encountered in a Headingley tram: 'a moustache, a pair of dog-shin gloves, two and a half inches of wrist linen, a pair of gaiters, a bull-dog's head pin, a circumference of stiff collar, and a circuitous hat'.[38] Gentlemanliness represented the yardstick by which all other forms of masculine appearance were judged. In Birmingham in the late 1870s the *Owl* ran a series of articles entitled 'People One Doesn't Care to Meet', male 'types' encountered at the social club or at church whose behaviour failed to live up to the standards expected of the 'true' gentleman.[39] But most ire was expended on 'swells', 'mashers', 'cads' and 'counter-jumpers', young men associated with marginal status, such as warehouse clerks and shop assistants: 'He is the man who during the week consents to appear in the seediest and most threadbare garments, but on Sundays emerges in all the glories of gaiters, "masher" collars [and] a crutch stick'.[40] It was predominantly men who were depicted as 'social types' in this manner, but observation was not restricted to them. Women in public were classified, for instance, according to 'types of beauty' – the 'languishing', the 'dressy', the 'genteel', and so on –, while a sense of social hierarchy was provided by the portrayal of 'shopping ladies', 'showy shopgirls' and barmaids as distinct species of femininity.[41]

This brand of journalistic caricature was used to reinforce particular notations of gender and sexuality, which themselves helped to underwrite the perception of social difference. As an expert in appearances, the street philosopher was skilled in deciphering the prostitute from the 'true' lady. The former could be identified by details of style or gesture: 'Mark how she struts and stalks along, thinking that she is gracing the room with an elegant and refined style of locomotion'. 'Ladies' were distinguished by naturalness of appearance and manners, which were invariably seen as artificial and contrived in prostitutes, even of the most fashionable kind.[42] Equally, an over-attention to dress among 'swells' and 'mashers' disqualified them from gentlemanliness; as a Leeds journal put it, by their appearance and behaviour such 'types' forfeited 'any claim to be considered *men* in the ordinary and best acceptation [*sic*] of the term'.[43] Indeed, anxiety about the sexual as well as the social identity of young men was a repeated motif in the periodical press of the 1880s. The association of 'mashers' with prostitutes was seen to compromise not only their moral standing but also their masculinity; both groups were identified with surface and illusion as against substance and 'character'. In Birmingham the presence of Oscar Wilde impersonators in New Street and transvestites in Aston Lower Grounds, alluded to in the press, was connected with a larger trend in which a younger generation of men was seen as corrupted and 'feminised'.[44] Such concerns focused on groups who could themselves be regarded as new social actors in the 1870s and 1880s: the sons of established middle-class families yet to acquire a responsible position in business or the professions and young white-collar males whose social status was inherently precarious. Representations of sexuality were thus entwined with perceptions of class and status, moral and social qualities complimenting one another at each point in a hierarchy of respectability.

Social 'types' were also categorised according to specific locations in and around the city. A Birmingham commentator satirised Edgbaston as the home of the 'wretched rich' whose 'miserable conditions' were related to the number of 'at homes' and dinner-parties such families were forced to hold. A series on 'types' observed on Leeds tram routes allowed for disquisition on the different social character of suburbs: 'Chapeltown Varieties', 'the Perambulatory Gallery of Mixture' (Headingley), 'Humanity in the Rough' (Hunslet).[45] In Leeds, in particular, the connotations of individual streets or districts were brought out by means of visual and literary caricature, the prosperous Jew representing the Leylands, a fashionable woman and chaperone Commercial Street, a female factory worker Hunslet Lane, and so on.[46] Such descriptions rendered the city knowable in a way that differed from statistical investigation and abstract maps. They both reflected local knowledge and reconstituted that knowledge by depicting in specific and increasingly stereotyped ways an image of the city as socially zoned. While presenting the city as a 'living panorama', they sharpened the idea of bounded social differences coexisting in a seemingly unchanging social order.

As Pierre Bourdieu has argued, such classificatory schemes are part of a practical knowledge of the social world, organising that knowledge on the principles of 'vision and division'.[47] The visual and literary representation of the social order conveyed by the periodical press in Birmingham, Leeds and Manchester was essentially harmonious and hierarchical; its predominant tone was comic or ironic rather than contestatory or overtly class-based. Nevertheless, it organised local society in a manner which was implicitly classed. The higher echelons were seen as graded by a series of coteries and status divisions. In the old days, a Birmingham correspondent lamented, dances were a 'merry meeting' of young people; but from the 1850s they had become fashionable events where 'to have anything to do with a partner outside the correct "set", is a thing not to be thought of'.[48] By contrast, little direct attention was given in the periodical press to workers or the poor as part of urban society. While Jews, street arabs and factory workers were identified in passing, they were conventionally described only in relation to the presence of the well-to-do. Moreover, by contrast with statistical surveys there was limited attempt at hierarchisation and division within or between elements of the 'lower classes' and little or no reference to the 'intelligent artisan' or to the distinction between the 'rough' and the 'respectable' found in other forms of contemporary literature.[49] Where such groups were described, it was generally in the visceral terms noted earlier: beggars who 'follow you with their whining appeals' and 'clutch you by the coat-sleeve', or workers in the trams whose presence was registered by the smell of 'the rough cut and the shag'.[50] Thus, the society of the well-to-do was presented as complex and finely graded, that of workers and the poor as comparatively simple and uniform.

Ostensibly hierarchical, the view of the social order projected in the periodical press was intrinsically dichotomous. It was predicated on an implicit division between a population whose resources derived from 'non-manual' occupations, the families of clerks as well as of employers, and the bulk of the urban population dependent on physical labour of different kinds. This division was reproduced in a multiplicity of forms: between those with legitimate access to the city centre and others whose presence was viewed as threatening and transgressive; between consumers as 'subjects' and those who were represented as 'objects' of the largesse of the well-to-do; between those identified as possessing education and culture and the 'Great Unwashed' upon whom the benefits of education were wasted.[51] At its most fundamental, the division between mental and manual labour was rooted in analogies between the human and the social body. In 1892 the president of the Birmingham and Edgbaston Debating Society defined the aristocracy, the middle class and the working class as respectively 'the belly, the brain and the bone of modern society'. In the periodical press the well-to-do were identified by the outward signs of mental discernment, taste and refinement. By contrast, workers and the poor were distinguished by their physicality, by sensual excess, as in the figure of the prostitute, or by bodily grossness, as in the caricatures of 'Smowler', the eponymous 'working-man's candidate'.[52] In these ways, the seemingly diverse and hierarchical representation of social 'types' developed between the 1860s and the 1890s turned on a latent dichotomy between mental and manual categories which was to continue to be a staple element in the representation of class and the social order into the twentieth century.[53]

Ritualisation and performance

The significance of the portrayal of social 'types' lay in the attempt to fix social boundaries and meanings in an environment that was seen as

especially prone to flux and change. Yet there were also other means
by which a suburban middle-class population sought to register appearance in the city. The most notable of these was the highly stylised ways
in which the wealthy transacted movement to and from the centre and
registered their presence within it during the mid- and later Victorian
decades. Such behaviour was ritualistic in the sense that it was repeated,
standardised and performative, but it also encompassed less formal
modes of conduct, defined as 'routine' and 'habit'. In reviewing the vexed
problem of defining ritual the anthropologist Catherine Bell has proposed the use of the term 'ritualisation' to refer to a 'way of acting that
is designed and orchestrated to distinguish and privilege what is being
done in comparison to other, usually more quotidian, activities'.[54] Such
a broadened concept of ritual is useful in that it incorporates a wide
range of events and modes of behaviour which were designed to appear
as 'strategically distinguished' in relation to the everyday and the
cultures of popular life. These forms ranged from the elaborately staged
rites associated with civic ceremonial to the regular and regulatory acts
of urban life such as the activity of 'High 'Change' or the Saturday
promenade on the main shopping streets. It was not only the former
which were widely commented upon in literature and the press, but also
the latter, suggesting that such performative events were significant and
intended to be visible to a wider population than merely the participants.

The routinisation and stylisation of modes of appearance in the city
centre was partly related to suburbanisation. Withdrawal to the suburbs
meant that visits to the city centre had to be planned in advance,
involving considerations of travel and dress. Visits were also likely to
be intermittent, and therefore special, particularly for middle-class
women who might only make the trip into 'town' once or twice a week.
These factors were magnified where suburbs lay at a distance from the
centre, which could be relatively short, as in the case of Chapeltown in
Leeds or Edgbaston in Birmingham, but was often substantial. By the
1860s a large proportion of established Manchester employer and professional families were living in outlying towns and villages such as
Altrincham, Bowdon and Alderley up to twelve miles from the
centre.[55] In Manchester the appearance and activities of the wealthy in
the city centre were given more systematic attention in the press than
in Birmingham or Leeds, suggesting that the significance of such occasions was linked to the pace and extent of suburbanisation in the second
half of the nineteenth century.

The act of travelling to and from the centre was not, of course,
merely occasional, but also performed daily during the week by those

engaged in business. A tidal metaphor was commonly applied to the life of the mid-Victorian city, the ebb and flow of population marking its diurnal rhythm. In the first half of the nineteenth century it was not uncommon for industrial and commercial employers to use the journey to work as a public demonstration of self-discipline and punctiliousness, not merely to the workforce, but to all in business and the urban community who were witness to it. The phaeton which daily took the Manchester cotton master Joseph Leese from Ardwick to his warehouse in Portland Street was known as the 'Polygon Diligence' by virtue of its unvarying punctuality. Manufacturers who did not have their goods ready for inspection by 7 a.m. would be barred from business dealings 'until they came to their senses and amended their manners'.[56] More generally, the display of carriage and horses continued to serve as a symbol of wealth and prestige throughout the Victorian period. In the 1880s, according to W. H. Mills, they 'not only signalled a considerable social consequence, but specified many of its gradations'. These varied from the 'estate and twilight condition of dowagerdom, unmistakably notified in the elderly white horse and coachman, to noontide family splendour indicated in buckskin and cockades, flying foam and bevelled glass, behind which some great personal force could be seen communing with itself as it drove home'.[57]

The advent of the train as the favoured methods of middle-class commuting after 1850 left less scope for performative display. However, some of the earlier features of the journey to work persisted. As part of a 'suburban way of life', Mark Girouard has noted, the act of commuting took on an air of 'almost ritual sanctity'. By the 1860s a Manchester journal commented on the 'wonderful regularity' that commuting imposed upon businessmen. Not only did the same men travel by the same train each working day, but 'particular seats in the compartment are considered by the regular occupiers to be as clearly their right as the head of the dinner table at home. No stranger at all aware of the etiquette in these matters would rashly occupy any corner of which he did not feel quite sure.'[58] In Birmingham women travelling on the commuter trains were urged to 'keep to the right places' lest they upset the customary seating arrangements.[59] This powerful sense of routinised order differentiated the commuter train from the democratic free-for-all of the tram and omnibus. It also reflected a new emphasis on privacy and physical containment in public; the silence of first- and second-class railway compartments contrasted with the hubbub of the third-class carriages as well as with the sociable character of coach travel in an earlier era.[60] More than this, however, descriptions of commuters' behaviour signified bodies habitualised to self-presentation, as in the figure of Wemmick in Dickens's *Great Expectations* 'who every morning becomes less human and more mechanical as he approaches work in the central city, and every evening reverses the process as he approaches home in an outlying suburb'.[61]

These characteristics of self-presentation were carried over into the workplace. Guides for clerks emphasised punctuality, diligence and attention to appearance, and also appropriate manner and bodily demeanour in front of employers: 'if you would associate with, and be acknowledged by gentlemen, you must comport yourself accordingly'.[62] The business day itself was highly regulated with working hours in counting houses between 8 a.m. and 8 p.m., and a dinner hour between one and two o'clock in Manchester in the 1840s. 'Business becomes a habit' a guide to the city explained.[63] Even by the 1860s when business habits began to relax among certain commercial and professional groups, the day appears to have been routinised. 'We had our dozen of port' the Manchester lawyer James Crossley was reported to have remarked; 'no smoking, no hurry; we dined at three o'clock, had copious talk, and went home at seven'.[64]

The high-point in the weekly cycle of business was 'Change day, especially in Manchester where up to 7,000 manufacturers, merchants and agents from the city and cotton districts would descend on the Exchange. From the 1830s High 'Change on Tuesdays was one of the sights of Manchester, a time when the Exchange was transformed from a state of listlessness into a 'community of dancing dervishes' as bargains were made and deals struck.[65] Outwardly chaotic in appearance, the ritual of High 'Change was underpinned by rules governing its operations. Individuals and firms were located on the floor according to a grid system; business was conducted by gesture – 'nods, winks, shrugs' – in an atmosphere of 'silence and perpetual motion'; custom dictated that all goods were excluded from the floor, that payment was by cash and that verbal contracts were binding.[66] At the peak hour of High 'Change, one observer remarked, 'the floor seemed to be pervaded by a quasi-electrical stream of intelligence, transmitted between perfectly-adjusted business machines moving as purposively as bees within a hive'; after an hour or so of activity, 'the meeting gradually but noiselessly melts away'.[67] Descriptions of High 'Change provide a reminder that the market was always in part a cultural construct, as Robert Gray has emphasised.[68] The representation of business conduct reassured the observer that although the market might appear to be a random process of chance, it was a system governed by laws of supply and demand as well as by code and custom. At the same time, the spectacle of High 'Change provided a powerful visual metaphor of the business middle class as an entity, of regulated conformity and self-discipline.

Significantly, many of the behavioural characteristics associated with the world of work were also evident in the public display of bourgeois leisure, most notably the promenade. In Birmingham, Leeds and Manchester, midday on Saturdays was identified with the weekly parade of 'gilded youth' in the most fashionable shopping streets, New Street, Commercial Street and St Ann's Square respectively. Accounts of the Saturday promenade stressed its status as a time-honoured 'institution'. 'Among the many institutions of Manchester, there is none perhaps so extensively patronised as that wherein the gentle blood of Cottonopolis delights to air its gentility', a commentator stated of the St Ann's Square promenade in the 1870s, dating its inception from the later eighteenth century.[69] The informality of the occasion and its brevity were especially noted. 'From about eleven to one, they flock hither and thither, and promenade backwards and forwards', indicated a Leeds observer, but 'in very little time they will be gone and Bond Street and Commercial Street will be empty'. Similarly, in Manchester 'Doing the Square' was seen to consist of 'a saunter past certain aldermanic art repositories, a measured pacing of the Square flags, a leisurely crush through the Passage, and a lounging survey of the millinery Eden of King Street'. Taking shape 'of its own accord', the promenade was also 'transient in duration', the participants soon returning to their carriages and the suburbs.[70]

Like High 'Change, the seeming informality of the Saturday promenade was underpinned by codes and customs which regulated its form. The weekly promenade was seen to unfold by involuntary yet definite means, 'stealthily, tacitly, neither *sub rosa* nor yet open and above board, but more effectually for all that'. It was also strongly territorial in character. In Leeds, it encompassed the fashionable shopping streets, but stopped short of 'busy Briggate, crowded by the vulgar herd'. King Street was the extremest limit of the Manchester promenade; 'once it rubs shoulders with the commonalty of Cross Street, or profanes its garments with Deansgate mud, it is lost'.[71] The Saturday promenade thus recognised and reinforced socio-spatial boundaries between the fashionable and the vulgar, the domains of respectability and those of moral danger. It acted to reclaim certain streets, in symbolic and provisional terms, from the invasive presence of prostitutes, hawkers and beggars. In David Scobey's phrase the bourgeois promenade represented a 'performative utterance of gentility' which envisioned social position by the act of embodying it symbolically in the city centre.[72] A rite of class it was also a rite of age and gender in which middle-class youth held centre stage and which women controlled. In the promenade, a journal asserted, women were 'in their vocation'. It was they who acted as the arbiters of ritual competence – nodding, bowing, and removal of the hat – on which 'recognition' was based, and which was crucial in defining the lines of inclusion and exclusion.[73] Thus, in a single event, the promenade condensed key elements of the bourgeois rite: visibility, social exclusivity, demarcation of space and of gender roles, and bodily mastery of tacit codes of behaviour.

Promenades in the industrial cities were not confined to the centre. From the 1830s recreational areas were developed away from the noise and bustle of the city streets. Here it was possible to incorporate men and women of different ages and to set promenades in a park-like setting, some socially exclusive, as in the Botanical Gardens, others socially mixed, as at Woodhouse Moor, Leeds or Aston Lower Grounds, Birmingham. Yet they did not displace the Saturday morning promenade; indeed, in some cases attempts were made to replicate its exclusivity. In 1882 there were vociferous complaints in Leeds at the Corporation's decision to ban popular sports on Woodhouse Moor, and to construct purpose-built parades known as 'Walking-Stick Avenues'. The Moor, it was complained, 'will eventually be so much "improved" that working men will be prohibited from entering its sacred precincts, and it will be entirely reserved for the class of society who do the Commercial Street "crawl" on Saturday mornings'.[74] Promenading was seen not only to improve the health and morals of the population, but also to provide a model of orderly behaviour in public.[75] More generally, the example of the promenade highlights the importance of middle-class women in signalling respectability and status in the city. If, as Judith Walkowitz has argued, women remained 'bearers of meaning, not makers of meaning' in the later nineteenth century, then women of wealthier families still carried considerable social influence. In the provincial cities, it was women's patronage that determined the fashionable character of certain shops and streets, their presence that confirmed the desirable exclusivity of public events such as classical concerts and promenades.[76]

During the second half of the nineteenth century, therefore, the wealthier, suburban sections of society in the provincial cities announced their presence in the city centre by means of certain stylised modes of behaviour and a series of repeated, visible displays of wealth and authority. Both these forms of public appearance were ritualised. They were normative, designed to serve as a model of behaviour, and strategically distinguished, in that they sought to differentiate middle-class behaviour from everyday and 'popular' appearance on the street, identified with the figures of workers and the urban poor. They were performative in the sense that they were public, carried out in front of a variegated urban audience, and embodied, predicated on a discipline of the body which emphasised restraint, uprightness and a mastery of the composite range of gestures which designated respectability. The public presentation of the Victorian middle class was, to an important degree, symbolic, designed both to conceal the inner person and to project an idealised, moral self to others through details of dress, demeanour and behaviour.

Ritualised performance did not, of course, resolve issues of social order. Rather, it deferred such issues, transposing them from one register to another, from the sphere of social relationships to those of the symbolic.[77] At the same time, ritualisation of all kinds was used to celebrate the durability of social forms and their continuity of meaning. The themes of time, space and recurrence in the literary representation of the industrial cities were used to create a social imaginary that was, in certain respects, organicist. By defining social life in terms of 'ebb' and 'flow', and behaviour in terms of underlying, involuntary mechanisms, the forms of middle-class presentation in public were naturalised, rendered part of a seemingly inevitable and unchanging order of things. In these ways, the transitory and provisional character of ritual was translated into larger, more permanent categories of meaning.

In different ways, the types of ritualised performance described here sought to make social difference visible, to assert control over public space and to define its uses. They drew on older cultural forms, such as the promenade and specific codes of deportment and gesture, to reinforce their authority. Yet the context and meaning of these was changing. The eighteenth-century promenade was confined to specifically designated walks or parks, and aimed to affirm status and solidarity within a relatively narrow social elite. But in the mid-Victorian city the purpose of the promenade was to make hierarchy and social order visible to an anonymous 'public', to make wealth and status apparent in a public sphere based on formal equality of access and use.[78]

More generally, the description of social 'types' and the enactment of ritualised performance were centrally concerned with the delineation of boundaries of gender, status and class. These boundaries were moral and social in character, and charged with cultural connotations. Perceptions of class difference were defined by reference to cultural criteria such as taste, rationality and mental ability. 'We are of the middle class', a Birmingham surgeon proudly proclaimed, 'and in the individual labours of our day our minds play a more leading part than either our mouths or our muscles'.[79]

The heyday of the portrayal of middle-class 'types' and rituals was the years between 1860 and 1890. From the later date they ceased to be so prominent in descriptions of life in the provincial cities. In part, this reflected the decline of the periodical press. Many of the satirical journals had closed down by 1890 and were not replaced by equivalent journals as at an earlier period.[80] Where such journals did continue, they increasingly submitted to commercial pressures, carrying advertisements for shops and businesses in the form of descriptive articles and reports of mass spectator sports such as cricket and football.[81] But the decline of the particular types of representation and modes of behaviour described here can also be connected to a number of more general factors. Firstly, it occurred simultaneously with the waning of civic ceremonial and processions, and of journalistic interest in them, from the later 1880s, a development that is examined more fully in Chapter 7. In this sense, it was linked to a wider decline of ritual expression among the middle classes in the industrial cities. Secondly, if a literature of social 'types' and ritual performance were related to fears of crime and social mixing in the city centre, then one would expect them to diminish in importance once these fears abated. The reduction of crime rates in the provincial cities by the 1890s, noted earlier, together with the development of a more self-sufficient and commercialised workers' culture from the 1880s, suggests that the need to intervene, practically or symbolically, in the city centre was commensurately less pressing.[82] Finally, there was a tendency among all social groups in the last decades of the century to move from outdoor forms of leisure to those pursued indoors or in enclosed spaces. In popular culture these forms comprised the music hall, professional sport and the pub; in bourgeois culture they included the concert hall and the social club. By the 1890s the street was no longer so significant a site of leisure and display as it had been in earlier decades. It is with the development of one of these interior forms of bourgeois culture, the gentlemen's social club, that the next chapter is concerned.

Notes

1   The best-known example is Henry Mayhew's *London Labour and the London Poor* (London, 1851), but intense and detailed speculation on the appearance and conditions of urban populations was a feature of fiction, the press and medical and statistical reports.

2   These issues are discussed variously in the following: M. Berman, *All That is Solid Melts into Air* (London: Verso, 1984); R. Fishman, *Bourgeois Utopias: The Rise and Fall of Suburbia* (New York: Basic Books, 1987); S. Marcus, *Engels, Manchester and the Working Class* (London: Weidenfeld and Nicholson, 1974); M. Nava, 'Modernity's disavowal: women, the city and department store' in M. Nava and A. O'Shea (eds), *Modern Times: Reflections on a Century of English Modernity* (London: Routledge, 1996); R. Sennett, *The Fall of Public Man* (London: Faber, 1993).

3   The literature is extensive but see in particular P. Bailey, *Leisure and Class in Victorian England* (London: Routledge, 1978); M. Hewitt, *The Emergence of Stability in the Industrial City* (Aldershot: Scolar Press, 1996); P. Joyce, *Visions of the People: Industrial England and the Question of Class, 1840–1914* (Cambridge: Cambridge University Press, 1991).

4   R. Williams, *The Country and the City* (St Albans: Paladin, 1975), pp. 178–80.

5   L. Faucher, *Manchester in 1844* (London, 1844), p. 26.

6   'Leeds at night', *Toby the Yorkshire Tyke*, 17 November 1883.

7   For examples of such literature see J. T. Slugg, *Reminiscences of Manchester Fifty Years Ago* (Manchester, 1881); T. Swindells, *Manchester Streets and Manchester Men* (Manchester, 1889).

8   'Manchester slums', *Freelance*, 12 March 1870; 'Improved Birmingham', *Owl*, 29 September 1882.

9   E. W. Clay, *The Leeds Police, 1836–1974* (Leeds: Leeds City Police, 1975), pp. 59–60.

10   C. Emsley, *Crime and Society in England 1750–1900* (Harlow: Longman, 1996), p. 70. For examples of this type of reportage in the three cities see the *Owl*, 20 October, 1882; 'A Deansgate tragedy', *Freelance*, 20 April 1867; 'Leeds at night', *Toby the Yorkshire Tyke*, 17 November 1883.

11   'The ruins of Birmingham', *Owl*, 3 November 1882; 'Birmingham cribs', *Lion*, 7 June 1877; *Leeds Mercury*, 16 July 1863; 'A Sunday promenade', *City Lantern*, 6 August 1874; 'Oldham Street on a Sunday night', *Freelance*, 6 August 1870.

12   F. Engels, *The Condition of the Working Class in England* (London, 1844); *The Builder*, vol. xxiv (1866), p. 292; Emsley, *Crime and Society*, p. 103.

13   S. J. Davies, 'Classes and police in Manchester 1829–1880' in A. J. Kidd and K. W. Roberts (eds), *City, Class and Culture: Studies of Cultural Production and Social Policy in Victorian Manchester* (Manchester: Manchester University Press, 1985), pp. 36–8; Clay, *Leeds Police*, pp. 39–40; *Yorkshire Busy Bee*, 1 April 1882, p. 297.

14   'Manchester police returns, 1847–65', Manchester Central Library Archives Department. For studies of Birmingham and Leeds see D. Philips, *Crime and Authority in Victorian England* (London: Croom Helm, 1977) and Clay, *Leeds Police*.

15   'Birmingham cribs', *Lion*, 10 May 1877.

16   S. Burt and K. Grady, *The Illustrated History of Leeds* (Derby: Breedon

Books, 1994), p. 169; D. Jones, *Crime, Protest, Community and Police in Nineteenth-Century Britain* (London: Routledge, 1982), pp. 164–5.

17 J. R. Walkowitz, *Prostitution and Victorian Society* (Cambridge: Cambridge University Press, 1980).

18 'Boar Lane', *Yorkshire Busy Bee*, 7 October 1882; 'Birmingham cribs', *Lion*, 17 May 1877.

19 'At the Volunteer ball', *Freelance*, 8 January 1875. On the identification of prostitutes with fashionable middle-class youth in Birmingham see the series on 'cribs' in the *Lion*, April–May 1877; in Leeds see *Yorkshire Busy Bee*, 27 January 1883, p. 52.

20 'Social laxity', *Toby the Yorkshire Tyke*, 1 December 1883.

21 Jones, *Crime, Protest, Community and Police*, pp. 161–7; Davies, 'Classes and police', pp. 36–40; Clay, *Leeds Police*, pp. 39–40.

22 'Hoots', *Owl*, 29 September 1882; 'Policemen', *Toby the Yorkshire Tyke*, 17 November 1883.

23 Jones, *Crime, Protest, Community and Police*, p. 167; C. Rowley, *Fifty Years of Ancoats* (Manchester, 1899), p. 15.

24 The issue of whether the modern city expanded or contracted opportunities for women's involvement in public life in the nineteenth century has been debated by feminist historians. For a classic statement of the pessimistic view see J. Wolff, 'The invisible *flâneuse*: women and the literature of modernity' in Wolff, *Feminine Sentences* (Cambridge: Cambridge University Press, 1990). For more optimistic (and plausible) views of the increasing participation of middle-class women, especially from the 1880s, see Nava, 'Modernity's disavowal' and J. R. Walkowitz, *City of Dreadful Delight: Narratives of Sexual Danger in Later Victorian London* (London: Virago, 1992).

25 C. Breward, *The Culture of Fashion* (Manchester: Manchester University Press, 1995), pp. 156–61, 174–5.

26 Carlyle cited in Sennett, *Fall of Public Man*, p. 153; E. Wilson, *Adorned in Dreams* (London: Virago, 1985), p. 137.

27 'The Botanical', *Freelance*, 27 May 1871; Slugg, *Reminiscences of Manchester*, p. 316; J. Harvey, *Men in Black* (London: Reaktion, 1997), pp. 24–7.

28. 'Social humbug', *Yorkshire Busy Bee*, 3 February 1883.

29 Walkowitz, *City of Dreadful Delight*, ch. 2.

30 'Feminine apparel', *Yorkshire Busy Bee*, 24 February, 1883.

31. 'A masher routed', *Owl*, 15 October 1884.

32 H. Taylor, *Our Clerks* (Manchester, 1874); J. Tomlinson, *Some Interesting Yorkshire Scenes* (London, 1865), p. 22; G. Anderson, *Victorian Clerks* (Manchester: Manchester University Press, 1976).

33 Harvey, *Men in Black*, p. 19.

34 'In City Road', *City Lantern*, 21 May 1875.

35 'Phases of "life" in Manchester', *Comus*, 13 December 1877; 'Leeds shop windows', *Yorkshire Busy Bee*, 10 December 1881; 'From my window', *Yorkshire Busy Bee*, 18 February 1882; 'In City Road'.

36 Sennet, *Fall of Public Man*, p. 160.

37 Mills, *Sir Charles W. Macara, Bart.: A Study in Modern Lancashire* (Manchester, 1917), p. 25.

38 'The professional man', *Yorkshire Busy Bee*, 7 April 1883; 'Riding in the trams', *Yorkshire Busy Bee*, 22 April 1882.

39 See the *Owl*, 29 May and 5 June 1879.

40 'Mis-spent Sundays', *Yorkshire Busy Bee*, 28 April 1883. For descriptions of such 'types' in Manchester and Birmingham see *inter alia* 'Manchester swells', *City Lantern*, 11 February 1876; 'The natural history of the cad', *Dart*, 31 March 1877.

41 'Types of beauty', *Yorkshire Busy Bee*, 21 January 1882.

42 'A midnight dance', *Comus*, 17 January 1878; 'Birmingham cribs', *Lion*, 19 April 1878.

43 'A word to the young', *Town Crier*, January 1884; 'Respectable blackguardism', *Yorkshire Busy Bee*, 10 March 1883.

44 'The "club"', *Lion*, 5 April 1877; 'Talking of Oscar', *Owl*, 8 September 1882; 'Chilli Chutnee', *Owl*, 6 October 1882. For more general comments of lower middle-class 'manliness' see A. J. Hammerton, 'The English weakness?' in A. J. Kidd and D. Nicholls (eds), *Gender, Civic Culture and Consumerism: Middle Class Identity in Britain 1800–1940* (Manchester: Manchester University Press, 1999).

45 'The wretched rich', *Town Crier*, February 1884; 'Riding in the trams', *Yorkshire Busy Bee*, 14 January and 11 February 1882.

46 See, for example, 'Studies from the streets' and 'Leeds street types', *Yorkshire Busy Bee*, 28 January and 18 March 1882.

47 Bourdieu, *Distinction: A Social Critique of the Judgement of Taste* (London: Routledge, 1992), p. 467; *Practical Reason* (Cambridge: Polity, 1998), ch. 1.

48 T. Wemyss Reid, *A Memoir of John Deakin Heaton* (London, 1883), p. 157; 'A word to the young'.

49 See, for example, the discussions in F. M. L. Thompson, *The Rise of Respectable Society* (London: Fontana, 1988), pp. 181–2; N. Kirk, *Change, Continuity and Class* (Manchester: Manchester University Press, 1998), pp. 115–37.

50 *Yorkshire Busy Bee*, 27 January 1883, p. 51; 'Riding in the trams', *Yorkshire Busy Bee*, 14 January 1882.

51 'Ladies public houses', *Owl*, 10 April 1879; 'The pursuit of literature', *Yorkshire Busy Bee*, 15 April 1882.

52 J. Lloyd, 'Errors of civilisation from a medical standpoint' [1892], *Birmingham and Edgbaston Society Addresses 1877–1927* (Birmingham, 1927), p. 11. For the figure of Smowler see 'A tavern parliament', *The Lion*, 11 January 1877; *Owl*, 4 June 1884.

53 B. Waites, *A Class Society at War* (Leamington Spa: Berg, 1987), esp. ch. 2; G. Stedman Jones, *Languages of Class* (Cambridge: Cambridge University Press, 1983), ch. 5.

54 C. Bell, *Ritual Theory, Ritual Practice* (Oxford: Oxford University Press,

1992), p. 74. For other helpful discussions of ritual and its definition see S. Lukes, 'Political ritual and social integration', *Sociology*, 9 (1975), pp. 289–308; E. Muir, *Ritual in Early Modern Europe* (Cambridge: Cambridge University Press, 1997), introduction.

55   S. Gunn, 'The Manchester middle class, 1850–1880' (Ph.D. thesis, Manchester University, 1992), ch. 4.

56   'Kershaw, Leese, Sidebottom and Co.', *Manchester City News*, 21 January 1865.

57   Mills, *Sir Charles Macara*, p. 27.

58   Girouard, *The English Town*, p. 286; 'To and fro on the Bowdon line', *Freelance*, 14 December 1867.

59   'To the ladies', *Lion*, 19 April, 1877.

60   W. Schivelbusch, *The Railway Journey* (Leamington Spa: Berg, 1986), pp. 73–7.

61   Marcus, *Engels, Manchester and the Working Class*, p. 154.

62   W. S. Richardson, *How to Attain the Position of Managing Clerk and How to Keep It* (Manchester, 1856), p. 10.

63   Love and Barton, *Manchester As It Is* (Manchester, 1839), p. 38; Wemyss Reid, *Memoir of John Deakin Heaton*, pp. 101–2.

64   C. Rowley, *Fifty Years of Work Without Wages* (London, 1911), pp. 43–4.

65   Love and Barton, *Manchester As It Is*, p. 192; 'On the Rialto', *Sphinx*, 25 July 1868; D. A. Farnie, 'The commercial development of Manchester in the later nineteenth century', *Manchester Review*, 7 (1956), pp. 327–33.

66   R. J. Allen, *The Manchester Royal Exchange* (Manchester, 1921), p. 27; W. C. Taylor, *Notes of a Tour in the Manufacturing Districts* (London: Frank Cass, [1842] 1968), pp. 10–13; D. A. Farnie, 'An index of commercial activity: the membership of the Manchester Royal Exchange, 1809–1948', *Business History*, 21 (1979), pp. 98–9.

67   Farnie, 'Index of commercial activity', p. 98; Taylor, *Notes of a Tour*, p. 13.

68   R. Gray, *The Factory Question and Industrial England, 1830–1860* (Cambridge: Cambridge University Press, 1996), p. 98.

69   'The square', *City Lantern*, 6 November 1874.

70   'In Commercial Street', *Yorkshire Busy Bee*, 27 August 1881; 'Doing the Square', *Freelance*, 3 April 1869.

71   'In Commercial Street'; 'On the Square', *Freelance*, 9 January 1874.

72   D. Scobey, 'Anatomy of the promenade: the politics of bourgeois sociability in nineteenth-century New York', *Social History*, 17, 2 (1992), pp. 219–20.

73   'The Botanical'.

74   *Yorkshire Busy Bee*, 28 October 1882, p. 678.

75   Girouard, *The English Town*, pp. 271–4.

76   *City of Dreadful Delight*, p. 21. For evidence of women's influence on shopping see 'Modern shopping', *Owl*, 6 February 1884; 'Boar Lane'. On women at concerts see ch. 6 of this study.

77   For further comments on ritual and deferral see Bell, *Ritual Theory*, p. 106.

78 For eighteenth-century promenades see P. Borsay, *The English Urban Renaissance* (Oxford: Clarendon Press, 1991), pp. 162–72.

79 Lloyd, 'Errors of civilisation', p. 11.

80 In Manchester, for example, the *Freelance, City Lantern* and *Momus* had all disappeared by 1890.

81 See, for example, the *Owl* in the mid-1890s.

82 For the development of a commercialised working-class culture in the later nineteenth century see E. J. Hobsbawm, 'The making of the working class, 1870–1914' in *Worlds of Labour* (London: Weidenfeld and Nicholson, 1984); G. Stedman Jones, 'Working-class culture and working-class politics in London, 1870–1900' in *Languages of Class*; C. Waters, *British Socialists and the Politics of Popular Culture, 1884–1914* (Manchester: Manchester University Press, 1992).

4

Clubland: the private in the public

In the Victorian city the lines dividing public and private domains were multiple and shifting. Other lines of territorial and ideological demarcation cut across the conventional middle-class opposition between a public world of work and politics and a private world of family and domesticity. Thus while the city centre was recast, at one level, as a domain of pleasure accessible to an anonymous public, the city contained its own private domains reserved for subscribers or initiates. Of all urban institutions the most exclusive and impervious to change was the gentlemen's club. Throughout the 'long nineteenth century' male social clubs remained select and private institutions at the heart of an expanding public sphere.

These fraternities extended from the freemasons, whose activities became increasingly closed and secretive in the course of the nineteenth century, to the growing number of more open clubs and societies whose purpose was to provide an arena for eating, drinking and socialising for middle-class men.[1] It is the latter group of institutions with which this chapter is concerned. Private associations in the heart of the city, they became a significant presence in urban life, forming a distinct social world known as 'clubland' and involving an increasingly wide cross-section of the male business, professional and white-collar population. Clubs came to occupy a strategic position in bourgeois culture. They represented an important focus of bourgeois leisure in their own right, while also providing a gateway for middle-class men to other opportunities and pleasures that the city had to offer. Clubland defined a world of male homosociality, predicated on the absence of women. Yet it comprised different forms of middle-class male sociability, corresponding to the diverse cultural styles of particular clubs and societies. How clubland developed and how it was internally differentiated are therefore important issues in understanding the construction of a bourgeois culture in the industrial cities during the second half of the nineteenth century.

The development of clubland

A now extensive literature has emphasised the centrality of clubs and societies in eighteenth-century urban culture, both in London and the provincial towns.[2] They were an integral part of what Peter Borsay has termed the 'English urban renaissance' between 1660 and 1770, the extensive refashioning of provincial town life around the imperatives of culture, consumption and fashionable leisure. Clubs and societies were a constituent part of the eighteenth-century concept of 'sociability'; whether their purpose was political or cultural 'they were also treated as social institutions in which ties of friendship and good company could be cultivated'.[3] Social and cultural attributes, distinct from those of birth, became increasingly important to the definition of gentility after 1700, allowing for greater ease of interaction between middle and upper ranks in a range of settings from the learned society to the spa. While these characteristics were most marked in fashionable resorts and county towns like Bath and York, they were also evident in the newer industrialising centres. John Money's study of later eighteenth-century Birmingham depicts a flourishing urban culture organised around the assembly rooms, the music festival, libraries, and associations like the Bean Club, where the elites of town and county came together for the purposes of pleasure and influence.[4] Eighteenth-century Leeds lacked the size and wealth of Birmingham or Manchester, but it too possessed an assembly rooms from 1726, one of the finest provincial subscription libraries, a public concert series from 1762 and its own clubs and societies.[5]

This broad-based associational culture, rooted in concepts of sociability and cultivated gentility, did not survive the political upheavals of the 1790s wholly intact. Significantly, those institutions which possessed an unbroken record of existence in Birmingham and Manchester between the early eighteenth and nineteenth centuries were Tory clubs, the Bean Club and John Shaw's, established in 1660 and 1738 respectively.[6] The politicisation of public life which accompanied the resurgence of the movement for parliamentary reform and the French Revolution left few urban societies untouched. In the climate of Tory reaction many institutions of liberal culture, like the Manchester Literary and Philosophical Society and the Birmingham Lunar Society, found themselves suppressed or neutralised.[7] In Thomas Bewick's Newcastle, where according to John Brewer there were fifty clubs and societies by the turn of the century, the tenor of these associations remained liberal though no less politicised. Bewick himself was 'an astringent critic of autocratic government, proud aristocrats and narrow-minded clerics of the Church of England'.[8] The predominant tone of clubs established from the 1790s in Manchester, by contrast, was Tory Anglican, whether social in inspiration such as the Billiard Club (1792) and Scramble Club (1801), or political as in the case of the Church and King Club (1791) and the Pitt Club (1812).[9]

An analysis of the membership of the leading Manchester Tory club, John Shaw's, in 1825 shows how tightly it was linked to the existing network of the town's political, social and cultural institutions. Of the fifty-seven members in 1825, thirty-eight had been involved in branches of the cotton trade. Over half the membership held public office in the Tory-dominated institutions of local government, such as the court leet and police commission; nine served as churchwardens or sidesmen at the Collegiate Church (later Manchester Cathedral), emphasising the Tory connection with Anglicanism. Two-thirds were also members of clubs or societies other than John Shaw's, notably cultural bodies such as the Literary and Philosophical Society, the Natural History Society and the Portico Library. The figures for institutional involvement, it should be noted, are likely to be underestimates since the information was not comprehensive.[10] What they emphasise is the high degree of inter-connection between the memberships of elite institutions in early nineteenth-century Manchester. Indeed, if kinship and Nonconformity were the principal forces for cohesion in the town's Whig/Liberal elite at the period, it was the network of clubs and societies, together with Anglicanism, that seems to have played an equivalent role in local Toryism.[11]

However, this configuration was not stable. The widely noted development of middle-class societies in the 1820s and 1830s was mainly confined to elite scientific and cultural bodies, and has obscured other aspects of associational change.[12] From the later 1830s the older Tory clubs like John Shaw's and the Bean Club went into steady decline. In 1836 the minutes of the Birmingham Bean Club lamented the committee's failure 'to increase its members and promote its general interest, particularly at a time when it is highly important that the principles of the club should be promulgated and fostered'. Between the 1820s and the early 1850s the membership of John Shaw's more than halved, and the seepage continued inexorably over the next two decades.[13] Decline mirrored the disastrous electoral fortunes of urban Toryism following municipal reform in 1835. At the first municipal elections after incorporation Tories won no council seats in Manchester or Birmingham, and only six of the forty-eight seats in Leeds.[14] Yet decline was not restricted to political clubs alone. In Manchester, institutions of sociability like the assembly rooms and the Billiard Club, formerly the 'recognised resort of the wit, the fashion, the intelligence, and the learning of the district', were defunct by the 1850s. Similarly in decay was the Leeds Old Club, founded in 1796 and patronised by members of Leeds' Liberal merchant families, such as the Luptons and Luccocks, in the earlier part of the century.[15] The reasons for the waning of an older club culture by 1850 thus went wider than politics. Leonore Davidoff and Catherine Hall have argued that evangelical imperatives for men to return to home and family after work influenced men to abjure the pleasures of clubs and associations in early nineteenth-century Birmingham.[16] The gradual suburbanisation of the wealthy, especially in Birmingham and Manchester, reduced the attractiveness of older associations that had relied on a regular evening clientele. More important than the blunt fact of out-migration, however, were the ways in which the city centre was reconstituted from the mid-century as a site not only of business and public affairs, but also of consumption and private pleasures. In this context, what was significant about the decades after 1850 was the development of a fresh generation of clubs and societies that came to constitute an important part of a new world of male leisure and sociability.

In many ways the pioneer institutions were the significantly titled Union clubs, designed to attract the male elite on the basis of wealth, not political or sectarian affiliation. Manchester's Union Club set up in 1825 was proto-typical. By the mid-1830s it had a clubhouse, an entrance fee of thirty guineas with an annual subscription of five guineas, and a membership of over three hundred, including the largest employers of the city and region, Liberals like the Gregs, Heywoods and Ashtons, Tories like the Birleys, Houldsworths and Loyds.[17] The elite social clubs were more commonly established later, however; the Leeds Club, which later added 'Union' to its title, in 1847, Birmingham's Union Club in 1856. What such institutions shared were not only high entrance fees and a non-sectarian admissions policy, but also a strong emphasis on comfort and privacy embodied in purpose-built clubhouses. They were thus distinguished from the old elite political associations, like John Shaw's or the Bean Club, peripatetic institutions based in traditional inns and taverns. The social clubs of the 1850s created a new kind of space for the rich, permanent private zones in the centre of the urban public sphere where bourgeois men could drink, dine and converse surrounded by the luxuries of urban modernity.

The elite social clubs were only one aspect of the expansion of associational life in the mid-Victorian years. More representative of the wider middle classes were the numerous cultural associations established in these years. In 1866 Birmingham counted, among others, a Debating Society, Literary Association, Shakespearean Reading Society, Art Union, Society of Artists, and several musical societies and libraries.[18] Entrance to these societies was usually by ballot and involved a relatively modest fee; the Birmingham and Edgbaston Debating Society, for example, had a 5s. entrance fee and a 5s. annual subscription. In addition to their closed proceedings, they also held 'semi-public' evenings and conversazioni, to which friends and relatives of members were invited, again at a modest charge. While such bodies were therefore able to control entry, they nevertheless had a broader (and often younger) membership than social clubs like the Union. Both the Central Literary Association and the Birmingham and Edgbaston Debating Society had a membership of over two hundred in the 1860s. The Birmingham and Midland Institute's 'General Department', which provided weekly lectures on literary and scientific topics, a newsroom and an annual conversazione for one guinea per annum, had over twelve hundred members by 1870. Yet there were limits to the popular character of such bodies. When in 1858 the MP C. B. Adderly commended the Birmingham and Edgbaston Debating Society to the House of Commons as an example of a rational association of 'skilled artisans', the Society's secretary speedily responded: 'It is in no sense a working man's institution, but comprises amongst its nearly two hundred members many graduates of both Universities, physicians, architects, lawyers, manufacturers and tradesmen'.[19]

Manchester, too, spawned a range of new cultural associations from the mid-nineteenth century designed to appeal to a wider propertied population than simply the elite. The Athenaeum aimed to cater for the city's 'middle classes', the amorphous population of clerks and young men – often the sons of wealthy families – apprenticed to professional and commercial firms. Originally opened in 1839, it was effectively relaunched, following financial difficulties, in the early 1850s, with an annual subscription of 24s. (16s. for those under twenty). By the mid-1860s, with billiard room, restaurant and newsroom, as well as classes, lectures and debates, and a membership approaching two thousand, it was increasingly depicted as a 'middle-class club' rather than a centre for education and improvement, despite objections to this trend by older members.[20] Other associations developed more closely attuned to the cultural interests of specific groups. The Manchester Literary Club (1862) represented a formalisation of the earlier Sun Inn group of artisan poets; it included journalists committed to dialect literature and anti-quarian pursuits, such as J. H. Nodal, editor of the *Manchester City News* and several satirical journals, and W. E. A. Axon of the *Manchester Guardian.*[21] Most important was the Brasenose Club, founded in 1869 'to promote the association of gentlemen of Literary, Scientific or Artistic Professions, Pursuits, or Tastes'. Self-consciously 'bohemian' in style, the Brasenose was to be a club in which 'there would not be too much respectability or too much wealth, but in which there would be good fellowship'.[22] Combining cultural interests with a jovial and inclusive sociability, clubs such as these distinguished themselves not only from elite institutions, like the Union, but also from professionalised scientific societies, like the Manchester Natural History Society (1821), and pro-fessional bodies, such as the Manchester Architectural Association (1837).[23]

Leeds was slower than Manchester or Birmingham to develop a network of social and cultural associations, though here also new in-stitutions took root from the late 1840s, such as the Conversation Club and the Archers Society. Yet opportunities for social and cultural activity were clearly extensive in the 1850s and 1860s, as is revealed by the diaries of Benjamin Barker of Bramley near Leeds. The son of a woollen manufacturer, and employed in the firm's warehouse from the late 1850s, Barker's diaries are filled with accounts, not of work or politics, but of events attended. His world appears to have been composed of concert-going, visits to hear lectures and sermons in Leeds and Bradford, debating society evenings at the Bramley Mechanics Institute, trips to the theatre in Manchester, and parties at the houses of local elite families, such as the Luptons, Illingworths and Heatons. That such a pattern of behaviour was considered aberrant is indicated by the upbraiding that Barker received from his father and brothers for neglect of business. Nevertheless, it is suggestive of the extensive social and cultural oppor-tunities open to young men of relatively modest middle-class means by the period.[24]

It was out of this matrix of institutions that the efflorescence of provincial club-life occurred between 1870 and 1900. 'Clubland', as it was termed, became a distinct sphere, indicating both a particular social space in the city and distinct modes of behaviour and ways of life associated with it.[25] The new political clubhouses from the 1870s set the pace in terms of scale and expenditure. In Manchester, the new Reform Club was opened in 1871 at a cost of £60,000; the Conservative Club followed in 1876, built at a cost of £110,000. In Birmingham, the new Liberal Club, opened in 1885 as part of the complex of political, cultural and educational institutions known as the Forum, was so lavishly fitted that it proved too expensive for the party to maintain, standing uninhabited in the late 1880s.[26] Established by subscribers and run as private companies, the political clubs catered for members on an ample scale. The Manchester Conservative Club, which had eleven hundred members by 1885, was staffed by 'three tribes' of servants, pages, liveried footmen and black-coated waiters, while the Reform Club, with over two thousand members, employed sixty-five staff by the early twentieth century.[27] The general increase in the size and wealth of many clubs at the period also encouraged the movement to more permanent and luxurious surroundings. Manchester's Brasenose Club was symptomatic of the trend. Starting out in one room in 1870 with an annual subscription of two guineas, the club's popularity with major employers like Sir William Bailey, James Kershaw and the Galloways compromised its bohemian credentials. By the early 1890s the membership had risen to over three hundred and its subscription to eight guineas. In 1892 a permanent clubhouse was established in the former building of the National and Provincial Bank in Mosley Street, a move that supporters of the old bohemian ethos, like the architect Alfred Darbyshire, viewed with alarm: 'I feared the Poor Artist element would have to go and that Bullion would reign supreme'.[28]

While the size and scale of the larger social and political clubs did much to define provincial clubland in the last quarter of the nineteenth century, it was also characterised by an increase in the number and variety of institutions. In the 1890s the directories of Birmingham, Leeds and Manchester listed over twenty clubs and societies in each city, excluding the large number of ward associations of the political parties. They included 'Ladies' clubs and associations, newer cultural societies like the Birmingham Ruskin Society and the Leeds Arts Club, and a host of sporting clubs.[29] Yet the true number was much higher since the directories ignored the more modest or transient social clubs occupying rented rooms in hotels or inns, such as that recommended in a Manchester periodical in 1870:

> The chief room was supplied with newspapers and magazines, and an empty bookcase always reminded members with odd volumes to spare of its unfurnished state. The second room had its card-table and chessboard, with pigeon-holes for members' letters, and a stationery case filled with club note-paper. The subscription was fixed at two guineas per year, with a guinea entrance fee after the first fifty.[30]

Claims that urban social life was in decline by the later nineteenth century, such as J. W. Hunter's assertion in 1870 that 'as a social institution the club must now be regarded as a thing of the past', were wide of the mark.[31] It was in the decades between 1870 and 1914 that social clubs enjoyed their heyday. The precise number of participants is impossible to calculate, given the semi-private nature of such institutions and the facts of plural membership. But the numbers affiliated to the array of Institutes, Athenaeums and gentlemen's clubs, as well the clubhouses of the main political parties, indicates that it involved many thousands of middle-class men. In this period, clubs formed part of something akin to a mass bourgeois culture of sociability that paralleled developments in popular urban leisure. As clubs and societies became clustered in the city centre, so clubhouses became a visible part of the institutional fabric. As early as 1876 a commentator remarked that Manchester's Mosley Street was now dominated by the headquarters of banks and clubs like the Union and the Clarendon, 'sedate' establishments inhabited by elderly men, and identifiable by the presence of 'servitors in livery' outside.[32] Moreover, they had become organised within a distinct field of urban sociability in which institutions took on social connotations as 'bohemian', 'select', 'swagger' or 'cribs', defined in relation to one another in a loose hierarchy of prestige according to scale of entry fees and degree of exclusivity. Thus in late nineteenth-century Manchester, a contemporary recalled, the Union Club 'was to the other Manchester clubs what the Guards are to the army', while in contradistinction to the Union, the Brasenose in 1870 considered itself the home of an intellectual elite, a club which 'subordinates brass to brains'.[33] 'Clubland' designated a world apart, but also a world that was internally differentiated by wealth and status, and by specific modes of sociability.

Gender, status and sociability

The changing pattern of modes of male sociability over time is difficult to delineate, not least because the outward forms of club life, such as the rules of subscription, governance and conduct, remained relatively constant through the nineteenth century. Clubs sought to cling to time-honoured rituals, such as dinners and archaic toasts ('Church and King and Down with the Rump!'), as a means of asserting a male esprit de corps and traditions that were seen as embodying their unique character.[34] Yet changes there clearly were, whether measured in terms of notions of masculinity, sociability or the private/public division. Richard Sennett has argued that private clubs were neglected in mid-eighteenth-century London in favour of the tavern or coffee-house, because the cult of sociability demanded a more equal and open exchange of information than exclusive institutions could provide; put bluntly, the 'limitations of the club soon produced boredom'. Yet by the mid-nineteenth century privacy had come to rule over sociability: 'people went to clubs so that they could sit in silence, without being disturbed by anyone; silence had become a right'. Although a regime of silence was restricted to certain London clubs, such as White's, and was not typical in the provinces, from the mid-century the provincial social club was nevertheless conceived as a refuge from aspects of city and suburban life, a charmed circle sealed off from private cares and public duties.[35]

The male club was first and foremost a retreat from women, a 'masculine sanctuary' in Katherine Chorley's phrase.[36] While urban space as a whole was demarcated by gender in the nineteenth century, no institution was so carefully and persistently safeguarded against women's intrusion as the male social club. In the 1860s and 1870s women might occasionally be invited to conversazioni, debates and lectures at cultural associations such as the Birmingham and Edgbaston Debating Society or the Manchester Arts Club. On sporting occasions women's attendance could prove vital to the event's success, as the Leeds Archers Society acknowledged in 1879 when lack of public interest at open meetings was attributed to the 'absence of the magnetic influence and the charm which accompany the presence of the ladies'.[37] Yet women's presence at middle-class clubs and societies was permitted only in so far as women constituted a passive audience for male prowess, or were directly invited by male relatives. The women's clubs and societies formed in provincial cities from the 1880s were strictly separate organisations, as their names indicated: the West Riding Ladies Club, the Birmingham Ladies Association for Useful Work, the Manchester Ladies Literary Club.

Significantly, the higher the status of a male club, the less likely it was to tolerate women's participation on any count. In 1875 the Manchester Brasenose Club held a conversazione and art exhibition to which 'ladies' were invited. Yet when a similar event was proposed at the expensive new clubhouse twenty years later, it was rejected on the grounds that it might 'injure the prestige' of the Club.[38] The profound ambivalence that marked men's attitude to women's appearance in public, as alternately raising or lowering the tone of male proceedings, was thus used to preclude women's involvement. Although in the 1890s women did enter the more culturally and politically progressive provincial societies, such as the Leeds Arts Club, on a formally equal footing with men, this was itself a statement of the self-conscious radicalism of such bodies. There was no necessary weakening of the bar on women in more established clubs. Indeed, examples such as that of the Brasenose Club suggests that by the late nineteenth century the total exclusion of women came to be seen by middle-class men as a fundamental criterion of a club's standing and repute. As Katherine Chorley recalled of the Manchester Union Club before the First World War: 'The community quarters of a monastery are not more jealously withdrawn from outsiders than was the Union Club from feminine penetration. No one among our ladies would have dared enquire for her spouse at its portals'.[39]

Clubs were also viewed as a refuge for men from a feminised domesticity. As Joseph Hunter forcefully put in 1876, they enabled men 'to step outside the circle of domestic cares, and discuss masculine topics in a masculine atmosphere'.[40] Yet this was not an unproblematic view at the period, contravening as it did the evangelical tenet that once work and public duties were finished, men should return to the domestic hearth.[41] The force of such moral invocations may have been waning by the mid-Victorian period, as middle-class women themselves became an increasingly visible part of the urban public, but they lingered on in the 1870s and 1880s in the form of a persistent uneasiness about the respectability of club life. Even in bohemian clubs, which sought most strongly to promote the virtues of homosocial fellowship over those of home and family, it was deemed normal for office-holders to resign their post on marriage. Similarly, in describing a model club in 1870, a Manchester periodical reassured its readers that the majority of members were unmarried. Transmuted into a haven for widowers, bachelors and young men (who would thereby be spared the temptations of the tavern), the club could be depicted as providing a surrogate domesticity, supplying 'the comforts of a home' and a 'happy family' to single men or visitors to town. 'An Englishman's club for the time being is his private house. The members represent his family and friends.'[42]

Much of this was a shallow fiction, as the numbers of married men in membership lists demonstrated, but that it was felt necessary at all is suggestive of the liminal position of the male social club in the construction of the public and private well into the nineteenth century. For the club not only offered an escape from women, domesticity and business life, but also a way in to the social life of the city. Entry into the world of clubs and societies was an important rite of passage to adulthood for middle-class men from the 1850s; it signalled material independence and, with it, an emotional detachment from the parental home. Club membership not only lent a veneer of substance and sophistication to the individual, but also gave access to the rituals of drinking, dining and companionship, as well as to other pleasures of the city that lay beyond the clubhouse doors. Here, however, it is necessary to differentiate between types of club and the specific, if overlapping, modes of sociability and masculinity which they promoted.

The most sedate establishments in later nineteenth-century clubland were the Union clubs and their slightly less prestigious imitators, the Albion and the Victoria in Leeds, the Clarendon, the Princes' and the Trafford in Manchester. Also included in this category were the political clubhouses, the Conservative and Reform, whose committees were composed 'of club-men rather than politicians – of men who have known how to organise and improve the Kitchen as well as the Reading Room and the Library'.[43] Frequently advertised as 'dignified and secluded' the sedate social club was intended, in Sennett's words, to be 'cut off from the confusion, smoke and noise of the city', to represent 'security against the city's complexity'.[44] Substantial expenditure was lavished on the interior furnishings – carpets, panelling, lighting – designed to create an interior of 'elegance and comfort', a 'soothing influence' as a visitor to Manchester's leading clubs observed in 1869.[45] A studied opulence in the surroundings was complimented by plentiful food and drink, the scale and magnificence of the dining room and the quality of food being indices of the importance of the establishment. The Conservative Clubs in Birmingham and Manchester were regularly referred to as 'gastro-political' institutions, yet the emphasis was widely shared among the elite city clubs. As one commentator averred: 'after all, it is in the kitchen that much of the success of the club is to be looked for'.[46] The consumption of food and drink was crucial to the financial prosperity of institutions, the accounts of the Leeds Club, for example, revealing that receipts from food and drink consistently outstripped those from membership fees between the 1850s and the 1890s, and by a steadily increasing proportion.[47] The elite clubs prided themselves on their range of amenities, the library, reading room and, above all, the billiard room. In the 1870s skill at billiards was considered to be evidence of a misspent youth according to Herbert Spencer, but thereafter it became *de rigueur* for all but the most highbrow establishments. At the Manchester Reform Club the billiard room was regarded as the most important room in the club and its social centre, while the Clarendon boasted the finest such room in the city.[48]

There is, therefore, some indication of a relaxed conviviality in elite establishments, but this should be balanced against persistent evidence of more formal codes of conduct. These codes extended from qualifications for entry to rules governing members' behaviour. There are signs that these stipulations grew more, not less, rigid in the later nineteenth century. While entrance fees and subscriptions rose substantially, entry requirements grew stiffer in many clubs judged by the rules of the 'blackball'.[49] All the elite clubs had strict rules on bankruptcy, which led to immediate exclusion, on gambling and on tipping servants. Clubs sought to intervene directly to uphold their dignified reputation. At Birmingham's Union Club, the committing of 'any act derogatory to the character of a gentleman, either in or out of the Club' rendered the offender subject to expulsion. In the 1880s the Club Committee strengthened its disciplinary powers by establishing a 'Special Meeting' to reprimand or expel any member judged culpable 'by reason of his conduct'.[50] The elite clubs therefore sought to marry their exclusivity and sedate character with a code of gentlemanly behaviour, itself designed to ease social interaction between diverse groups among the membership: urban employers and professionals, county gentry, army officers stationed nearby, judges and lawyers serving at the assizes.[51]

The discussion and debating associations provided a different sphere of sociability, marked by commitment to 'rational' exchange of views across a spectrum of educated urban opinion. The Birmingham and Edgbaston Debating Society, whose purpose was defined as 'Discussion of any subjects, literary, political, historical, social or otherwise', attracted large numbers of men interested in public affairs, including figures such as Joseph Chamberlain and J. T. Bunce, and held open as well as 'members only' debates.[52] The Leeds Conversation Club, on the other hand, had a strictly limited membership of twelve, met in private houses, and sought to promote conversation 'on any subject except controversial Politics and Religion' while disdaining the 'evil of set orations or debating society dialectics'.[53] The Club's members included not only Liberals like Edward Baines, W. E. Forster and the Unitarian minister Charles Wicksteed, but also the Tory banker, George Hyde, and a succession of Anglican vicars. From 1859 the Club sought to extend its influence on Leeds 'society' by inviting up to three hundred notables to annual parties, 'so as to make acquainted with each other the different little coteries into which [Leeds] is divided'.[54] Topics of discussion ranged across the arts, 'social' questions such as poverty, crime and education, and politics; by 1868 the Conversation Club had amended its rules on politics and religion, which in any case had never been strictly adhered to. In 1851–52, for example, the Club topics included discussions of international relations, currency reform, the taxes on knowledge, and the question of whether biography was 'conducive to sound historical realisations'. Similarly, the Birmingham and Edgbaston Debating Society's deliberations in 1865–66 included discussions of Byron's poetry, alpine climbing and the behaviour of Governor Eyre in the Jamaican rebellion.[55]

The rational associations saw themselves as firmly linked to a culture of improvement. Discussions at the Conversation Club were taken as the catalyst for the setting up of the Leeds Improvement Society and the Educational Council, and the Birmingham and Edgbaston Debating Society was likewise depicted as an essential part of the city's liberal culture:

> There cannot be the slightest doubt but that the free discussion of all questions which affect the progress and best interests of humanity, which is the principle which has animated this Society, has enabled its members to take a prominent and useful part in bringing about that change in popular opinion which is necessary to the establishment of all reforms, moral, social, intellectual, physical, political, and spiritual.[56]

Other societies like the Central Literary Association, sister society to the Birmingham and Edgbaston, shared similar aims, the Association claiming to cultivate 'individual judgement by fair and temperate discussion'.[57] This culture of rational exchange fostered an ideal of sociability identified with liberal education, eloquence and good fellowship. As such it was an easy target for critics who satirised the 'intellectual athlete' with his 'scraps of French and Latin, and a surface acquaintance with art, politics and literature, who lays down the law on every topic'.[58] Yet if the ideal drew on earlier notions of urban culture associated with rational knowledge, it also differed from them. Unlike the Lit. and Phils., and the scientific societies of the early nineteenth century, the later rational associations encouraged active participation and a generalised knowledge. Unlike the earlier social and political clubs, they were organised on non-sectarian lines, and sought consciously to connect their activities with a larger notion of urban and national improvement. At the same time, they retained a strong club identity, nurtured by means of an annual round of dinners, conversazioni and excursions.

The third significant milieu which provided a context for sociability, distinct from the elite clubs and the rational discussion societies alike, was that of the bohemian clubs like the Arts and Brasenose in Manchester and the Savage Club in Leeds. From the 1870s such clubs defined a distinctive urban realm and style, combining an assertive homosociality with a self-conscious aestheticism. As one devotee proclaimed, 'Bohemia is the country of universal brotherhood, united by a common sympathy with what is at once aesthetic and unconstrainedly social'.[59] Initiated by groups of journalists, artists and professionals, together with sympathetic businessmen, the bohemian clubs mixed culture and excess. While the activities of smoking, drinking and dining were ritually celebrated as part of a generalised 'good fellowship', impromptu performances were held by leading actors and musicians such as Irving and Hallé. A cultivated unrespectability was an important part of proceedings, Manchester's Brasenose Club styling itself 'the Abiding Place of Genius and the Home of Vice'.[60] High spirits often spilled out of the clubrooms and on to the street. In 1900 fifty members of the Manchester Arts Club met the actor Collette at the stage door of the Theatre Royal after his nightly performance: 'Collette headed the procession in theatrical costume, and, all wearing kilts, they marched via Peter Street, Mount Street and round Albert Square to the Club, Collette playing the bagpipes'.[61] In similarly stylised fashion, members took on specific, half-humorous identities within the club precincts: the Arch Druid, Parmiter, the Chief and his 'braves'. Bohemia thus represented an imaginary domain in which fantasy and sociability were allowed free rein within the liberal framework provided by an unregenerate masculine bonhomie.

Located by design on the margins of respectability, in practice bohemia faced two ways. One way led to the institutions of high culture – the concert hall, the institutions of fine art – to which many 'bohemians' were affiliated. The other led out to the pleasures of the city: saloons, dining rooms and 'low clubs' or brothels. Both the Manchester and the Birmingham periodical press provided weekly coverage of the increasing number and variety of such establishments from the late 1860s. Wine and luncheon bars, restaurants, hotels and fashionable inns were all described in graphic detail.[62] 'The good old-fashioned "smoke-room" is, unhappily for we men of Bohemia, a fast-decaying institution' one Birmingham correspondent complained in 1877; 'for we men of the present age rise the gaudy "luncheon bars" and taverns, where we "loaf" and stand about'.[63] Particular fascination was expressed with the 'low clubs' or 'cribs', where 'painted procuresses' and 'youths holding good appointments, whose flushed faces spoke of nights of debauch' made up 'an easy virtue society'.[64] Bohemia thus represented a point of access into the vicarious pleasures of urban life, embodied, in male form, by the figures of the 'loafer', the 'man about town' and the 'swell'.

Within clubland, therefore, there existed distinct milieux, which, while never wholly discrete, nonetheless corresponded to different modes of masculine sociability. The sedate elite clubs, the rational discussion

societies and the deliberate informality of bohemia represented different
ways for men to define or identify themselves in the later nineteenth-
century city. Yet the different milieux were also founded on shared codes
of class and gender. Entry into the fraternity was carefully bounded by
entrance fees and the balloting of applicants for membership, thus
preserving exclusivity and status. Manual workers were represented
only in the form of liveried servants or tradespeople catering to middle-
class needs. No less importantly, male clubs defined themselves not
simply by separation from women, but in opposition to them; the forms
of masculinity promulgated were predicated on what might be termed
a dialectic of women's absent presence. The codes of gentlemanly
conduct that characterised the elite clubs rested on the simultaneous
recognition and erasure of the feminine 'other'. The 'rational' discussion
of the debating societies was considered possible only in the context of
women's silence. Bohemia, which was arguably the most misogynistic
of all the club milieux, insisted on its status as a 'brotherhood' freed
from feminine 'constraints'. As a member of the Manchester Arts Club
put it, 'bohemianism' denoted 'behaviour not indulged in when women
were present'.[65] Clubland therefore rested on a double closure. It made
it possible for bourgeois men to live out an important part of their social
life in a private environment insulated, so far as was deemed desirable,
from the complex relations of class and gender pertaining beyond the
clubhouse doors.

The politics of clubland

If men's clubs represented a particular form of the private, this did not
mean they were set apart from other kinds of public activity. Recent
interpretations of urban bourgeois culture have argued that in the
mid-nineteenth century, clubs and societies, in line with culture generally, came to represent a neutral sphere where different politico-religious
sections of the middle class were able to interact and forge a shared
social identity.[66] Certainly, the clubs established in provincial cities from
the 1840s sought to attract members independent of sectarian affiliations
and to limit discussion of 'controversial' matters of religion and party
politics. This did not imply, however, that such associations existed
independently of party or wider political cultures. By the 1870s, if not
earlier, clubland represented a space in which political cultures were
refracted and reinforced in specific ways.

    This was most obviously the case with the great party clubhouses,
which served as organisational epicentres for Liberal and Conservative

activists of city and region after the Second Reform Act of 1867. It was from the Billiard Room in the Manchester Reform Club that Jacob Bright chose to launch his parliamentary election campaigns in 1876 and 1880, while council politics was represented by the existence of the 'Corporation Table' in the Club dining room. Yet outside election times it was the social functions of the Club which were uppermost; as the Liberal editor of the *Manchester Guardian* put it, 'you can always find someone who agrees with you, and plenty who disagree, to sit down with you at luncheon'.[67] In the party clubhouses social and political activities were inextricably meshed. In Birmingham the emergent Liberal caucus sought to establish a social base independent of existing political institutions, setting up the inappropriately named Arts Club in 1873, whose purpose was to facilitate 'the daily social intercourse of gentlemen holding Liberal opinions, who are interested in the public life of Birmingham'. Mainly used as a dining club, the Arts served as a focus for sixty or so key members of the caucus, including Chamberlain, Bunce, Kenrick, Matthews and Timmins.[68] By the 1870s club life was seen to underpin the political activities of all parties in Birmingham. 'Clubs, clubs clubs!' the *Dart* exclaimed at the opening of the Birmingham Conservative Club in 1877: 'they [the Conservatives] are going to thrash their opponents by clubs; they are going to eat and drink, and talk them into silence, and so win'.[69]

If the emphasis placed on politics in the 1870s and 1880s is notable, it was not unprecedented, nor restricted to the institutions of party. From the 1850s social and cultural associations were frequently seen as providing their members with a political education and an opportunity to influence civic affairs. The Birmingham and Edgbaston Debating Society saw itself as a 'training school in which the intellectual athlete has prepared himself for the more vigorous, if not the more difficult, conflicts of public life'.[70] For all its avowedly 'non-political' policy, the Leeds Conversation Club actively sought to intervene in public questions like smoke abatement and the Town Hall in the 1850s and 1860s, and consequently came into direct conflict with the Liberal town council. The Leeds 'elite', represented by the membership of the Conversation Club, was thus counterposed to what were defined as the 'philistine' ratepayer interests of the council.[71]

More generally, the cultures of party politics were refracted in associational cultures, no matter how firmly the latter professed their independence of political affiliations. The shibboleths of urban Liberalism were dutifully recited in the Birmingham Central Literary Association's review of its first ten years: 'It has given help and pleasure to many outside the ranks of its own members, it has sought help and patronage from none. Self-help and self-sustaining; all that it has gained, it has earned; and in the honest satisfaction of an honourable want, it has become useful and prosperous'.[72] Even in the bohemian clubs, the assumption of an unworldly aestheticism had political overtones. Despite the presence of a number of Manchester's Liberal councillors and MPs among its membership, the ethos of the Brasenose Club revealed itself as anti-municipal and anti-'improving'. Similarly, opposition to urban Liberalism was the unifying factor among the curious amalgam of groups that came to make up the Leeds Arts Club from 1893. According to its historian, the Club was 'a conjunction of Tory businessmen with Social-ist professional workers, the line of unity surfacing often as an intense antipathy to nineteenth-century Liberalism, with what they believed was its moral hypocrisy, its smug belief in perpetual progress, but mostly its philistinism'. In other cases pro-imperial sentiment was manifested, as at the Leeds Savage Club which marked the British army's victories at Ladysmith and Bloomfontein in 1900 with special celebratory 'pow-wows'.[73] A strong vein of Conservatism, whether instinctual or openly political, appears to have run through late nineteenth-century bohemian culture, just as the earlier discussion and debating circles were informed by an incipient or active Liberalism.

If clubland cannot be defined in simple political terms, neither did it constitute a 'non-political' sphere of bourgeois association. Social clubs were shaped by the wider political cultures of the provincial cities and in turn shaped them. Club and party shared masculine cultures of 'rational' debate and sociability, of dinners, toasts, and convivial bon-homie. They represented closely linked institutions enabling middle-class men to engage in the life of the city on their own terms while remaining, ostensibly at least, within established codes of class and gender. The conjunction of politics and club-life helped to define public forms of masculinity in the late nineteenth century and to give politics, in Denise Riley's words, 'an intensified air of privacy and invulnerability'.[74] Clubland, in short, was an important terrain on which the political cultures of the later Victorian period were formed.

The study of gentlemen's clubs is a reminder of the complex ordering of the public and the private in the nineteenth century, the lines between these spheres demarcating not simply home and work but also different spaces within the city itself. Clubs remained quintessen-tially private institutions, owned by subscribers or limited companies and governed by their own sets of rules, which in some cases were deemed to pre-empt civil law.[75] The rituals by which clubs asserted their own fraternal identities were designed for private purposes, consolidating internal solidarities of class and status rather than contributing to the outward display of power and authority. Yet such institutions were more than merely private; they bordered the public worlds of politics and urban pleasure to which they gave privileged access. Unlike freemasonry, they proudly published their private proceedings and activities to an urban audience. Membership of clubs, both provincial and metropolitan, was represented as a badge of middle-class status, and recorded along with details of directorships and public offices in obituaries and collective biographies of local worthies.

Together with the increasing public visibility of women as a collectivity, this might suggest a gradual blurring of the boundaries between public and private domains in middle-class life in the decades after 1880. Yet the boundaries specific to clubland did not dissolve before the First World War. On Armistice Day in November 1918 Katherine Chorley broke with protocol and asked to see her father at the Manchester Union Club, an action she considered 'daring', 'absurd' and comprehensible only in the light of the extraordinary events: 'I brought my father out from lunch. I think he wondered, but he smiled and understood'.[76] The dissolution of clubland in the industrial cities only occurred once the social and economic foundations of the provincial middle class fragmented between the two world wars. By 1939 only a handful of the more inveterate or exclusive provincial clubs remained.[77] Clubland in cities like Birmingham, Leeds and Manchester was extinguished not so much by a direct challenge to the codes it represented as by the disintegration of provincial bourgeois culture as a whole in the early twentieth century.

Notes

1 J. Tosh, *A Man's Place: Masculinity and the Middle-Class Home in Victorian England* (New Haven: Yale University Press, 1999), p. 133.

2 See among others P. Borsay, *The English Urban Renaissance: Culture and Society in the Provincial Town, 1660–1770* (Oxford: Clarendon Press, 1991); J. Brewer, *The Pleasures of the Imagination: English Culture in the Eighteenth Century* (London: Harper Collins, 1997); N. McKendrick, J. Brewer and J. H. Plumb, *The Birth of a Consumer Society: The Commercialisation of Eighteenth-Century England* (London: Europa, 1982); P. Langford, *Public Life and the Propertied Englishman* (Oxford: Clarendon Press, 1991).

3 Borsay, *English Urban Renaissance*, p. 268.

4 J. Money, *Experience and Identity: Birmingham and the West Midlands* (Manchester: Manchester University Press, 1977).

5   Borsay, *English Urban Renaissance*, appendices, for details of provincial
    social and cultural institutions. For eighteenth-century Leeds see
    M. Beresford, *East End, West End. The Face of Leeds During Urbanisation,
    1684–1842* (Leeds: Thoresby Society, 1989).

6   For a full description of these clubs see F. S. Stancliffe, *John Shaw's
    1738–1938* (Timperley: St Ann's Press, 1938) and J. B. Stone, *Annals of
    the Bean Club, Birmingham* (Birmingham, 1904).

7   A. Thackray, 'Natural knowledge in cultural context: the Manchester
    model', *American Historical Review*, lxix (1974); R. E. Schofield, *The Lunar
    Society of Birmingham: A Social History of Provincial Science and Industry in
    Eighteenth-Century England* (Oxford: Clarendon Press, 1963).

8   Brewer, *Pleasures of the Imagination*, pp. 507, 525.

9   J. W. Hunter, 'The clubs of old Manchester', *Papers of the Manchester
    Literary Club*, vol. 2 (1876).

10 Figures based on information in Stancliffe, *John Shaw's*, ch. 5.

11 V. A. C. Gatrell, 'Incorporation and the pursuit of Liberal hegemony in
    Manchester 1790–1839' in D. Fraser (ed.), *Municipal Reform and the Indust-
    rial City* (Leicester: Leicester University Press, 1982), esp. pp. 29–32;
    R. G. Wilson, *Gentlemen Merchants: The Merchant Community in Leeds,
    1700–1830* (Manchester: Manchester University Press, 1971), p. 212.

12 M. Hewitt, *The Emergence of Stability in the Industrial City: Manchester,
    1832–1867* (Aldershot: Scolar Press, 1996), pp. 86–7; R. J. Morris, *Class,
    Sect and Party. The Making of the British Middle Class: Leeds, 1820–1850*
    (Manchester: Manchester University Press, 1990), chs 9–10; E. Hopkins,
    Birmingham: The First Manufacturing Town in the World, 1760–1840 (Lon-
    don: Weidenfeld and Nicholson, 1989), ch. 8.

13 Stone, *Annals of the Bean Club*, p. 10; Stancliffe, *John Shaw's*, pp. 242–53,
    316.

14 D. Fraser, *Urban Politics in Victorian England* (London: Macmillan, 1976),
    p. 124.

15 Hunter, 'The clubs of old Manchester', p. 19; 'Leeds Old Club correspond-
    ence 1879–1909', Thoresby Society, MS, Box III, 40.

16 L. Davidoff and C. Hall, *Family Fortunes: Men and Women of the English
    Middle Class, 1780–1850* (London: Hutchinson, 1988), pp. 416–18.

17 'Manchester Union Club papers', MSS, Manchester Central Library
    Archives Department.

18 *The Birmingham Red Book and Reference Almanac for 1866* (Birmingham,
    1866).

19 For details see J. A. Langford, *Modern Birmingham and Its Institutions*,
    vols 1 and 2 (Birmingham, 1873 and 1877); 'Birmingham and Edgbaston
    Debating Society circulars 1864–1903', Birmingham Central Library.

20 For accounts of the foundation of the Athenaeum and its place within
    urban culture see M. Rose, 'Culture, philanthropy and the Manchester
    middle classes' in A. J. Kidd and K. W. Roberts (eds), *City, Class and Culture:
    Studies of Cultural Production and Social Policy in Victorian Manchester*

(Manchester: Manchester University Press, 1985), pp. 111–12; P. Joyce, *Democratic Subjects: The Self and the Social in Nineteenth-Century England* (Cambridge: Cambridge University Press, 1994), pp. 165–73; Hewitt, *Emergence of Stability*. For the institution's development after 1850 see *Manchester Athenaeum Gazette*, 1852–1875, Manchester Central Reference Library.

21 J. H. Swann, *Manchester Literary Club: Some Notes on its History* (Manchester, 1908). For comments on this group see M. Beetham, '"Healthy reading": the periodical press in late Victorian Manchester' in Kidd and Roberts, *City, Class and Culture*, pp. 173–4.

22 'Rules of the Brasenose Club, Manchester, and a list of members, 1879', Manchester Central Library; The Lion [A. Darbyshire], *A Chronicle of the Brasenose Club, Manchester*, vols 1 and 2 (Manchester, 1892 and 1900).

23 R. H. Kargon, *Science in Victorian Manchester* (Baltimore: John Hopkins University Press, 1977).

24 'Diaries and recollections of Benjamin Barker, Bramley, near Leeds', Thoresby Society, MSS, Box XI, 2 and 3.

25 For examples of the phenomenon nationally see J. Hatton, *Clubland, London and Provincial* (London, 1890); J. Woode, *Clubs* (London, 1900); A. Griffiths, *Clubs and Clubmen* (London, 1908); R. Neville, *London Clubs* (London, 1911).

26 Anon., 'Clubs and club-houses', *Manchester of Today: An Epitome of Results* (Manchester, 1885); Hatton, *Clubland*, pp. 64–5.

27 H. France, 'A chapter in domestic economy' in W. H. Mills (ed.), *The Manchester Reform Club 1871–1921* (Manchester, 1921); *Manchester of Today*, p. 58.

28 *Chronicle of the Brasenose Club*, vol. 2, p. 11. The history of the club and a list of members are also found here.

29 See, for example, *City of Birmingham Red Book* (Birmingham, 1899); *Kelly's Directory of Leeds and Neighbourhood* (Leeds, 1897); 'Newspaper cuttings: societies, associations, clubs', Box 512, Manchester Central Library Archives Department.

30 'A model club', *Shadow*, 28 May 1870.

31 Hunter, 'Clubs of old Manchester', p. 31.

32 *Freelance*, 18 August 1876.

33 K. Chorley, *Manchester Made Them* (London: Faber, 1950), p. 135; *Sphinx*, 23 April 1870, p. 130.

34 The toast was that of John Shaw's Club, Manchester, carried on till 1938.

35 Sennett, *The Fall of Public Man* (London: Faber, 1993), pp. 81–3, 215–17.

36 Hunter, 'The clubs of old Manchester', p. 7.

37 'Birmingham and Edgbaston Debating Society addresses', Birmingham Central Library; 'Manchester Arts Club papers', Manchester Central Library Archives Department; G. D. Gaunt and D. H. C. Sillers, 'The Leeds Archers Society 1848–1892', *Journal of the Society of Archer Antiquaries*, 23 (1980), p. 8.

38 *Chronicle of the Brasenose Club*, vol. 1, pp. 32–3; vol. 2, p. 21.

39 Chorley, *Manchester Made Them*, p. 136.

40 Hunter, 'The clubs of old Manchester', p. 7.

41 Davidoff and Hall, *Family Fortunes*, pp. 416–19.

42 *Shadow*, 28 May 1870, p. 292; Hatton, *Clubland*, p. iii.

43 W. Robson, 'The twentieth century: a retrospect' in Mills, *The Manchester Reform Club*, p. 87.

44 R. Sennett, *The Conscience of the Eye: The Design and Social Life of Cities* (London: Faber, 1993), p. 33.

45 For comments and details of repeated expenditure on furnishings see 'Leeds Club annual reports, 1883–1896', MSS, Leeds Central Library. For comments on the internal arrangements of Manchester clubs, *Sphinx*, 27 March 1869 and 29 May 1869.

46 See, for example, *Dart*, 4 August 1877; *Sphinx*, 27 March, 1869; Hatton, *Clubland*, p. 64.

47 'Leeds Club, annual reports and abstracts of accounts', MSS, Leeds Central Library.

48 H. France, 'Billiards' in Mills, *Manchester Reform Club*, pp. 99–101; W. A. Shaw, *Manchester Old and New*, vol. 3 (London, 1894), p. 65.

49 Birmingham's Union Club had no blackball rule for candidates in 1858; by 1870 one blackball in five excluded, and one in seven by 1889. 'Rules and regulations of the Birmingham Union Club with a list of members, 1858–1909', Birmingham Central Library. For comments on anti-Semitism in selection procedures at the Manchester Union Club, see Chorley, *Manchester Made Them*, p. 135.

50 'Rules and regulations of the Birmingham Union Club, 1858 and thereafter', Birmingham Central Library.

51 See, for example, the membership lists of the Leeds Club and the Union Clubs at Birmingham and Manchester. 'Rules and regulations of the Leeds Club with a list of members, 1858 and thereafter', Leeds Central Library; 'Rules and regulations of the Birmingham Union Club with a list of members, 1858 and thereafter', Birmingham Central Library; 'Rules of the Union Club, Manchester, with a list of members, 1825 and thereafter', Union Club papers, Manchester Central Library Archives Department.

52 Langford, *Modern Birmingham*, vol. 1, pp. 235–48.

53 'Leeds Conversation Club minutes', vol. 1, 1849–1867, MS, Leeds Central Library; T. Wemyss Reid, *A Memoir of John Deakin Heaton* (London, 1883), p. 106.

54 For membership lists see Anon., *Conversation Club, Leeds 1849–1939* (Leeds, 1939); Reid, *Memoir*, pp. 157–8.

55 'Leeds Conversation Club minutes'; Langford, *Modern Birmingham*, vol. 1, pp. 241–2.

56 Reid, *Memoir*, p. 107; Langford, *Modern Birmingham*, vol. 1, p. 247.

57 Langford, *Modern Birmingham*, vol. 2, p. 179.

58 *Owl*, 29 May 1879. For similar caricatures see other satirical Birmingham journals of the 1870s, such as the *Dart* and the *Lion*.

59 'A night in Bohemia', *Freelance*, 22 March 1878.

60 *Chronicle of the Brasenose Club*, vol. 1, p. 21. See also G. Black, 'The Leeds Savage Club and its origins' in *Thoresby Society Publications*, vol. 54, part 4, pp. 298–304 for a description of bohemian activities in Leeds.

61 *Manchester City News*, 22 June 1879.

62 For Manchester see, for example, *Freelance*, 16 February, 2 March and 20 April 1867; for Birmingham, *Owl*, 6 February and 1 May 1879; *Lion*, 10 May 1877.

63 'At the Woodpecker', *Lion*, 4 January 1877.

64 *Lion*, 5 April, 12 April and 17 May 1877. For a description of similar events in Manchester see *Comus*, 17 January 1878.

65 'The Arts Club', *Manchester City News*, 29 June 1929.

66 See, for example, the essays by Alan White and Caroline Arscott in J. Wolff and J. Seed (eds), *The Culture of Capital: Art, Power and the Nineteenth- Century Middle Class* (Manchester: Manchester University Press, 1988); R. J. Morris, 'Middle-class culture, 1780–1914' in D. Fraser (ed.), *A History of Modern Leeds* (Manchester: Manchester University Press, 1981).

67 See the essays by Mills, France and Scott in Mills, *Manchester Reform Club*, pp. 33, 49, 80. For a discussion of the social and political role of the Manchester Reform Club see also P. Whitaker, 'The growth of liberal organisation in Manchester from the 1860s to 1903' (Ph.D. thesis, Manchester University, 1956), ch. 10.

68 'Birmingham Arts Club reports, 1873–1878/9', Birmingham Central Library.

69 *Dart*, 4 August 1877.

70 Langford, *Modern Birmingham*, vol. 1, p. 247.

71 Wemyss Reid, *Memoir of John Deakin Heaton*, pp. 107–8; G. Kitson Clarke, 'The Leeds elite', *University of Leeds Review*, 17 (1974–5), pp. 250–53.

72 *Central Literary Magazine*, 1 January 1873.

73 *Sphinx*, 23 April 1870; T. Steele, *Alfred Orage and the Leeds Arts Club 1893–1923* (Aldershot: Scolar Press, 1990), p. 4; Black, 'Leeds Savage Club', p. 301.

74 D. Riley, *'Am I That Name?' Feminism and the Category of 'Women' in History* (London: Macmillan, 1988), p. 51.

75 For example, the Birmingham Union Club rules of 1889 stated that the club committee retained the right to expel any member, and 'no appeal from this decision shall lie to any Court'. 'Rules and regulations of the Union Club with a list of members, 1889'.

76 Chorley, *Manchester Made Them*, p. 136.

77 See the comments in the article 'Manchester and its clubs', *Manchester Guardian*, 18 November 1925. Some clubs seem to have hung on until 1939, but were not revived after the end of the war.

5

Spiritual culture

If the nineteenth-century industrial city gave rise to conditions of fluidity, impersonality and disorder, it also saw the development of institutions that aimed to mitigate these conditions and to impose discipline on the rhythms of urban life. In the second half of the nineteenth century the most prominent of these were the institutions of Protestant religion, the Anglican and Nonconformist churches whose spires punctuated the skylines of the industrial cities and the extending suburbs. The presence of churches and chapels signaled the continuity of an older social order, yet their purpose was radically augmented in the mid-nineteenth century. In the 1840s and 1850s the parish organisation of the Church of England was overhauled in Birmingham, Leeds and Manchester to cope with the perceived needs of an expanding urban population. Both Anglican and Nonconformist denominations engaged in a massive programme of church building between 1840 and 1900.[1]

In their internal workings as in their external relationships, churches and chapels represented the attempt to regulate the urban environment. The churches embodied a continuous denominational tradition of spiritual and moral authority, and throughout the nineteenth century no urban institution with the exception of the pub attracted so large a population on a regular basis.[2] If manufacturing cities such as Birmingham, Manchester and Leeds were in the group with the lowest index of attendance on Census Sunday 1851, less than 30 per cent of the population attending church or chapel, then this was still a substantial figure. Moreover, the lower the figure for attendance in the population overall, the starker was the identification between organised religion and social order. Attendance at church or chapel was integral to definitions of respectability in all social classes, but above all in the most prosperous sections of urban society, where it remained obligatory until at least the 1890s.[3] For the urban middle class church-going was a social as well as a religious rite; in the mid- and later nineteenth century, churches and chapels served as important centres for the well-to-do. Here families gathered on a regular basis, while for the sons and daughters of the suburban middle classes the associations attached to church or chapel represented an important focus of recreational activity. The diversity of functions undertaken by churches and chapels, acting as the foci of missionary, philanthropic and community endeavour, underlines their importance in the reproduction of the social and cultural order in the mid- and later Victorian city.

At the centre of this order stood the figure of the clergyman or minister. As spiritual directors of their congregations, and coordinators of the increasingly complex set of auxiliary institutions that clustered around church and chapel, the influence of the leading Anglican and Nonconformist preachers in the industrial cities grew steadily from the 1840s. Anglican and Nonconformist leaders such as James, Dawson and Dale in Birmingham, Hook, Wicksteed and Reynolds at Leeds, and Fraser, Maclaren and Parker in Manchester, attained a national as well as a local celebrity. Such men moved on national circuits of denomination and participated in national associations for temperance, education and philanthropy. Within Nonconformity, ministers of the wealthiest urban congregations became figureheads of provincial bourgeois culture, embodying in their person, in their writings, and, above all, in their preaching, a specific ideal of 'spiritual culture'.

This chapter examines critically the idea of spiritual culture as it was espoused by leading Nonconformist ministers in the industrial cities between 1840 and 1914. Such men were not necessarily typical of the Nonconformist ministry as a body, nor were their beliefs shared by the whole of the propertied urban population, itself fragmented by denominational divisions.[1] Research on Birmingham and Manchester indicates that old Dissent, comprising Baptists, Congregationalists, Unitarians and Quakers, accounted for roughly half the population of major manufacturing, mercantile and professional families in Birmingham and Manchester at mid-century; the remainder were identified with the Church of England and, to a much lesser extent, Methodism. Within old Dissent, Congregationalism overtook Unitarianism after 1850 as the leading denomination of Nonconformist wealth in both Leeds and Manchester.[5] But if Nonconformist ministers could not claim to represent the middle class as a whole, their position at the head of a major sectarian interest, conscious of its historical exclusion from the religious and political nation, meant that they articulated the meanings and modalities of English middle-class life more strongly than their Anglican counterparts, or perhaps any equivalent group between 1840 and 1914. It was, indeed, the ministry who had been the first to promulgate the notion of the 'middle class' through the dissenting press of the turn of the century.[6] Here I shall emphasise in particular the cultural role of the ministry. As public figures, ministers not only acted as mediators between different social groups, they also served as exemplars of forms of 'mental' labour which were crucial to the idea of the middle class as a moral and cultural force, distinct from an idle aristocracy and a manual working class alike. In these ways, the Nonconformist ministry provided a nexus through which class was articulated and given a powerful cultural inflexion in the mid- and later Victorian decades.

The networks of the ministry

The ministry was not a group apart; it was bound into complex networks based on denomination, organisation and kinship that increasingly spanned cities, regions and the nation as a whole. Although these networks could not rival in longevity those of the Church of England, they nevertheless provided Nonconformity with a dense matrix of institutions and social relationships on which its growth as a religious and political force was predicated. In many cases the roots lay in the late eighteenth and early nineteenth century. This was the period, for example, when the major Baptist and Independent (Congregational) training colleges for the ministry were established: Highbury, Hoxton and Stepney in London, Spring Hill, Birmingham, Rawdon and Airedale Colleges near Leeds, and Lancashire Independent College at Manchester, their locations suggesting the identification of important sections of Nonconformity with London and the industrial centres. Approximately 80 per cent of Congregationalists and 50 per cent of Baptists who entered the ministry between 1820 and 1849 were trained at theological colleges. Others entered via the well-worn Nonconformist route from the Scottish universities, especially Glasgow. The connection between the colleges and the universities was to become close after 1840, mirroring the role of Oxford and Cambridge as a training-ground for the Anglican clergy. Highbury, Stepney and Airedale established links with University Collge, London in the 1840s, Lancashire Independent College with Owens, Manchester from the 1850s, and the trend continued, culminating in the decision to move Spring Hill from Birmingham to Oxford and the setting up of Mansfield College in 1889.[7] These networks, inspired by specific denominational needs for the supply of trained ministers, indicate the growing coalescence of Nonconformity as a whole and its insertion into both new and traditional centres of English cultural life.

Denomination continued to provide important lines of communication along which ministers moved. Appointments of ministers to the wealthier urban chapels were made on the basis of a reputation often established at a smaller, more provincial chapel. Joseph Parker's appointment to the wealthy Cavendish Street chapel, Manchester, in 1858 was based on his reputation as a promising preacher and organiser at the Congregational chapel, Banbury, and involved, among other agreements, a transfer fee of £700 to Banbury to pay off the debt of their new church.[8] As the reputation of individual ministers grew so they were drawn into regional and national circuits of denominational preaching, thus tapping a lucrative source of fees to supplement their income. It was in financial terms that leading Congregationalist divines were known to the treasurer of Albion Church at Ashton-under-Lyne in the 1860s: 'if it had been the day of the "annual sermons" he could tell us what exactly it had cost to have Dr Parker, and what it would have cost to have had not Dr Parker but Dr Dale. Others might have known divines by their doctrine; he knew them by their price'.[9]

Ministers moved easily on denominational networks. Among Unitarian pastors links between the major chapels at Leeds, Manchester and Liverpool were strong, as were connections between the provincial cities and London in Congregationalism. R. W. Dale, minister at Carr's Lane, Birmingham, between 1852 and 1890, 'was in London so often that he had no need to write about questions of lasting interest to Dr Allon, Dr Guinness Rogers, and his other friends'.[10] Links within Nonconformity were maintained on a formal basis by the denominational Unions, established nationally from the early 1830s, and regionally thereafter, bringing together religious leaderships on an annual basis. They were reinforced by the multiple associations which developed from the same period to promote the major Nonconformist causes; the Peace Society, the United Kingdom Alliance, and, most important, the weekly *Nonconformist* newspaper, established by Edward Miall in 1841, to which leading ministers regularly contributed. To these should be added the more local and short-lived Nonconformist associations, such as the Leeds Congregational Council, established in the 1860s, and the General Conference of Nonconformists, organised by committees in Manchester, Birmingham and Liverpool between 1872 and 1874, which assembled nearly two thousand delegates in the cause of Church disestablishment.[11]

As a result, during the second half of the nineteenth century Nonconformity developed networks of association that could claim to match those of the Church of England. If ministers themselves were the prime movers, they enjoyed support from wealthy employer and professional families in the industrial cities. Partnerships were forged initially in the close working relationships established at chapel level. But lay notables were increasingly drawn into wider denominational affairs. The ministers George Dawson, R. W. Dale and H. W. Crosskey sat alongside businessmen and local politicians such as Joseph Chamberlain on the Central Committee of the Birmingham Nonconformist Association in the 1870s. The building of Mansfield College, Oxford, a decade later, was underpinned by funds from Manchester cotton employers, such as Armitage, Haworth and Rylands, who also added organisational expertise.[12] Strong personal ties were common. The Congregationalist minister, Alexander Raleigh, lived for a year with the family of Sir James Watts, Mayor of Manchester, cotton magnate and self-proclaimed descendant of the Puritan divine, Isaac Watts. George Hadfield, Congregationalist, solicitor and MP for Sheffield, named thirty-six ministers among his 'friends and associates', more than the equivalent number of laymen.[13] The strength of these ties was cemented by kinship in the second half of the nineteenth century. At Leeds, Eustace Conder, minister of East Parade chapel, married the daughter of Edward Baines junior in 1871; at Manchester, the Baptist minister Alexander Maclaren was the brother-in-law of Frank Crossley, the engineering employer.[14]

From the 1830s the ministry of old Dissent emerged as a new profession. It was new not so much in function as in institutional and social context; it encompassed new forms of education and training, of intra- and interdenominational organisation and of social connection. One result was the elevation of the ministry, and especially its upper echelons, to a recognised position as part of an established urban middle class. These processes can be traced in the denominational histories of the later nineteenth and early twentieth century, but they are perhaps best exemplified by the role of ministers in the expansion of middle-class cousinhoods based on kinship, religious affiliation and economic interest.[15] Such clans included the Armitage and Rigby connexion, whose filiations traversed Liverpool, Manchester and the cotton districts, and the Baines–Willans nexus, which, in similar fashion, encompassed Leeds, Huddersfield, and Rochdale. Within these clan networks ministers occupied an important place as spiritual leaders and cultural guides, and as friends, husbands and family members. In effect, the professionalisation of the Nonconformist ministry was an integral part of the larger formation of the Victorian middle class at local, regional and national levels.

Chapel: the hierarchy of authority

If the expanding networks of the ministry in the Victorian period indicate its increasing influence and integration, the foundation of min- isterial authority continued to rest with the pastorate of the individual chapel. In the case of the best-known urban chapels, such as Cross Street, Manchester, East Parade, Leeds, or Carr's Lane, Birmingham, authority was part of the legacy of accumulated prestige derived from the celebrity of previous ministers and the inherited reputation of the chapel within denominational circles. When R. W. Dale was offered the role of assis- tant to John Angell James at Carr's Lane in the 1850s, he saw James's influence as providing the 'principle of cohesion' which made it the 'centre of Christian effort' in Birmingham. While Dale was critical of the prosperity and 'unduly satisfied' character of the congregation, the prestige of the chapel meant that he rejected other offers from across the Midlands and north and accepted the role as James's successor.[16]

Whatever the status of the chapel, the authority of the minister was conventionally represented as patriarchal; he was cast as the 'head' of the larger 'family' which comprised the membership and congregation of the individual church. For the Unitarian divine, James Martineau, the relationship between the minister and the lay congregation was equi- valent to that between parent and child, combining what he termed the 'two types of "authority": the rational, wielded by those who know more, and the religious, vested in the higher and larger personality'.[17] The parent–child model with its implications of a particular authority struc- ture was the dominant image and worked to reinforce the power of the minister over the congregation. However, it was not the only model. The relationship could also be expressed as a more democratic frater- nalism, as in the later nineteenth-century conception of the Church as a 'brotherhood'. On occasions, it even echoed the formal expressions of romantic love. It was in such terms that Henry Reynolds wrote to his congregation at East Parade during a voyage to the Holy Land in 1855: 'I may safely say that I fill up very much of my time with thoughts, and wishes, and intentions connected with you; and, therefore, I have re- solved to commence a letter which will, I trust, express for me some of the feelings I am now trying to cherish and deepen'.[18]

The intricate language of emotion in which the claims to ministerial authority were couched overlaid what was in fact a complex ordering of power within individual chapels. By contrast with the Church of England, where clergy were appointed by individual patrons or the Church hierarchy, within old Dissent the appointment of a minister was the responsibility of the deacons of the particular chapel, acting on behalf of the membership as a whole. The same body was responsible for setting ministerial salaries and conditions, and for matters of discipline and dismissal. Whatever their status in the wider world, therefore, ministers were dependent on a lay patriciate for their position. The inequalities of condition between minister and lay patriciate were often marked. At Manchester's Cavendish Street chapel in 1861 the deacons were composed entirely of prominent professional men and partners in major textile firms. At his initial invitation to preach at Cavendish in 1858, Joseph Parker envisaged the chapel as composed of millionaires: 'every man seemed to be looking at me over the top of a money-bag'.[19] While Parker exaggerated the wealth of his audience for literary effect, the disparity between ministerial salaries and lay members of the congregation was substantial. The annual salaries of ministers varied between £100 and £700 in the second half of the nineteenth century, according to the size and prosperity of the congregation, with the mean towards the lower end. When topped up with gifts, paid holidays and earnings from preaching or writing, this placed Nonconformist ministers between white-collar earnings at one end of the spectrum, and a comfortable professional income at the other. But even the most successful could not compete materially with the merchants, lawyers and manufacturers whose families made up an important part of their congregations, and on whose largesse ministers frequently depended.[20]

The existence of Nonconformist chapels was therefore structured by a complex set of power relations. The model of the chapel as a family gave the minister the authority to act as its head or 'spiritual director'. But the institutional structures of chapel life, which the language of family worked to obscure, potentially reversed this relationship: the minister was the 'servant' of the membership, who effectively 'owned' the church. In the most extreme cases, conflict led to the splitting of congregations and the founding of new chapels. At Birmingham the Baptist minister George Dawson, newly arrived at Mount Zion chapel, became embroiled in a doctrinal controversy with the deacons and resigned in 1845. He was fortunate to have wealthy supporters in the congregation who were prepared to secede and fund a new church, St Saviour, which remained Dawson's base for thirty years.[21] Such schisms were dramatic, but more common was the spasmodic or low-level tension which marked many prominent ministries, such as Dale at Carr's Lane, or Parker and his successor, Edwin Paxton Hood, at Cavendish Street.[22]

Yet despite these tensions, it is clear that many ministers wielded

considerable authority over their own congregations and a wider religious public. Their authority derived from the spiritual and cultural
resources that accrued to the ministry, its cultural and symbolic capital.
This capital was bound up with specific forms of intellectual and
rhetorical ability, embodied most visibly in the act of preaching, or
'pulpit power'. Following James Martineau, it was a combination of
mental and spiritual force that represented the foundation of religious
authority, personified in the ministry. 'Authority' argued R. W. Dale,
'rightly belongs to a clear brain and a resolute will'.[23] The notion of
'spiritual culture' was central to the identity of Nonconformist ministers.
It was this form of power that contributed substantially to ministers'
ability to hold sway over their congregations and the religious public
in the period between 1840 and 1914.

Intellectual and spiritual culture

An attachment to intellectual speculation and polite culture was not
peculiar to the Victorian ministry. It was inherent in the tradition of
puritan divines from the seventeenth century, and was the hallmark of
Unitarianism in centres like Manchester, Leeds and Liverpool from the
later eighteenth century.[24] But between the 1820s and the 1840s a
concern with the educational and cultural attainments of the ministry
was articulated more widely, notably among Congregationalists and
Baptists. At the opening of Lancashire Independent College in 1840 the
principal, Dr Vaughan, assured the assembled notables that the training
provided would favour 'an *educated* over an emotional ministry'. The
same point was persistently reiterated in the following decades. 'Ministerial education must keep up with the education of the time', a Baptist
minister warned in 1868. 'If the attention of the educated is to be secured,
and if our cultivated people are to be retained in the ranks of Nonconformity, the pastor must retain their confidence and respect'.[25] The
reasons for this emphasis were several. Firstly, there was a perceived
need to underline the respectability of old Dissent and to compete with
the Church of England for the allegiance of propertied urban opinion.
Secondly, the spread of a moderate evangelicalism, encompassing even
elements of Unitarianism by the 1850s, meant that doctrinal controversy
within Nonconformity was gradually declining in frequency and force.
In this context, the ministry began to focus more strongly on matters
of culture and ethics as well as abstract theological speculation.[26]

As a result of educational developments, ministers trained in the
theological colleges, academies and universities had come to predominate

in old Dissent by the 1850s, a shift that had taken place over the previous generation. The scope of the education offered to trainees was broad. At Unitarian Manchester College from the 1820s, a sound knowledge of Greek and Latin was a precondition for entry and students took ancient and modern history, mathematics, literature, philosophy and modern languages, together with divinity and theology. At the Congregationalist Spring Hill College in the 1840s the training included courses in European philosophy, logic, classics, literature and history. Ministers were expected to be 'abreast of modern culture', in the words of James Martineau, as well as versed in Nonconformist history and theology.[27] The significance of this education, however, lay also in the specific qualities it sought to foster in ministers. High value was placed upon the habit of abstract thought, inculcated through logic and philosophy and seen as an essential part of a minister's 'mental discipline'. A preoccupation with literary style was also encouraged, especially in the preparation of sermons; at Spring Hill students' sermons were evaluated for their literary as well as their theological merit.[28] Students were expected to extend their command of public oratory by attending the sermons of well-known ministers and by developing their own preaching skills in outlying chapels.

Habits of mind developed early remained with leading ministers throughout their lives. G. B. Bubier, minister of Hope Street chapel, Salford, considered his spiritual outlook to have been formed in boyhood by the dual influence of Calvin and Samuel Taylor Coleridge. At Leeds, the Unitarian minister Charles Wicksteed was president of the Philosophical and Literary Society, and gave papers on Homer, Milton and contemporary British poets.[29] The intense bookishness which historians have noted among many Nonconformist ministers was not a marginal attribute, as is often implied, but central to their private and public personae. It encompassed a catholic interest in literary culture (though stopping short of prose fiction before the 1890s) and a strong commitment to scholarship. According to his son, R. W. Dale's bedroom was a testament to his literary tastes: 'on the shelves above the bed, or upon the chair at its side, stood a pile of books – poets, historians – Wordsworth, Arnold, Froude; some of the great French masters of style – Pascal or Sainte-Beuve; but invariably, year after year, a volume or two of Burke in the familiar red covers might be found there'. In 1868 Dale moved to the suburbs to escape casual callers, and devoted mornings and, when possible, evenings to scholarly activity in his private study.[30] An enduring commitment to scholarship encouraged leading ministers to seek semi-retirement in the training colleges, where it was considered that there was greater time for intellectual reflection. Robert Halley left Cavendish Street, Manchester, in 1857 to become principal of New College, London; Henry Reynolds left East Parade, Leeds to take on the directorship of Cheshunt College in 1861; George Bubier moved from Hope Street chapel, Salford, to become professor at Spring Hill in 1864.

As this suggests, leading ministers were responsible for the wider transmission of 'spiritual culture' through teaching in the training colleges and new universities, and through writing. In the latter case, they were aided by the substantial demand for religious publications in the mid-Victorian period: before 1870 the number of new books on religious subjects outstripped those of any other variety, including fiction, while in 1875 some 37 per cent of all periodicals were defined as 'religious in tone'.[31] Ministers took full advantage of the opportunities on offer. Of those mentioned above, Wicksteed was co-editor of the Unitarian *Prospective Review* in the 1840s, with James Martineau of Liverpool and J.J. Tayler of Mosley Street, Manchester; Bubier was literary editor of Miall's *Nonconformist*; Dale was editor of the *Congregationalist* in the 1870s, and wrote a stream of articles on theology, politics and literature for journals such as the *Eclectic Review*, as well as books and pamphlets on a wide range of subjects. The dissemination of moral and cultural opinion, especially via the press, was part of the professional life of leading ministers and an essential factor in establishing their reputations. Between 1848 and 1871 George Dawson acted periodically as a newspaper editor, and on his death in 1876 was described by the *Spectator* as 'the most famous intellectual "middle-man" of his day'. The display of erudition was, indeed, often a form of self-publicity; John Angell James, for example, devoted several pages of his history of Nonconformity to a list of his own works, together with their estimated sales.[32] In these ways, ministers came to represent what Clyde Binfield has called an 'intermediate intelligentsia'. Moving between their congregations and a wider religious public, they served as nodal figures in the construction of a culture that was provincially based yet national in scope.[33]

Above all, ministers embodied spiritual culture in their persons and in their teachings. Figures such as R. W. Dale incarnated the belief that intellectuality and spirituality were indivisible, and that true religion required 'self-culture'. Aged fifteen Dale published an article in the *Evangelical Magazine* arguing that 'the moral and the spiritual results from a culture of the self', a theme which was to recur in his writings throughout his life.[34] Other ministers made a similar connection in their diaries and public writings; as with Dale, the combination of spirit and intellect formed a central theme of their subsequent biographies. For Charles Wicksteed, religious inspiration evoked 'a conscious intellectuality – a spiritualisation of our whole frame, mental and corporeal'. The faith of J. A. Macfadyen of Chorlton Road church, Manchester, a colleague recalled, combined a strong evangelicalism with an 'equal belief in the importance of spiritual culture. Puritan in mental build and habit, he had nothing of the Methodist about him'.[35]

The identification between the cultural and spiritual dimensions of ministerial religion was not espoused without ambivalence. An alleged disdain for 'intellectual preaching', for example, was commonplace, even among influential advocates of spiritual culture.[36] Towards the end of his life, R. W. Dale confessed: 'my preaching moved at a height – intellectual and spiritual – far above the congregation generally. Notwithstanding the kindness of the dominant element of the criticism – that the sermons have an intellectual, literary and spiritual quality which commands the sympathy of the best and most cultivated, it pained me a great deal at the time and kept me awake for many hours'. Significantly, however, Dale never altered his style of preaching, due no doubt to his acknowledged 'dread of the popular method'.[37] Caught between the 'dread of the popular' and the intellectual vanity of 'fine preaching', ministers tried to steer a middle course which in practice veered strongly towards the latter. This bias was inevitable given that the assertion of spiritual culture was an essential means by which ministers of old Dissent sought to distinguish themselves and their congregations from the excesses of popular Methodism and the complacency of the Church of England. According to a recent historian, throughout the nineteenth century the Methodist 'connexions were shot through with anti-intellectual prejudice'.[38] The same charge was levelled at important sections of the Anglican clergy in the industrial cities. In Birmingham, the predominant evangelical party 'paid greater regard to zeal and to orthodoxy than to intellectual force'. At Manchester, the leading figures in local Anglicanism in the second half of the nineteenth century, Canon Stowell and Bishop Fraser, were strongly populist in tone, countering 'polite culture' with a 'muscular', aggressive Protestantism.[39]

By conjoining intellect and spirituality, Nonconformist ministers laid claim to an older tradition of the cultivated Christian gentleman. At the opening of the largely Nonconformist Owens College, Manchester, in 1851, the theme was explicitly announced in the inaugural speech of the principal, A. J. Scott. For Scott, the influence of the religious ministry was essential to the education 'which should distinguish the man of

mental cultivation in general – what we mean, in short, by that characteristically English phrase, the education of a gentleman'.[10] It was a
tradition which leading ministers sought to personify, provincial figures
like John Angell James and George Dawson in the 1840s and 1850s as
well as the metropolitan James Baldwin Brown and Silvester Horne in
the later Victorian and Edwardian periods. Adopting the mantle of the
Christian gentleman implied a status that was at once social, intellectual
and spiritual. By appropriating the language of the Christian gentleman,
ministers projected themselves as models of conduct and cultivation. In
so doing they deliberately laid claim, for themselves and for Nonconformity, to a place at the symbolic centre of English bourgeois
culture.

Preaching and performance

More than any other aspect of the ministerial role, however, it was the
act of preaching which was taken as the measure of a minister's power,
the index of his spiritual culture and of his dominion over the faithful.
According to his biographer, the 'pulpit was the source and centre of
Macfadyen's influence' at Chorlton Road church.[41] The sermon formed
the focal point of the religious service, the central rite within the larger
ritual of chapel-going among prosperous families. W. H. Mills captured
this ritual aspect in his evocation of chapel-going among the wealthy in
Manchester during the 1870s: 'There were many Congregational and
Unitarian chapels in which the arrival in the street outside of carriages
drawn by horseflesh in its most mettlesome examples betokened with
certainty the approaching end of the sermon and was indeed as much
part of the order of worship as the collection or the concluding hymn'.[42]
It was the perceived quality of the minister's preaching which served as
a magnet for lay audiences, especially among the propertied, confirming
the authority of minister in the eyes of the congregation while extending
his reputation within and beyond the bounds of denomination. At
Alexander Maclaren's Union chapel the congregations were notable for
their heterogeneous character: 'They contained men of all classes and
creeds, rich and prosperous merchants, men distinguished in professional
life, and others working their way towards success. Strangers were
attracted in large numbers, among them clergymen and dignitaries of
the Established Church, nonconformist ministers, literary men, artists,
and students from the theological colleges'.[43] The better-known
preachers acquired a floating audience alongside the regular congregation; 'sermon-tasting' was a common pastime among those with the time

and the means to indulge. As a young man Benjamin Barker, the son of a Leeds woollen manufacturer, regularly attended sermons at different chapels before settling into the Church of England. 'It is the finest lecture I ever heard: eloquent beyond description' he noted of one preacher's address in 1855; 'this is I think the best treat I ever had'.[44]

Sermons were a cultural event, and an important part of the drama of urban life for large sections of the chapel-going public. The sermon was understood as a performance, the analogy between the pulpit and the stage being commonplace in the later Victorian period. In 1887 the *British Weekly* ran a poll of the most popular preachers in the five leading Protestant denominations, rendering explicit the idea of a ministerial star system. Among the most celebrated was Joseph Parker, who was reputed to model his performances on the actor Henry Irving, and who, according to Charles Booth, brought 'to the pulpit all the arts of the stage'.[45] The more self-consciously popular preachers were capable of attracting large audiences. In London, the disastrous meeting at Surrey Gardens in 1856 addressed by the Baptist Charles Spurgeon, which ended with seven deaths, was attended by an estimated twelve thousand people. In Manchester, the Baptist Arthur Mursell could attract several thousand to his Sunday afternoon lectures at the Free Trade Hall in the 1850s, and it was estimated that ten thousand applied for tickets to hear Dale speak on the politics of Nonconformity at the same venue in 1871. If many Nonconformists were deeply distrustful of religious populism – Spurgeon's preaching, for example, was dismissed by the Unitarian minister William Binns as 'the jokes of a circus clown' – it is clear that as a public performance sermons and religious lectures appealed to audiences across the social spectrum.[46]

Yet styles of preaching were highly contextualised. In urban and suburban chapels dominated by wealthier Nonconformist families, preaching was required to be stylish and demanding. The quality of preaching was seen to depend on the education of the minister and his capacity to embody the idea of spiritual culture: the dignity of the ministerial office, in the words of R. W. Dale, 'derived from the intellectual force and culture of the preacher'. Edward Miall, editor of the *Nonconformist*, spoke of the 'etiquette of preaching' as demanding a refined spiritual artistry.[47] The manner in which ministers were seen to give bodily form to the idea of spiritual culture is indicated by the attention paid to gesture. In the sectarian atmosphere of the mid-Victorian decades the smallest movement could take on symbolic significance. Attending an Anglican service conducted by W. F. Hook, Vicar of Leeds, Florence Nightingale observed critically that he exhibited 'the regular Catholic jerk of making the genuflection every time he approaches the altar'.[18] In higher status Nonconformist chapels the physical self-control of the preacher was an important sign of culture. The preaching of Arthur Stowell at Newton Park, Leeds, was reportedly marked by his 'fine ear for the music of words' and his minimal gestures. 'No piston finger or hammering fist. A shrug of a shoulder, a slow lifting of the hand are all the physical movement needed.'[49]

The adoption of this restrained, mannered style of preaching was a further means by which the denominations of old Dissent sought to distance themselves from forms of religious 'ranting' and the revivalism associated with Moody and Sankey in the 1870s. The high intellectual tone of sermons, however, did not preclude passion. The sermons of Alexander Maclaren at Union chapel, Manchester, were described as 'logic on fire': 'the speaker's *tout ensemble* gives one the best possible idea of etherialised matter, of spirit overpowering matter'. Dale's preaching at Carr's Lane was reported in similar terms: 'At times his denunciation of sin was overwhelming in its force. He never stormed; but his wrath, as it grew, glowed with passion at a white heat. It swept on in waves of living fire. It seemed to scorch, to shrivel, to consume'.[50] If the balance between rationalism and emotion in such descriptions is apparent, so too is the element of romantic vitalism. The combination of spiritual and physical power, attributed especially to Congregationalist and Baptist preachers, was frequently compared to a natural force. Sermons were regularly described as 'electric', and likened to 'torrents', 'waves' and 'fire'. While rationality was insisted upon, it was the infusion of controlled emotion that confirmed the authenticity of the religious sentiments conveyed and differentiated the performance from 'mere intellectual' preaching.

While allowance should be made for the hyperbole in such accounts, it is clear that preaching could exert an intense, even trance-like, effect on congregations. The extent to which respectable audiences were susceptible to the power of the word is suggested by the impact of a play reading in Leeds described by the Unitarian minister, Charles Wicksteed in 1852. 'It was interesting to observe the transmutations that took place in the hearers as the reading went on', he observed. 'A very well-behaved, proper-looking young girl began to forget herself, her still frigid and formal countenance giving way before the charm, the head uplifted and bent slightly forward, the lips opened, the eye bright and suffused, the finger lifted up towards the bosom and curved. At length, the elderly single ladies began to yield in the fixed and sharp outline of their countenances.'[51] If this account is significantly sexualised, it also indicates the extent to which formal spoken language possessed the power to overcome hearers, altering both mental and physical states. Like music, it was capable of inducing a state of rapture which, while registered individually, could overtake a whole audience. The discourses of religion were thus framed in a romantic idiom for much of the mid- and later Victorian period. Yet, to reiterate, in old Dissent the mystical was never divorced from the rational; spiritual culture was always an admixture of the two. It was precisely these qualities which attracted a young woman who attended Lyndhurst Road, Hampstead, under the Congregationalist minister R. F. Horton in the 1890s. 'His sermons interested me immensely. He made me think; he appealed to my reason, which surprised and pleased me. He frequently used the expression, "I am persuaded": he did "persuade". And yet he appealed to something else beyond one's reason. I began to discover the existence of a world of Truth, hitherto unsuspected. My eyes were opened by degrees to unseen Reality.' [52]

It was in the act of preaching that the cultural and symbolic capital of the Nonconformist ministry was concentrated. In the sermon, the cultural and intellectual faculties imbued in the individual minister through education and training, as well as the spiritual qualities inherent in his privileged relationship to the Word, achieved their full expression. Given that Protestantism in general and Nonconformity in particular rejected the notion that the ministry was divinely ordained or sanctioned, it was essential that spiritual authority be demonstrated. The act of preaching therefore represented a public performance of spiritual authority, derived not simply from its rhetorical quality, but also from its invariable, repeated character as part of the ordered temporality of middle-class life. It symbolised the power of the minister over the congregation. "A man who holds for years unquestioned supremacy in a congregation and is as absolute in his sphere as a feudal sovereign, inevitably acquires more or less the tone of dominion", a Manchester journal observed in 1866. [53] 'Pulpit power' and the public influence of the ministry rose together, both reaching their height in the industrial cities during the second half of the nineteenth century.

The message of the pulpit

Given the influence of the pulpit, it is not surprising that recent historians have seen church and chapel as a fulcrum for discourses bearing on diverse areas of moral, social and economic life. [54] The sermon was the principal vehicle for these discourses and even a cursory assessment of the content of sermons among Baptists and Congregationalists indicates their wide-ranging character. Theological matters were naturally to the fore, preachers regularly debating from the pulpit the successive issues of the day: biblical criticism from the 1840s; the doctrine of the Atonement, and its declining importance in evangelical religion, from the 1860s; and, from the 1880s, the challenge of agnosticism.[55] Social and ethical questions were also directly broached, particularly in the mid-week sermons which chapel members were urged to attend. By the late nineteenth century this dimension became uppermost, especially in Congregationalism, under the influence of a new generation of ministers such as Baldwin Brown, Silvester Horne and Alexander Raleigh; in Unitarianism, it had always been a significant feature of sermons.

R. W. Dale's *Weekday Sermons*, given in the late 1860s and going through six editions by 1895, is a good example of the genre. Sermons on subjects such as 'The discipline of the body' and 'The perils and uses of rich men' were addressed directly to a prosperous audience. A persistent theme was the need to regulate consumption as a condition of the legitimacy of wealth: 'One reason, then, for which men are born to wealth, and for which they are able to accumulate wealth, is this, not that they may spend it in vulgar and offensive ostentation or self-indulgence, but that they may have the opportunity of cultivating their own intellectual nature'.[56] An important feature of ethical sermons, drawing on a tradition of puritan abstinence, was to link capital accumulation to personal moral capacities, including intellectual 'self-culture'. The effect was to underline the distinction between mental and manual labour and to affirm the position of the minister as the model of the moral intellectual.

Alongside the market, the other important theme in ministerial discourses on the social was family and gender relations. John Seed has noted the manner in which, within early nineteenth-century Unitarian chapels, all kinds of relations, including those between employer and employee, were construed according to a model of master and servant, extending an analogy based on the household to wider social and economic spheres.[57] The same set of metaphors continued to be used in the discourses of Nonconformity for much of the century. I have argued above that the conception of the chapel as a family was commonly used to rationalise the unequal distribution of power within the congregation and to assert the authority of the minister over the membership. Gender was one specific aspect of this ordering. Thus, the 'masculinity' of spiritual culture remained an essential, largely unquestioned element in its articulation up to the First World War. Alexander Maclaren sought to promote a 'masculine type of Christian life'; according to Silvester Horne, R. W. Dale was notable for his 'masculine intellect', a phrase which would be applied in turn to Horne and Baldwin Brown after their deaths.[58] Among other things, masculinity here denoted a broad intellectuality, free of pretension and capable of expression at a variety of levels, as well as a distinguished and dominating presence. As an integral part of the patriarchal ordering of chapel life, it served to naturalise the subordination of women. Despite their indispensability to the functioning of the chapel community – to home-visiting, Sunday School and philanthropic work, for example – women occupied a marginal position in relation to the key activities of office-holding and decision-making. They were denied a say in the election of ministers: 'the women voted with their souls', as John Angell James put it. While women could serve as deaconesses in the Church of England from 1862, and as preachers among Quakers and Bible Christians, in Congregationalism they were not admitted to the meetings of the Congregational Union before the 1890s and many chapels did not allow women deacons before 1914.[59] Whatever the professed views of Nonconformist ministers and the lay male hierarchy – and many Unitarian and Congregationalist men were in the vanguard of Liberal campaigns for women's rights – the discourses and practices of chapel tended to endorse a sharply dichotomous and hierarchical view of gender relations.

Just as Nonconformist ministers were expected to pronounce on public events in their sermons, so the pulpit was a key site for the production and circulation of ideologies impacting on the social and economic lives of their congregations. Yet the main influence emanating from the pulpit was arguably neither doctrinal nor social, but historical. An essential role of ministers, and one which they embraced, was as guardians of the historical patrimony of the denomination in particular and of Nonconformity in general. Ministers were not alone in promulgating this inheritance, lay employers and professionals also participating in a culture of puritan remembrance. Nor indeed was an historical consciousness confined to Nonconformity, elements in the Church of England in the industrial cities drawing sustenance from a specific version of the English Protestant tradition.[60] But the ministry had a special part to play in the representation of the Nonconformist past. It was apparent, firstly, in the numbers of historical works published by leading ministers, James's *Protestant Nonconformity* (1849), Dale's *The Rise of Evangelical Nonconformity* (1880), and Horne's *Popular History of the Free Churches* (1903) being notable examples. Still more publicly, ministers took a leading part in the main commemorative celebrations of later nineteenth-century Nonconformity, the Bicentenary of the Ejection of Ministers in 1662 and the Cromwell Tercentenary in 1899, which were accompanied by memorials, services and lectures in all the major cities.[61]

The elements of the Nonconformist version of the past were relatively simple and unvarying. While in some cases a history was traced back to the early apostles, the key event seen as initiating the rise of Protestant Nonconformity was the Reformation; as Dale put it, 'The true glory of the nation began with its great controversy with Rome'.[62] The fortunes of Nonconformity were then charted in terms of successive periods of progress and reversal, the rule of Elizabeth and Cromwell identified with the former, the latter with the reigns of Mary, Charles I and the Restoration of 1660. Only with the Glorious Revolution did the development of 'civil and religious liberty' become irreversible. At this point the rise of Nonconformity conjoined with other forms of social, economic and political advance:

> The revival of earnest religion through the preaching of Whitfield and Wesley – the growth of large towns with their industries, associations, and interchanges of thought – the diffusion of education – the removal of restrictions and taxes that had impeded the circulation of the discussions of the press – the increase of rapid movement from place to place – and the greater dependence of the different classes of society on each other for mutual labour and enjoyments, have all contributed to deprive intolerance of its former power and to promote the common interests of truth and justice'.[63]

In effect, 'progress' since the late seventeenth century was presented as a single, upward historical movement, encompassing all aspects of national life.

As the principal promoters of this historical narrative, the ministry gave themselves a prominent part in it. Key events encompassed not only the Reformation, but also the Ejection of 1662 and the repeal of the Test and Corporation acts; leading actors included puritan divines, like Owen and Howe, and figures associated with the evangelical revival such as George Whitfield and Isaac Watts. By reading the history of England through the lens of religion, Nonconformists stressed their own role in the creation of national identity. While Protestantism remained integral to the nineteenth-century representation of Englishness, this version of history located Nonconconformity at the centre of English Protestantism. As Dale proclaimed to a Nonconformist audience at Exeter Hall in 1874: 'Our Protestantism has become one of the chief bonds of our national unity; the achievements of our ancestors in the Protestant cause have been cherished among our most glorious national traditions'.[64] At the same time, the rise of Nonconformity was also identified with the growth of a particular social force, the 'middle class', which Silvester Horne described as 'the stronghold of commerce, morality and religion'.[65] Thus the strength of the Nonconformist version of history, espoused by ministers, lay in its capacity to integrate diverse developments – a history of civil and religious exclusion, the rise of new moral, economic and social forces – into a single narrative of the national past.[66]

Part of the appeal of this version of the past was that recent political events could be appropriated to it. It was in these terms that Dale greeted parliamentary reform in 1867: 'The history of our country has been a long and magnificent battle for freedom, and I believe that the recent extension of the franchise will render more secure the victories we have already won, and make fresh victories possible'.[67] Other campaigns, notably the movement against the alliance of Church and State, encompassing education, church rates, burials, and disestablishment, similarly drew succour from an historical vision in which Anglicanism was identified variously with pro-Catholic sentiment, the aristocracy and a hidebound, unjust state.[68] Equally, the 'municipal gospel', preached most fervently in Birmingham by ministers such as Dawson, Dale and Charles Vince, rested on an idea of the city as a bio-historical entity, an organism whose 'functions grow in range and in importance as the city rises from its humble beginnings, and advances in power and dignity and fame'.[69] If the Nonconformist conscience of the later Victorian period was heavily identified with the ministry, then this itself was a radically historicised conscience. An integral part of the role of ministers was to link platform and pulpit, and to imbue the politics of the moment with a deeper sense of Nonconformity's historical mission to recreate England in its own moral and cultural image.

Spiritual directorship

The considerable cultural as well as spiritual resources that many ministers possessed meant they dominated their congregations. In consolidating this authority, organisational flair was important as well as force of personality. At Cavendish Street chapel, Joseph Parker insisted on the 'presidentship of the Church', including chairing all committees. At Chorlton Road, J. A. Macfadyen exerted similar dominion: '"Good generalship" was one of the qualities which he displayed in the vestry and the committee room. Men of affairs, skilled merchants and bankers, heads of departments in the large Manchester houses of business, professional men, leading tradesmen, and many richly graced and gifted women recognised in him one fit to direct their religious zeal.'[70] The growth of auxiliary bodies around churches and chapels after 1850 meant that the directive skills of ministers came increasingly to the fore. By the 1880s the site of Chorlton Road church covered almost two acres, including schools, a library, mission and numerous clubs and societies.[71] Together with the large inner-city missions, established from the same period, churches and chapels represented major enterprises in their own right, often employing in a voluntary capacity over a hundred people.

Chapels served, firstly, as social centres for the well-to-do. In the suburban settings in which Baptist and Congregationalist chapels were increasingly located after 1840, chapels represented the focus for, and embodiment of, middle-class 'community'. While business and professional men served as deacons or trustees, their wives were active in domestic visiting and philanthropy, and youth of both sexes took Sunday School classes. Diaries and other records provide ample testimony of the centrality of chapels in suburban social networks, especially among the young. At Headingley, a fashionable suburb of Leeds, the Congregational church, opened in 1866, established mutual improvement and discussion societies, conversazioni, lectures and art exhibitions, all intended to encourage 'high mental culture and scientific research'. The Union church at Newton Park, Leeds, generated its own magazine, *Manefti's Moon*, in 1889. Written in an arch literary style, professionally printed and sold in local shops, the magazine presented the chapel as the focal point in the lives of suburban youth, with its tennis club, singing classes, dances and debating societies.[72]

Chapel fostered sociability, an example set by the minister's 'At Home', held on a weekday afternoon. But the minister's impress was also felt in other aspects of the community life of chapel. The emphasis on a high cultural and intellectual tone in chapel societies often derived directly from the minister. At the women's reading group attached to the Union church, Manchester, in the 1870s the Baptist minister Alexander Maclaren insisted on selecting the books to be read, demanding that they be 'good all round (including the literary form), not merely well-intentioned as to motive'.[73] The minister wielded considerable power as a symbol of discipline. Within the chapel community discipline was encouraged by the presence of associations, such as temperance and provident societies, concerned with abstinence and restraint. But it was also a function of standards directly imposed from above. Attempts to establish a drama society at East Parade chapel in 1883 were blocked by ministerial fiat, justified by reference to the long tradition of Non-conformist opposition to the theatre.[74] As the fount of spiritual culture, ministers policed the boundaries of taste and morality, acting with the deacons to censure or, if required, to expel members. In these ways, the outlines of chapel as a disciplined community were maintained.

At the same time as chapel and its satellite institutions were established as the focus of community among the well-to-do, the networks were extended outwards in the form of the 'civilising mission' to reclaim the mass of the urban population for organised religion. This involved not only continual fund-raising and expenditure on churches, missions and improving agencies, but also new types of bureaucratic organisation at local level which ministers supervised and coordinated. Home-visiting, which encompassed an older style of pastoral responsibility and newer types of missionising, involved complex, large-scale forms of voluntary organisation. The system under Macfadyen at Chorlton Road was described as a 'specimen of methodical exactness', based on the division of the surrounding area into districts, each of which was under the supervision of an elder or deacon responsible to the minister for a team of visitors.[75] Wealthier chapels also set up their own branch churches. In 1865–66 East Parade chapel funded the building of two churches in Leeds, one 'in the democratic suburb of Beeston Hill', the other 'in the somewhat aristocratic suburb of Headingley Hill'. By 1891 Chorlton Road had founded four missions in Ancoats and other industrial districts of Manchester, complete with branch church, Sunday School, temperance society and philanthropic agencies, as well as establishing congregations in the outer suburbs of Withington and Chorlton-cum-Hardy.[76] Significantly, branch churches were frequently located in 'frontier' zones, on the urban fringe where the suburbs met the countryside, and in workers' enclaves which bordered on the commercial centre or on areas of middle-class housing. Together with other philanthropic agencies, churches and chapels worked to create lines of communication across the city which served to mark out social differences by defining relationships of activism and dependency, responsibility and need. The growth of unified religious organisations from the later nineteenth century, such as the Leeds Congregational Council and the Manchester Free Church Council, encouraged the process. It enabled ministers and prominent laymen to co-ordinate their efforts and to envisage the city in terms of a grid of religious endeavour in ways similar to those delineated by charitable and educational agencies.

Under the spiritual directorship of ministers the major denominational chapels became the nexus of a burgeoning organisational complex.

Chapels focused both inwards and outwards, enjoining sociability and social action. In this sense, the 'civilising mission' was a dual process: the reclaiming of a regenerate population for the purposes of religion, morality and social order was dependent on the creation of a community which could itself be seen to exhibit these virtuous characteristics. Among prosperous sections of Nonconformity, therefore, the culture of chapel was integral to the institutionalisation of the middle class as a distinct and recognisable social force. Within this culture, ministers had a strategic part to play. Not only did they embody in their person the conception of spiritual culture and historical tradition, but they also provided the focus for discipline and organisation essential to the maintenance of the community and to its insertion in the larger networks of urban social relationships. Through institutions such as chapel it was possible to mobilise the middle class, to give an amorphous propertied population a continuous social identity and presence.[77]

In the period between 1840 and 1914, therefore, Nonconformist ministers came to occupy an increasingly prominent position in the life of industrial towns and cities. While many, like Dale and Fairbairn, became national figures in the configuration of 'militant Dissent', their public names – Dale of Birmingham, Maclaren of Manchester – emphasised that their identities were ultimately tied to a specific urban locale. More intimately still, the reputation of ministers was imprinted on specific districts of the city. W. H. Mills observed how, from the 1870s, 'The Sunday suburbs were apportioned out among a hierarchy of powerful theologians', while tram stops were referred to by ministerial names: 'Maclaren's chapel', 'Mursell's chapel', 'Finlayson's chapel'.[78] By virtue of their public visibility and influence, which itself rested on their authority as bearers of a distinct spiritual culture, such men acted, in Gramsci's phrase, as the 'organic intellectuals' of provincial bourgeois culture.[79] In the absence of a recognised, secular literary or academic intelligentsia in nineteenth-century provincial cities, it was the ministry which took on this role. They did so by virtue of their claim to scholarship and intellectual culture, their existence as a close-knit group based on common networks, and their high-profile commitment to the major causes of Liberal Nonconformity. The decline of the Nonconformist ministry as a force in the decades before and after the First World War was the product of many factors. Yet it is significant that the Bloomsbury group, which defined itself in opposition to Victorian evangelicalism, was also in certain ways the heir of old Dissent. Maynard Keynes was the grandson of the minister John Brown, chair of the Congregational Union in 1891. 'Perhaps no one who was not brought up as an evangelical or a nonconformist', Keynes considered, 'is entitled to think freely in due course', a view with which Leslie Stephen, himself of evangelical stock, would have concurred. Even Lytton Strachey, the most ardent critic of Victorian religiosity, termed Bloomsbury 'the mysterious priests of a new and amazing civilisation'.[80]

Yet for most of the nineteenth and early twentieth century, organised religion with Nonconformity at its head was the touchstone of respectable bourgeois culture in provincial, industrial England. Located between the public and private, chapel represented the link between the suburban world of family and the competitive individualism of the city. It stood in opposition not only to the disorderly world of the streets and slums, but also to the unrespectable face of bourgeois culture, the bohemian informality of the more relaxed gentlemen's clubs and the insalubrious world of drink and prostitution which lay beyond. In this sense, religion involved more than simply belief or ideology. Like the promenade or High 'Change, chapel-going represented one of the performative rituals of bourgeois life. Its unvarying place in the Victorian Sunday, the carriage procession before and after the service, and the highly-charged act of preaching, all made chapel-going a shared experience, a demonstration of the collective self-discipline of the middle-class community. As ritual and performance, it also connected to other sites where cultural distinction and middle-class authority were publicly displayed. Of these, one of the most important from the mid-Victorian period was the concert hall.

Notes

1 The reform of parish organisation was undertaken by a series of prominent early Victorian clergymen such as Walter Hook at Leeds, J. P. Lee in Manchester and J. C. Miller in Birmingham. See H. W. Dalton, 'Anglican church life in Leeds during the early Victorian resurgence, 1836–51, with special reference to the work of W. F. Hook' (Ph.D. thesis, Leeds University, 1993); W. R. Ward, *Religion and Society in Industrial England* (London: Batsford, 1978), p. 221; A. Briggs, *History of Birmingham*, vol. 2 (London: Oxford University Press, 1952). For church and chapel building see S. J. D. Green, 'Religion in the industrial town, with special reference to the West Riding of Yorkshire, c.1870–1920' (D.Phil. thesis, Oxford University, 1989); S. Gunn, 'The Manchester middle class, 1850–1880' (Ph.D. thesis, Manchester University, 1992), ch. 6.

2 D. W. Bebbington, *Evangelicalism in Modern Britain* (London: Routledge, 1995), p. 113.

3 K. S. Inglis, 'Patterns of religious worship in 1851', *Journal of Ecclesiastical*

History, xi (1960); H. Mcleod, *Class and Religion in the Late Victorian City* (London: Croom Helm, 1974); A. D. Gilbert, *Religion and Society in England, 1850–1914* (London: Macmillan, 1976).

4 For comments see K. D. Brown, *A Social History of the Nonconformist Ministry in England and Wales, 1800–1930* (Oxford: Clarendon Press, 1988), pp. 11–12; R. J. Morris, *Class, Sect and Party. The Making of the British Middle Class: Leeds, 1820–50* (Manchester: Manchester University Press, 1990), ch. 6.

5 L. Davidoff and C. Hall, *Family Fortunes* (London: Hutchinson, 1987), p. 82; Gunn, 'The Manchester middle class', p. 259; C. Binfield, *So Down to Prayers: Studies in English Nonconformity, 1780–1914* (London: J. M. Dent, 1977), p. 60.

6 A point made earlier, following Asa Briggs, in ch. 1 of this study.

7 Brown, *Social History of the Nonconformist Ministry*, chs 2–3; J. Thompson, *Lancashire Independent College* (Manchester, 1893); W. B. Selbie, *Mansfield College, Oxford: Its Origin and Opening* (London, 1890). In examining ministers' networks more generally, see also R. Gray, 'The platform and the pulpit: cultural identities and civic networks in industrial towns, c. 1850–70' in A. Kidd and D. Nicholls (eds), *The Making of the British Middle Class? Studies of Regional and Cultural Diversity Since the Eighteenth Century* (Stroud: Sutton, 1998).

8 J. Parker, *A Preacher's Life* (London, 1899), p. 199.

9 W. H. Mills, *Grey Pastures* (London: Chatto and Windus, 1924), p. 7.

10 R. H. Wicksteed (ed.), *Memorials of the Rev. Charles Wicksteed, B.A.* (London, 1886), p. 45; A. W. W. Dale, *The Life of R. W. Dale of Birmingham* (London, 1898), p. v.

11 E. A. Payne, *The Baptist Union: A Short History* (London: Carey Kingsgate Press, 1958); R. Tudor Jones, *Congregationalism in England, 1662–1962* (London: Independent Press, 1962); D. A. Hamer, *The Politics of Electoral Pressure* (Brighton: Harvester, 1977); 'Manchester Nonconformist Association pamphlets 1872–4', Dr Williams Library, London.

12 *General Conference of Nonconformists, Held in Manchester, January 23, 24 and 25, 1872: Authorised Report of Proceedings* (Manchester, 1872); Selbie, *Mansfield College*.

13 Watts papers, Manchester Central Reference Library Archive Department.; G. Hadfield, 'Personal narrative', MS, Manchester Central Reference Library Archive Department.

14 Binfield, *So Down to Prayers*, p. 76; E. T. Maclaren, *Dr Maclaren of Manchester* (London, 1911).

15 Further examples of these cousinhoods can be found in Gunn, 'Manchester middle class', ch. 5; P. Joyce, *Work, Society and Politics: The Culture of the Factory in Later Victorian England* (Brighton: Harvester, 1980), ch. 1; Binfield, *So Down to Prayers*. For other viewpoints on the development of the ministry as a profession see Gray, 'The platform and the pulpit';

R. O'Day, 'The men from the ministry' in G. Parsons (ed.), *Religion in Victorian Britain*, vol. 2 (Manchester: Manchester University Press, 1988).

16 Dale, *Life of R. W. Dale*, pp. 76–87, 116.

17 Rev. J. Martineau, *The Seat of Authority in Religion* (London: [1875] 1898), p. xii. For further discussion of the model of the family in discourses of the Nonconformist chapel see J. Seed, 'Theologies of power: Unitarianism and the social relations of religious discourse, 1800–50' in R. J. Morris (ed.), *Class, Power and Social Structure in British Nineteenth-Century Towns* (Leicester: Leicester University Press, 1986), pp. 136–142; Davidoff and Hall, *Family Fortunes*, ch. 2.

18 Letter from Rev. H. R. Reynolds to East Parade Congregation, 23 December 1855, East Parade file, Leeds City Archives.

19 'Our Own', *Cavendish Street Manual* (Manchester, 1861); Parker, *Preacher's Life*, p. 143.

20 Brown, *Social History of the Nonconformist Ministry*, pp. 155–8; J. A. Banks, *Prosperity and Parenthood* (London, 1954) for the classic discussion of middle-class incomes.

21 A. W. W. Dale, 'George Dawson' in J. H. Muirhead (ed.), *Nine Famous Birmingham Men* (Birmingham, 1909), pp. 79–81.

22 Dale, *Life of R. W. Dale*, p. 174; T. T. James, *Cavendish Street Chapel, Manchester* (Manchester, 1948).

23 R. W. Dale, *Weekday Sermons*, 6th edn (London, 1895), p. 35.

24 J. Seed, 'Gentlemen dissenters: the social and political meanings of rational dissent in the 1770s and 1780s', *Historical Journal*, 28, 2 (1985).

25 J. Harris, *The Importance of an Educated Ministry* (London, 1843); Thompson, *Lancashire Independent College*, p. 84; B. Davies, 'Ministerial education' in *Cardiff Memorial: Five Papers Read at the Autumnal Sesssion of the Baptist Union of Great Britain and Ireland* (1868), p. 6.

26 S. Gunn, 'The ministry, the middle class and the "civilising mission" in Manchester, 1850–1880', *Social History*, 21, 1 (January 1996), pp. 30–2; B. Hilton, *The Age of Atonement* (Oxford: Clarendon Press, 1991), part 3.

27 L. Burney, *Cross Street Chapel, Manchester and Its College* (Manchester: Morten, 1983), pp. 19–20; Dale, *Life of R. W. Dale*, pp. 39–42; Martineau cited in McLeod, *Class and Religion*, p. 137.

28 Dale, *Life of R. W. Dale*, p. 44.

29 Obituary, Manchester Central Reference Library Biography Index; Wicksteed, *Memorials*, pp. 42–3.

30 Dale, *Life of R. W. Dale*, pp. 44, 511.

31 Bebbington, *Evangelicalism*, p. 141; P. Keating, *The Haunted Study* (London: Fontana, 1991), p. 34.

32 Maclaren, *Dr Maclaren*, pp. 90–3; Dale, 'George Dawson', pp. 93–4; J. A. James, *Protestant Nonconformity: A Sketch of Its General History* (Birmingham, 1849), p. 133.

33 C. Binfield, 'The story of Button Hill: an essay in Leeds Nonconformity' in A. Mason, *Religion in Leeds* (Stroud: Sutton, 1994), p. 83.

34 'Self-culture', *Evangelical Magazine* (June 1845), pp. 296–7.

35 Wicksteed, *Memorials*, p. 93; A. Mackennal, *The Life of J. A. Macfadyen* (London, 1891), p. 87.

36 See, for example, the derogatory comments of the Baptist minister Alexander Maclaren of Union chapel, cited in Maclaren, *Dr Maclaren of Manchester*, p. 62.

37 Dale, *Life of R. W. Dale*, pp. 591–2.

38 Brown, *Social History of the Nonconformist Ministry*, p. 84.

39 Dale, *Life of R. W. Dale*, pp. 139–40; J. B. Marsden, *Memoirs of the Life and Labours of the Rev. Hugh Stowell* (London, 1868); J. W. Diggle, *The Lancashire Life of Bishop Fraser* (London, 1890). For similar comments on Hook at Leeds see S. Gilley, 'Walter Farquhar Hook, Vicar of Leeds' in Mason, *Religion in Leeds*, p. 44.

40 A. J. Scott, *Introductory Lectures on the Opening of Owen's College, Manchester* (London, 1852), p. 6.

41 Mackennal, *Life of J. A. Macfadyen*, p. 114.

42 W. H. Mills, *The Manchester Reform Club, 1871–1921* (Manchester, 1921), p. 8.

43 Rev. James Slater of Watford cited in Maclaren, *Dr Maclaren*, p. 106.

44 'Diaries and recollections of Benjamin Barker, Bramley, near Leeds', MS, Box XI, 2 and 3, Thoresby Society.

45 Cited in McLeod, *Class and Religion*, p. 162.

46 For Mursell see M. Hewitt, *The Emergence of Stability in the Industrial City* (Aldershot: Scolar Press, 1996), pp. 145–6; Dale, *Life of R. W. Dale*, p. 285; W. Binns, 'The religious heresies of the working classes', *Westminster Review*, 21 (January 1862), pp. 60–97.

47 Dale, *Nine Lectures*, p. 37; E. Miall, *The British Churches in Relation to the British People* (London, 1849), pp. 212–13.

48 Cited in Gilley, 'Hook', pp. 56–7.

49 Cited in Binfield, 'Button Hill', p. 96.

50 Maclaren, *Dr Maclaren*, pp. 70–1; Dale, *Life of R. W. Dale*, p. 315.

51 Wicksteed, *Memorials*, p. 132.

52 Miss G. M. Campbell cited in A. Peel and J. A. R. Marriott, *Robert Forman Horton* (London: Allen and Unwin, 1937), pp. 177–9.

53 *Freelance*, 29 December 1866, p. 9.

54 The best discussions of this theme are to be found in Seed, 'Theologies of power' and Davidoff and Hall, *Family Fortunes*.

55 The main lines of these various shifts can be traced in Bebbington, *Evangelicalism in Modern Britain*. For examples of sermons on the topics mentioned see R. W. Dale, *The Old Evangelicalism and the New* (London, 1889); A. Mackennal, 'Agnosticism – sceptical and Christian' in *Bowdon Downs Church Manual* (1883).

56 *Weekday Sermons*, p. 172.

57 'Theologies of power', pp. 136–8.

58 Maclaren, *Dr Maclaren*, p. 62; C. S. Horne, 'R. W. Dale' in Muirhead, *Birmingham Men*, p. 260.
59 Dale, *Life of R. W. Dale*, p. 90; Binfield, *So Down*, p. 222. While the admission of women to chapel offices was a matter for the membership of individual chapels to decide, many did not allow this to occur until after the First World War. See, for example, V. Green and D. Figures, *Headingley Hill Church, 1866–1978* (Leeds, 1985), pp. 18–20.
60 A classic example is the Low Church Rev. Hugh Stowell of Christ Church, Salford, whose speeches are excerpted in Marsden, *Memoirs.*
61 R. Quinault, 'The cult of the centenary, 1784–1914', *Bulletin of the Institute of Historical Research*, 71, 176 (October 1998).
62 Dale, *Protestantism: Its Ultimate Principle* (London, 1874), p. 10.
63 Rev. W. Mckerrow, *Lectures on Voluntaryism* (Manchester, 1861), p. 21.
64 *Protestantism*, p. 11.
65 Binfield, *So Down to Prayers*, p. 196.
66 For further commentary on this type of history see P. Joyce, *Visions of the People: Industrial England and the Question of Class 1840–1914* (Cambridge: Cambridge University Press, 1991), pp. 181–3; J. Vernon (ed.), *Re-Reading the Constitution: New Narratives in the Political History of the Long Nineteenth Century* (Cambridge: Cambridge University Press, 1996).
67 R. W. Dale, *The Politics of the Future* (Birmingham, 1867), p. 18.
68 See *inter alia* Dale, *Protestantism* and *The Politics of Nonconformity* (Manchester, 1871); Mckerrow, *Lectures on Voluntaryism*; Rev. A. Maclaren, *Religious Equality in Its Connection with National and Religious Life* (Manchester, 1871); Rev. S. A. Steinthal, *Sermon at Cross St Chapel, Manchester* (Manchester, 1878).
69 Dale, 'George Dawson' in Muirhead, *Birmingham Men*, p. 100.
70 W. Adamson, *Life of the Rev. Joseph Parker D.D.* (London, 1902), p. 68; Mackennal, *Macfadyen*, p. 113.
71 Mackennal, *Macfadyen*, p. 110.
72 Green and Figures, *Headingley Hill*, p. 28; Newton Park Congregational Church file, Leeds City Archives. For an illuminating account of the importance of chapel for the children of a prosperous Unitarian family in Sale, Manchester in the 1880s, see the 'Diary of Clara Alcock', MS, Manchester Central Library Archives Department.
73 Maclaren, *Dr Maclaren*, p. 112.
74 'East Parade Sunday School, Senior Scholars Manuscript Magazine', vol. 1, no. 2 (1883), Leeds City Archives.
75 Mackennal, *Macfadyen*, p. 142.
76 *Official Handbook, Congregational Union of England and Wales* (Leeds, 1928), p. 45.; Mackennal, *Macfadyen*, p. 110.
77 These arguments are developed more extensively in Gunn, 'The ministry', esp. pp. 35–6.
78 *The Manchester Reform Club*, p. 22.

r>cusure*133

79 Q. Hoare (ed.), *Selections From the Prison Notebooks of Antonio Gramsci* (London: Lawrence and Wishart, 1982), pp. 5–14.
80 R. Skidelsky, *John Maynard Keynes* (London: Weidenfeld and Nicholson, 1991); Binfield, *So Down*, p. 92; N. Annan, *Leslie Stephen* (London: MacGibbon and Kee, 1951), ch. 3; M. Holroyd, *Lytton Strachey: A Critical Biography*, vol. 1 (London: Heinemann, 1967), p. 198.

6

Music and the constitution of high culture

If religion was one axis of the culture of middle-class respectability, then art was another. Indeed, the two were seen as closely linked in the mid-Victorian period, as the *Guardian* suggested at the opening of the Manchester Art Treasures exhibition in 1857: 'Art and religion have ever been found together, have grown with each other, and have declined together'; the opening of the Exhibition was thus an 'essentially religious ceremonial'.[1] Of all the arts, it was music that was most obviously associated with religion in the nineteenth century. It was not merely that many of the most widely accepted musical forms, such as oratorio, grew directly out of religious tradition and maintained this association. It was also the case that the 'classical' music which emerged as a distinct form in the second third of the nineteenth century took on many of the trappings of religious discourse and practice. Music became the 'divine art' and during the second half of the nineteenth century the concert hall was constructed as a sacred space for the performance of a cultural rite. The conjunction of the artistic with the sacred was commonly endorsed by the leading figures of the music world. Thus the founder and conductor of the celebrated Manchester concerts, Charles Hallé, declared: 'The art which I profess has been a sort of religion for me. It has certain influences beyond those of any other art'.[2]

Yet it would be misleading to construe art solely or even mainly in these terms. It is a commonplace of cultural history that art as a whole sought and gained increasing autonomy from other dimensions of social life during the nineteenth century, while different art forms took on an independent existence from each other and laid claim to distinct historical traditions. Music in particular came to the forefront of cultural attention. In the eighteenth century it ranked low in the scale of the arts, Kant, for example, considering music 'more a matter of enjoyment than of culture'. But during the nineteenth century it underwent a dramatic transformation of style and status. According to the historian

William Weber, music experienced a 'cultural explosion': 'no other cultural area experienced so remarkable a history'.[3] While this efflorescence was registered generally across Europe and the West, music came to have a particular importance in the culture of the provincial middle class in England. The triennial music festivals in Birmingham and Leeds and the Hallé concerts in Manchester occupied an unrivalled position as the cities' principal cultural events in the second half of the nineteenth century, achieving a national and even international celebrity. Within each of the cities these institutions had a major part to play in the foundation of a public high culture, open in the sense of being accessible on the basis of payment, yet also socially and culturally exclusive. By the 1870s the classical concert stood at the apex of a new cultural hierarchy, representing the model of aesthetic value against which other public forms of cultural expression, from opera and theatre to music hall and variety, could be judged and ranked.

How classical music came to stand as the epitome of urban high culture in Birmingham, Leeds and Manchester during the second half of the nineteenth century was not simply a matter of the social composition of concert audiences or the qualities inherent in the music itself. It depended upon a series of factors: the creation of forms of organisation able to provide stability and continuity for concert life; the identification of the concert hall with urban 'high society'; and the implementation of categories of judgement which enabled distinctions to be drawn between art and entertainment, 'high' and 'low' cultures. It was, in short, a complex process that came about in particular ways and according to different time-scales in the three cities. But in each city, I shall argue, music became central to the construction of a high culture after 1870 that was recognisably bourgeois in form and character.

Music and the organisational basis of high culture

The concert-hall world of the mid- and later Victorian period grew out of musical forms and traditions that took shape at least a century earlier. By the mid- and later eighteenth century concerts were an established part of the culture of consumption of the aristocracy, gentry and 'middling sort'. London was the undisputed centre of musical life nationally, but concerts also formed part of the social calendar of provincial towns, often linked to assizes, race meetings and assemblies. They included growing industrial centres no less than county and market towns: Leeds, Birmingham and Manchester all held music festivals between 1768 and 1777. An increasingly varied musical repertoire was established, made

up of opera, instrumental music and choral singing, by composers such
as Purcell, Corelli, Haydn, and, above all, Handel, whose oratorios were
acclaimed as the acme of sacred and patriotic music from the 1780s.[4]
From this there developed a variegated musical culture in the industrial
centres during the first half of the nineteenth century. Leeds in the 1840s
offered orchestral concerts at the Music Hall in Albion Street, organ
and choral music at churches and chapels, and chamber music concerts
held in the private houses of the wealthier families. In Manchester there
was the Gentlemen's Glee Club, the Harmonic Society which presented
large-scale oratorios, and the Gentlemen's Concert Hall, where opera,
songs and excerpts from the works of composers such as Beethoven and
Mendelssohn were performed seasonally.[5] In all three cities 'people's'
concerts were also initiated from the 1840s under the auspices of the
corporation, and voluntary bodies such as the Leeds Rational Recreation
Society, in the name of popular improvement.[6]

A diverse music culture was therefore well established in the industrial cities by the mid-nineteenth century. The London journal
Harmonicon in 1831 considered the 'community of Manchester' to be
'constantly in advance of all other parts of the Kingdom in their musical
taste and knowledge'. Likewise, early nineteenth-century Birmingham,
according to the Liberal spokesman J. T. Bunce, was 'decidedly a musical
town'.[7] Recent research has gone some way to bear out this picture of
the provincial cities as important musical centres. In 1861 Manchester
was second only to London in the number of full-time musicians resident
in the city; Liverpool ranked third, Birmingham fourth and Leeds fifth.[8]

However, the musical culture to be found in the provincial cities
during the first half of the nineteenth century differed in a number of
significant ways from the concert-hall world that was to take shape
thereafter. Firstly, it lacked a stable and continuous organisational basis.
Concerts by star soloists such as Jullien or Paganini were part of an
emergent touring circuit and attracted large audiences, but they were
infrequent. Locally organised concert series tended to be short-lived,
mainly for financial reasons caused by the decline of aristocratic patronage from the late eighteenth century and the difficulties of attracting
well-to-do audiences on a regular basis. At Leeds, for example, Walton's
Music Saloon opened in 1837, specialising in chamber music, but failed
financially and was sold in 1845.[9] Secondly, much of polite music culture
was organised on a private or semi-private basis. Concerts were often
held in the homes of the wealthy, as with the Leeds Musical Soirées
established by professional and employer families like the Heatons,
Kitsons and Marshalls in 1848. Glee clubs and madrigal societies,

meanwhile, demanded entrance fees and limited their membership. Similarly, 'public' concert series were organised as subscription societies, a limited number of members paying a substantial fee in advance for the whole 'season'. At Manchester in the early 1850s the annual subscription for the Gentlemen's Concerts was five guineas and there was a waiting list of over three hundred potential subscribers. The subscription lists read like a roll-call of the city's wealthiest professional and employer families – Greg, Philips, Peel, Heelis – independent of political and religious affiliations.[10]

Unlike the people's concerts for which tickets were sold individually at comparatively cheap prices, polite musical culture was therefore a more expensive and exclusive affair. Again in contrast to the concert-hall world of the later nineteenth century, concert programmes tended to mix musical genres: selections from 'classical' composers such as Beethoven and Mozart would be interspersed with extracts from operas, popular ballads and instrumental pieces. Termed 'miscellaneous', such programmes remained standard concert fare in the provincial cities up to the 1860s and in some cases beyond.[11] In so far as musical boundaries existed they lay between sacred music, identified with oratorio and choral singing, and music which served as an incentive to, or a diversion from, the business of socialising. The idea that music existed as an art in its own right, disassociated from religious or social ends, appears to have been held only by a minority of devotees, mainly identified with chamber music in the first half of the nineteenth century. In the 1850s the Gentlemen's Concert Hall resembled 'rather a fashionable lounge than a society for the enjoyment or cultivation of music', a Manchester journal caustically recalled.[12] One important effect of this was that types of music were weakly socially classified; the programmes for people's concerts and those performed at elite subscription concerts differed only to a limited degree either in their format or in the repertoire played.

From the mid-nineteenth century, however, there was a significant shift in the organisational basis of concert life. The world of semi-private concerts was opened up in the industrial cities, creating a secular public sphere for music while simultaneously maintaining and even augmenting the prestige of classical concerts as the cornerstone of high culture. The most striking and successful example of this process was the Manchester Hallé concerts.[13] Charles Hallé was a well-known concert pianist who was invited to Manchester in 1849 to conduct the Gentlemen's Concerts. Hallé, whose experience had been gained in the musical capitals of Paris and London, was critical of the closed character of the musical culture in Manchester. 'The Gentlemen's Concerts were an exclusive society', he asserted. 'None but subscribers were admitted and no tickets sold. Before my advent they had never published programmes of their concerts, and the directors had only done so since 1850 because I objected to conducting concerts of this clandestine sort.' [14]

It was not until the advent of the Art Treasures Exhibition in 1857, for which Hallé organised a number of concerts, that he considered there existed a sufficient audience in Manchester to support a regular series of orchestral concerts independent of the existing subscription system. The first season of concerts was inaugurated in 1858 and with a brief interruption in 1860–61 continued annually during the winter months thereafter at the Free Trade Hall. Season tickets were offered at £1, but Hallé also instituted a policy of cheap tickets available for each individual concert, ranging from 1s. upwards. A permanent, professional orchestra was formed and rigorous touring schedules undertaken, sometimes involving concerts on eight successive nights in different towns and cities. [15] By the late 1860s the Hallé concerts had achieved financial stability and were established in Manchester as an 'institution'. By contrast, the Gentlemen's Concerts waned in popularity among the city's middle class and came to be seen as musically inferior to their counterparts at the Free Trade Hall. 'With the introduction of Mr Hallé's concerts in the Free Trade Hall, the Concert Hall began to die', a local journal commented; 'the monopoly has broken down'. [16]

These developments were novel and significant, but the Hallé concerts were not unique in providing regular public orchestral series with cheap tickets available for each performance. In London August Manns established the Crystal Palace concerts in 1855, charging 2s. 6d. to hear new and demanding classical music, 1s. tickets being introduced from 1869. [17] Nor was the Hallé typical of provincial musical life in the mid-Victorian period. In Birmingham a small number of subscription concerts were held each winter in the 1850s and 1860s, but it was only with William Stockley's concerts in 1873 that the city obtained a lasting orchestral series, and even so the organisers were heavily reliant on subscribers for the concerts' survival. [18] In Leeds there was no equivalent orchestral series before the Leeds Symphony Society was established in 1890, the main events before this being the Tuesday and Saturday evening recitals by the municipal organist, William Spark. 'Eighteen months have elapsed since there was a concert of any importance in Leeds', a local journal complained in 1883; 'the old concert-givers have ceased to cater for musical Yorkshire owing to the lack of interest on the part of the public'. [19]

In Birmingham and Leeds, therefore, it was the triennial music festivals that occupied centre-stage in local musical culture. This pattern was early established in the case of Birmingham. The first festival was held in 1768 with the purpose of raising funds for the General Hospital, a philanthropic connection that was to persist until 1912. In the late eighteenth century the festival was strongly associated with the county aristocracy: in 1787, for example, the earls of Aylesford and Plymouth, and Viscount Dudley, were prominent on the committee, while the concerts themselves were a 'major rendezvous for the Quality of the West Midlands'.[20] Birmingham's Anglican establishment was also involved, festival performances being held at St Philip's church. From the early 1800s, however, the influence of the county and the Church began to wane. The organisational driving force behind the festivals between 1802 and 1849 was Joseph Moore, a button manufacturer and friend of Matthew Boulton. From 1834 the festival was held in the new Town Hall, itself importantly designed to serve as a concert hall. Through the association with Mendelssohn between 1837 and 1846, the festival became a cultural event of national significance, identified with Birmingham rather than the county as an institution representative of a 'liberal and enlightened people'.[21] In the second half of the nineteenth century, responsibility for the organisation of the festival resided with two committees, a small orchestral committee, appointed by the governors of the General Hospital, and a larger general committee, consisting of 'gentlemen of position and influence in the town'. In both cases, such men were drawn from the upper echelons of Birmingham society, and increasingly from its Liberal wing. While the names of the regional aristocracy continued to be found among the Presidents and Vice-Presidents of the festivals, their role had become purely honorific.[22]

The festival movement in Leeds, by contrast, was a product of the mid-Victorian period. While a music festival had been held in 1769, it was not built upon, and by the 1850s the town compared unfavourably in musical terms with Bradford, where a brief attempt to establish regular festivals was made between 1853 and 1859, held at the newly-built St George's Hall.[23] The role of civic rivalry with Bradford in the building of the new Leeds Town Hall is well known; what is less often recorded is that it also encompassed music. The opening of the Town Hall by Queen Victoria in 1858 was immediately followed by a music festival, the first of its kind in nineteenth-century Leeds. Like the Town Hall, it was at the outset a 'Corporate institution': the idea for the festival originated in the Corporation and half the committee in 1858 was made up of town councillors.[24] As at Birmingham, the festival was linked to philanthropic ends, profits going to the Leeds Infirmary. But plans to establish a triennial series were dashed in 1861 by conflicts over status and precedence between the two main choral societies in Leeds.[25] It was not until 1874 that the festival was revived, initiated by the Mayor, but now with limited council representation: of the forty-five members of the general committee in 1874 only four were councillors.[26] Thereafter the festivals continued on a triennial basis, rapidly acquiring a national reputation for sacred music second only to Birmingham, and representing the city's major cultural institution.

Outwardly, therefore, the organisation of the principal musical institutions developed on different lines in Manchester, Birmingham and Leeds. The Hallé concerts remained the private property of Hallé himself, the conductor/owner seeking to maximise revenues not only from the concerts, but also from the sale of programmes, tutorial manuals and sheet music. Hallé was lauded in Manchester as an entrepreneur who had single-handedly effected a 'musical revolution'.[27] The festivals in Birmingham and Leeds, on the other hand, were effectively owned and directed by the urban elite. In Birmingham the festival committees were made up of nominees of the General Hospital and 'gentlemen of position and influence in the town'.[28] In Leeds it was the Corporation which was instrumental in instigating the festivals in 1858 and 1874. From the later 1870s, however, control passed to an independent general committee, elected by some two hundred guarantors, each subscribing on average almost £50. The result was a cross-party group composed of the most powerful Leeds families: Baines, Barran, Beckett, Fairbairn, Harding, Kitson, Marshall and Tetley.[29]

Despite the outward differences, however, the musical institutions all had a fundamentally similar impact on the organisation of high culture in the three cities. Firstly, they effected the transposition of classical music from the semi-private realm of club and society to a public sphere of art deemed representative of the urban community as a whole. In Manchester, Hallé was depicted as the harbinger of 'free trade in music', opening music to a new urban public: 'Thanks to the enterprise and efforts of Mr Charles Hallé, all classes of society may enjoy, or learn to enjoy – for music is, in the majority of cases, an acquired taste – the works of the best masters'.[30] From the 1850s the festivals in Birmingham and Leeds were likewise seen as a means of achieving the 'support of all classes' for the public performance of sacred, classical music in a new and grandiose setting.[31] At the same time, the institutions themselves remained firmly in middle-class hands. In 1883 a Leeds journal spoke of the 'millionaires' who sat on the festival committee, while Hallé was forced to rely on the support of wealthy backers to offset losses in the early 1860s.[32] Importantly, too, the various concert series were organised on voluntary lines, despite their public character. Even at Leeds, where the influence of the Corporation was most marked, a direct link with the municipal authorities was severed in the 1870s. The festivals, like the Hallé concerts, developed in the second half of the century in tandem with an emergent civic culture, but organisationally they stood apart from the town councils and the trend to municipalisation that overtook art galleries and museums between 1880 and 1914.

The second significant feature of the organisation of classical music as a component of high culture was its status as a non-profit activity. Whatever his reputation as a business entrepreneur, Hallé remained firmly opposed to musical 'commercialism'. Before his death in 1895 he sought ways to 'avoid the calamity of the concerts falling into the hands of an impresario, whose chief object would be to exploit the undertaking for his pecuniary benefit'. As a result a Hallé Society was founded, consisting of fifty members who would guarantee the maintenance of the concerts as a non-profit enterprise, reinvesting any annual surplus in the orchestra and covering any losses.[33] At Birmingham and Leeds profits from the festivals were distributed to the cities' medical charities, a tradition which was maintained despite the escalating cost of performances. Increasingly, therefore, the highest forms of music in the provincial cities were seen as autonomous of the market. Even philanthropic motives receded in importance before cultural imperatives. As a correspondent to the *Yorkshire Post* put it in 1880, 'to raise money for the charities of the town is not the principal object of the Leeds Musical Festival, but the advancement of Art'.[34]

By the 1870s, therefore, a stable organisational framework had been established for classical music in Birmingham, Leeds and Manchester, enabling the principal musical institutions to secure a position as the central components of a high culture that was to endure until the eve of the First World War. The Hallé concerts and the musical festivals were instrumental in carving out a public realm for art, even if an older culture of private and subscription events was never wholly displaced. Unlike the majority of earlier concert series in the three cities, financial and organisational stability was ensured by the presence of guarantors or donors prepared to underwrite losses, and by the effective independence of the main musical institutions from other urban bodies, such as the corporations and the hospitals, which might seek to control them for different ends. To all intents and purposes the Hallé and the festivals had become autonomous voluntary institutions whose self-professed aims were defined by Art alone. As non-profit organisations insulated from the market they represented what Pierre Bourdieu has called an 'economic world reversed', in which the authenticity of classical music as art was guaranteed by its apparent distance from, and opposition to, the market relations which obtained in other spheres of economic and cultural life.[35]

The concert hall and 'high society'

The organisational changes in classical music during the mid-Victorian years brought with it certain tensions in the social definition and meanings of the concert-hall world. On the one hand, the institutions of the Hallé and the festivals were intended to represent the urban community as a whole, rather than a narrow county or urban elite. Music was to be opened up to an anonymous 'public', made accessible to substantial, if not all, sections of the population. On the other hand, the inherited associations of classical music as part of polite culture meant that despite its transposition from the private to the public sphere it retained an aura of exclusivity. This exclusivity in fact remained essential to the construction of classical music as a cornerstone of high culture. The cultural status as well as the financial viability of the principal musical institutions was fundamentally dependent on the identification of the concert-hall with urban 'high society'.

These tensions were reflected in the ticket policy for classical concerts. In 1863–64 prices for individual concerts at the Hallé ranged from 1s. to 7s. 6d., with private boxes at £3, while season tickets were £5. Such a policy was designed to construct concert audiences as a mirror image of the liberal social order, hierarchical yet open. As the *Musical World* put it in 1860: 'Mr Charles Hallé's Manchester concerts are becoming the vogue with all classes, from the rich merchant and manufacturer to the respectable, thrifty, albeit humbler artisans'.[36] Yet concert prices need to be placed against evidence of wage rates at the period; in the Manchester district in the 1850s cotton spinners earned on average 23s. a week, and these were generally accepted to be the best-paid group of workers in the industry. As David Russell has noted the 1s. entrance was a high price for industrial workers in the mid-Victorian period, requiring 'acts of considerable self-sacrifice'.[37] The ticket policy at the Birmingham festival by comparison was unequivocally exclusive. In the 1790s prices of individual concerts ranged between 2s. and 10s. 6d.; by 1846 the cheapest ticket was 8s., the highest one guinea.[38] Pricing at Leeds was pitched somewhere between Manchester and Birmingham. At the 1858 festival, tickets for the main concerts cost between 7*s*. 6*d*. and a guinea, depending on the seat, while 'serial' tickets could be bought at four guineas. However, the Leeds committee added a separate 'People's Concert' to the event, with cheap tickets set at 1*s*. and 2*s*. 6*d*.[39] In general, prices for concert prices were high in the industrial cities, if the small number of cheap tickets is disregarded. Whereas a season ticket for the Hallé stood at £5, the equivalent cost for the London Philharmonic was one to three guineas, at Crystal Palace two guineas in the later 1860s. Equally, the figure for average receipts per head at Birmingham and Leeds was higher than that at the Bristol festival in 1879–80.[40]

Moreover, ticket prices tended to rise over time, and the policy of cheap seats was concomitantly squeezed. At Birmingham by 1900 the most expensive festival seats had been raised from one guinea to 25*s*. and serial tickets from £5 to £6. Similarly, serial tickets for the Leeds festival rose from four guineas to £5 in 1874 and five guineas in 1883.[41] Although the price-bands for seats at individual concerts increased slowly during the second half of the century, the balance between different types of ticket holder altered. At the Leeds festival between 1874 and 1886 the proportion of serial ticket holders, those wealthy enough to afford to purchase seats for all the festival concerts, increased from just over a third to over half the audiences as a whole. No less indicative of the drift to exclusivity was the increase in prices for the People's Concert to between 2*s*. 6*d*. and 7*s*. 6*d*. in 1883 – sums which, a local journal argued, 'will keep "the people" out' – and the dropping of the title 'People's Concert' altogether by the 1890s.[42] Similar tendencies were apparent at the Hallé concerts in Manchester. After an effective doubling in the cost of all seats, except those of the 'shilling freeholders', in the early 1860s and of programmes in 1871, prices remained stable to the 1890s. The major shift occurred in the relative proportions of different groups within the concert-going public. The proportion of season ticket-holders increased from 33 per cent of audiences in 1861–62 to 60 per cent by 1882–83, while that of the 1*s*. entrants fell from 39 per cent to 18 per cent. Between 1861–62 and 1882–83, the contribution of season ticket-holders to the total revenue from the concerts rose from 55 per cent to 68 per cent.[43] In all three cities, therefore, the tension between exclusivity and accessibility was resolved in favour of the former. Classical music concerts increasingly drew, and depended on, the support of the wealthiest sections of the urban population.

This was the impression conveyed, and indeed enhanced, in the press. The classical concerts were portrayed as the major social ritual of the well-to-do, the audiences as the pinnacle of fashion. According to the *Freelance* the concert hall on Hallé night represented 'the most gorgeous and dazzling sight that is anywhere to be seen in Manchester, at one glance'. At the opening night of the 1858 festival, the *Birmingham Daily Post* enthused, 'the Hall looked brilliant in the extreme, forming a picture worth half of the money to look upon'.[44] Audiences at the Hallé and the festivals were conventionally identified as the 'middle and upper classes', the 'swells', the 'leading families of the district', except at special events such as the Christmas *Messiah* in Manchester and the People's Concerts in Leeds when these elements were temporarily displaced by the 'hard-handed sons of toil' and the 'popular classes'.[45] The idea of the leading concert series as a social ritual was augmented by the provision of special trains from prosperous suburbs such as Bowdon and Altrincham, in the case of the Hallé, or from outlying towns like Warwick and Leamington for the Birmingham festival. At Leeds in the early 1890s it was observed that the festival 'has become a social institution as well as a musical gathering. All the well-to-do-citizens receive into their houses relatives and friends from a distance'.[46] The status of the festivals as a magnet for high society was enhanced by the presence of royalty and land. The Duke of Edinburgh attended the festivals at Birmingham in 1873 and at Leeds in 1880. The *Birmingham Daily Post* noted that the audience at the opening concert in 1858 included 'members of nearly every county family of distinction', and the press in both cities provided full lists of notable visitors at every festival between the 1850s and 1914.[47] Yet though the appearance of visiting luminaries was observed as a matter of local pride, what was celebrated at the concerts was essentially an urban high society. It was signalled not only by the presence of local notabilities, the mayor and major employers, but also by the assembled ranks of men and women whose fashionable dress was taken to symbolise the scale, wealth and taste of the urban middle class. In describing the 'fair spectacle' of a Town Hall concert in 1873, the Birmingham press proudly commended 'our Festival *belles,* who have acquired a renown for their own rich and tasteful dressing', and the 'splendour of *ensemble* and elegance of detail' which rendered 'the sartorial aspects of the gathering remarkable'. At the Manchester Hallé, the absence of royal or landed visitors did not prevent the concerts becoming the recognised assembly of the city's own 'aristocracy' and a regular source of both encomium and satire in the periodical press.[48]

As in the promenade, it was the presence of fashionable femininity that conferred on the concert hall its 'brilliance' as a social occasion. Here also the middle-class family was reconvened in public, attendance at the leading concert series representing a rite of passage for sons and daughters into the adult world of cultivated society.[49] All this did not imply that the concert hall was an undifferentiated space; particular parts of the hall were distinguished by cost and status, and by separate entrances. But here the conventions were shifting. Whereas seating arrangements at Birmingham Town Hall followed aristocratic precedent in the 1840s, the galleries representing the locus of the 'quality', the floor that of the 'people', from the later 1850s the situation was reversed. Refurbishment in the 1890s, with the installation of 'crimson plush seats in gilt bronze frames', confirmed the trend, making the floor 'the most luxurious part of the hall'. By the later nineteenth century, in the concert hall as in the theatre, the stalls had become the 'home of the bourgeoisie'.[50] Representations of the concert-hall audience, moreover, dwelt not so much on the evidence of social difference as on the outward signs of collectivity and conformity. The clearest manifestation of these was the dress codes governing attendance at major concert events. Before 1914 evening dress remained *de rigueur*, a 'class uniform' in the words of George Bernard Shaw, and even after this date, when the concert as social ritual was in decline, dress codes remained stricter than for any other cultural event in the provincial cities. Thus Katherine Chorley evoked the Hallé audiences between the wars: 'low-cut dresses and opera cloaks, boiled shirts and dinner jackets with an occasional tail-coat on the floor of the hall'.[51]

Above all, the concert-hall was represented in the press as a public spectacle. At the festival concerts in Leeds and Birmingham crowds of onlookers gathered to watch the audience arriving. In Leeds in 1892 'the Town Hall was half surrounded by a crowd, who gazed at their more fortunate fellow-townspeople who were privileged to attend the performance. Most of the latter seemed to arrive in carriages, which having deposited their burdens, overflowed into the neighbouring streets, to wait until the performance was over.' On concert nights the hall was depicted in highly visual terms which stressed its romantic qualities: 'In the evening the Victoria Hall was packed to the doors and when the half-light of the gas paled before the bright glow of the electric light, there could be seen as brilliant an assembly of men and women as ever met within those stately walls'.[52] With its plush carpets, luxurious seats and electric lighting, the concert hall became a prime site for bourgeois display by the last quarter of the nineteenth century. It provided an elaborate setting in which an audience of several thousand men and women could regularly envisage themselves, and be envisaged by others, as high society. More than any other cultural event the classical concert enabled the provincial middle class to be collectively represented, in public and bodily form, as an assemblage of wealth, fashion and taste.

The concert as cultural rite

However, the classical concert was more than merely a social occasion; it was also, pre-eminently, a cultural rite. From the 1850s, indeed, the provincial concert-world developed in ways that gave precedence to the latter over the former. At Birmingham and Leeds the society ball with which music festivals had conventionally closed was dropped in 1858, breaking the eighteenth-century tradition of linking concerts with the social calendar.[53] In Manchester, Hallé's frequently proclaimed mission to create an 'educated' musical audience involved abolishing the idea that music was the background to fashionable socialising. From the outset, the Hallé concerts were marked out by a seriousness of cultural purpose: 'Those for whom a concert was only a social reunion, and who considered music of any kind nothing much better than a lively accompaniment to conversation, were harassed by the restrictions imposed upon them. For if anyone ventured to display Concert Hall manners [at the Hallé], he would be the centre of frowning observations from all sides, and it was impossible for the most daring to resist the indignant "Hush!"'.[54] During the second half of the nineteenth century, classical music in the provincial cities increasingly cast off its former associations with sociability, religion, philanthropy and moral improvement. An essential aim of the education of the musical public was to convince audiences of the superiority of music that had no function other than aesthetic.[55]

The result was the creation of a new concert-hall regime during the second half of the nineteenth century, in the English provincial cities no less than in London, Paris and Vienna.[56] The first aspect of this was the increasing professionalisation of musical performance itself. When Hallé arrived in Manchester in 1849 his verdict on the quality of the Gentlemen's Concerts was damning; he accepted the conductorship only 'on condition that the band should be dismissed and its reorganisation left entirely in my hands'.[57] In the late 1850s Hallé established the first professional symphony orchestra in Britain, attracting musicians from London and the Continent as well as locally, and over a hundred strong by the 1880s. By the latter date the orchestra had acquired a national reputation. George Bernard Shaw, in London, considered it the finest in the country and the success of the Hallé was held up as a model for concert series in provincial cities such as Birmingham.[58] Neither in Leeds nor Birmingham was there a musical grouping to match the Manchester

Hallé for professionalism; at the festivals, for example, the rehearsals of orchestra and chorus were restricted to two days at most. Nevertheless trends at the festivals were in a similar direction. Celebrated musicians such as Michael Costa and Arthur Sullivan were engaged as conductors; professional musicians from London and elsewhere were hired to perform; and the choral societies at both Birmingham and Leeds were placed on a permanent footing, enabling them to vie for the position of 'champion singers' of England.[59] The professionalisation of musical performance was reflected in growing capital expenditure on concert series. Between 1817 and 1837 festival expenditure at Birmingham doubled, and the problems of keeping down costs, particularly of star performers, was a major concern for all festival organisers throughout the second half of the century. In 1880 Mme Albani, a famous singer of the day, was paid 550 guineas for four performances at the Leeds festival. In the 1870s the French composer, Gounod, demanded a fee of £4,000 for a new oratorio; the offer was initially rejected by Birmingham and Leeds, but subsequently accepted.[60] In effect, the drawing power of the major composers and performers and the demand by audiences for 'music of the highest character' meant that organising committees were forced to deal in the increasingly market-driven musical world. Even the Hallé, which gave pride of place to orchestral and symphonic music, engaged celebrated singers such as Sims Reeves and virtuosi musicians like the violinist Joachim in the knowledge that such performers had a direct effect in raising attendances.[61]

All this was evidence not only of the penetration of the market into the non-profit world of classical concerts but also of the growing importance of musical performance in and of itself. The point is further underlined by the spatial rearrangement of the concert hall, emphasising the visibility of the musicians. At the Birmingham Festival of 1849 the conductor, Michael Costa, brought the orchestra to the front of the stage, where previously it had been hidden between the chorus and the organ. Similarly, whereas at the Gentlemen's Concert Hall in Manchester the audience sat facing each other in two blocks, at the Hallé concerts in the Free Trade Hall the audience confronted the performers in serried rows in the style of the modern auditorium.[62] In this reordered environment the conductor emerged as the focal point of attention for both performers and audience. Cyril Ehrlich has pointed to the first appearance of Hans Richter in England in 1877 as marking the moment when conducting came to be seen as an art worthy of critical attention.[63] Yet public fascination with the conductor/leader developed earlier, originating with the 'Mendelssohn mania' of the 1830s and 1840s, based substantially on the composer's appearances at the Birmingham festival, and continuing through the figures who dominated English musical life in the mid-Victorian decades, Costa, Hallé, Sterndale Bennett and Sullivan. By the 1850s no festival was deemed likely to be successful without such a figure at its helm; the conductor became a 'personality' before conducting itself came to be seen as an art.[64] Increasingly, the conductor was viewed as the fulcrum of discipline and authority in the concert hall. Thus the Vicar of Leeds in 1889 was moved to compare the concert-hall with a natural hierarchy in which 'all work for all and with all, and all are swayed together by the conductor's wand'.[65]

It was not merely the style of concert life that changed in the course of the mid-Victorian period, but also the musical repertoire. In the industrial cities the shift from the 'miscellaneous' concerts of the first half of the nineteenth century to a modern concert repertoire, centred on works by a limited number of recognised composers, was evinced in the programmes of the major musical institutions. The change was gradual. In London and Paris the emergence of classical music as a specific art form with a repertoire distinct from opera and salon music occurred in the 1830s and 1840s, and only took hold subsequently in the provinces.[66] As part of his mission to educate the Manchester public in the 1850s, Hallé attempted to wean audiences from a concert-hall diet largely made up of sections of orchestral works interspersed with ballads and operetta, but it was no easy task. 'To the public at large symphonies and overtures were *terra incognita*', he noted in his *Autobiography*, 'and it was not to be expected that they would flock to them at once.'[67] It was only from the mid-1860s that 'miscellaneous' elements were expunged and a modern concert programme took shape at Manchester, based on the performance of whole symphonies and oratorios, together with overtures and concertos. From this period, too, a familiar concert-hall canon became discernible, incorporating Bach, Handel, and, above all, Beethoven, whose symphonies were played in their entirety in the 1870–71 season. Yet this was not a frozen repertoire. On the contrary, new and contemporary composers were continually introduced, Brahms and Wagner in the 1870s, Grieg and Dvorak in the 1880s. 'No London programmes [of the 1880s] can match this for range and variety', the Hallé's historian has claimed, a verdict to which other music historians have cautiously assented.[68]

The repertoire at the Leeds and Birmingham festivals might have been expected to be more conservative, given that they were strongly identified with the tradition of sacred choral music. Certainly, grand-scale oratorios such as *The Messiah* and Mendelssohn's *Elijah*, first triumphantly performed at Birmingham in 1846, became staple elements of concert series, at the Hallé no less than at the festivals, and remained such to 1914. But concentration on traditional oratorio obscures the innovative aspects of festival programmes, especially between 1870 and 1900. From 1873 it became standard practice at Birmingham to introduce two new choral works at each festival, by contemporaries such as Wagner, Dvorak and Gounod and English composers like Parry, Coleridge-Taylor and Elgar.[69] Under the conductorship of Sullivan from 1880 there was less enthusiasm for Continental masters at Leeds, but this was compensated by an explicit commitment to the commissioning of new works by English composers. The 1886 festival included four new oratorios or cantatas by Mackenzie, Stanford, Dvorak and Sullivan himself, in each case conducted by the composer. By this date, Birmingham and Leeds were judged to be the nation's leading festivals of music and 'a sort of Royal Academy for the exhibition of new compositions'.[70] Moreover, from the 1870s there was a marked shift away from 'miscellaneous' evening concerts to the performance of whole works, including symphonies. At Leeds there was grumbling in 1901 about the quantity of orchestral music performed, but at Birmingham a year earlier the same tendency was seen as cause for celebration. 'What a contrast to the miscellaneous concert of thirty years ago! Then the band did little beyond accompanying the selections from Italian opera of the lighter sort, with an occasional Rossinian overture thrown in, and more rarely a symphony. Now at the evening concerts orchestral music has full recognition.'[71] In effect, the creation of classical music as the embodiment of high culture involved both modern and traditional elements. The existence of a canon, epitomised by the cult of Beethoven, ensured veneration, while the continuous introduction of contemporary Continental and English composers enabled classical music to be represented as 'serious' and demanding, distinguishing the concert hall from promenade and people's concerts.[72]

The construction of the classical concert as a cultural rite was evidenced most forcibly, however, in the new ways in which the music itself was appropriated. This applied both to the concert-hall environment and to the behaviour of the audience as listeners. The concert hall was increasingly constituted as a sacred space, sealed off from the outside world. In 1892 the *Leeds Mercury* commented on the refurbishing of the Town Hall for the festival: 'A thick carpet of crimson cloth in the corridors and staircases made footfalls noiseless. Heavy curtains fell over every door, so that no unhallowed sound could enter the great chamber that had been made sacred to music'.[73] Far from encouraging

social intercourse, concert protocol discouraged movement in or out of
the hall during the performance. Beating time with the foot was frowned
upon and attempts were made to regulate and limit applause. At
Birmingham in 1846 the festival committee earnestly requested that
'the Audience will not indicate approbation by any audible expression
of applause', and the same rule was applied at oratorios at Leeds.
Throughout the second half of the century only the President of the
Birmingham Festival possessed the right to demand an encore.[74] Such
restrictions were initiated by committees and conductors, but by the
1860s it is clear that audiences were policing themselves: in 1867 it
was reported that 'aristocrats' forced to leave a Hallé concert early to
catch the last train to the suburbs were publicly hissed.[75] The discipline
of collective silence in public was a relatively new phenomenon, first
noted at the concert hall in Paris between 1800 and 1830, and associated
with the growth of a middle-class audience.[76] In English provincial
cities it was imposed on the emergent concert-hall world between the
1850s and the 1870s. What the new attentiveness betokened was
reverence for Art and recognition of the classical concert as the principal
rite of a new, public high culture.

   The elevation of classical music to the apex of the cultural hierarchy
in the provincial cities was underpinned by an aesthetic that emphasised
its emotional and transcendent qualities. As the programme of the 1855
Birmingham Festival explained: 'Music is a suggestive, not a positive
art; it is essentially the language of passion, but it less represents the
emotions of the artist than stimulates our own, and its vagueness – the
quality in it which especially raises it above every other medium of
poetical expression – gives to it the ideality that is the highest characteristic of works of the imagination.'[77] Such ideas were indicative of the
perceived proximity of musical to religious experience, indicated at the
beginning of this chapter. Yet, increasingly, music was seen as inducing
states of experience independent of religious associations. Choral and
symphonic works were conventionally represented as a narrative leading
from uncertainty to struggle and ultimate triumph. Thus at Manchester
in 1876, Beethoven's *Moonlight Sonata* was reported to depict a movement from 'gloom' and 'grief' to glory and the 'impetuous outflow of
feeling', while the great oratorios involved a biblical transition from trial
to redemption.[78] This narrative, based on sequential 'rites of passage',
was mirrored in the imaginative states and behaviour of the audience.
Music was held to induce in listeners a state of 'self-forgetting' and
'rapture', of being cast 'under a spell', only broken by the spontaneous
effusion of pent-up feeling manifested in the 'torrents of applause' which

greeted the music's conclusion.[79] For much of the period between 1850 and 1914, therefore, the reception of classical music was framed within a neo-Romantic aesthetic that stressed its inward and individualised character. It emphasised 'feeling' as both a touchstone of the authenticity of music as art and an indication of the refined sensitivity of the listener. Yet concert-hall 'form' demanded that feeling be interiorised and held in check, and that collective self-absorption in the work of art take precedence over the individual display of emotion. It was in such terms that the *Leeds Mercury* justified the bar on applause at the 1858 Festival: 'we are convinced that the great bulk of the audience would have preferred fixed attention (as the index of their feelings) to this outward demonstration'.[80]

If audiences needed guidance in the protocol and aesthetics of the concert hall, this was provided by music criticism, which dispensed cultivated opinion to a public wider than those who attended classical concerts. Nationally, the growth of music criticism occurred from the 1840s, associated notably with the London-based *Musical Times*. Birmingham was close behind, however; the *Birmingham Musical Examiner*, established in 1845, claimed to be the first such periodical outside the capital, while the daily *Birmingham Morning News* had its own music critic from 1849.[81] By the 1860s all Manchester's leading newspapers had appointed music critics, the *Guardian* later laying claim to a proud tradition from the cotton spinner, George Fremantle, to Ernest Newman, Samuel Langford and Neville Cardus.[82] Moreover, from the 1850s programme notes to concerts became increasingly voluminous and self-consciously analytical.[83] 'Our art has theory and criticism within it as a condition of its existence', a German music critic asserted in 1852, a claim given literal substance by the *Manchester Guardian* whose morning editions in the 1870s produced explanatory notes for the music to be performed at the evening's Hallé concert.[84] The growth of criticism concurrent with the development of the classical concert hall was thus an essential component of the education of the musical public, setting music within a specific aesthetic framework. By casting classical music in technical language and contextualising it within a wide set of cultural references, criticism helped to transform the terms in which concert audiences were perceived. By the later 1870s those who attended the Hallé or the festivals were no longer depicted simply as the 'wealthy' or the 'upper and middle classes', but as 'initiates in the divine art', 'apostles of music' or, more commonly, the 'cognoscenti'.[85]

During the second half of the nineteenth century, therefore, the classical music concert took on all the appurtenances of a cultural rite.

It represented a new mode of appropriating art, marked by a clearly defined repertoire of works and composers, a strict etiquette of behaviour and a distinct aesthetic framework. As a rite it borrowed from the discourses of religion, yet it also demonstrated the growing independence of art from its earlier roots in the cultures of organised religion, sociability and philanthropy. By the later nineteenth century music provided the most striking example of the autonomy and sacred character of Art in the provincial cities, and its capacity to attract a wide audience among the urban middle class, including, but also extending beyond, the narrow circle of elite families.

Apotheosis and decline

In the industrial cities the highpoint of the concert hall occurred in the period between 1870 and 1900. During these years 'high-class' classical music concerts, incarnated in the Manchester Hallé and the Birmingham and Leeds festivals, represented the cities' most prestigious cultural institutions. The fine arts attracted considerable middle-class patronage and interest, and events such as the Leeds Polytechnic exhibitions between 1839 and 1845 and the Manchester Art Treasures Exhibition of 1857 had an important role in creating a public sphere of art in the mid-nineteenth century across social, political and religious boundaries.[86] However, exhibitions, especially on this scale, were not regular events. More common were the conversazioni organised by Societies of Artists in which works were displayed to guests in an atmosphere that mixed art appreciation with sociability.[87] In this sense, fine art represented a complement rather than a rival to classical music in the creation of a public high culture in the second half of the nineteenth century.

The theatre was likewise unable to compete with the concert hall, though for different reasons. Manchester, Leeds and Birmingham all possessed a number of theatres, but opposition to the stage remained strong in elements of Nonconformity. The *Leeds Mercury*, owned by the Congregationalist Edward Baines, refused to publish notices of the theatre before the 1880s. At East Parade chapel the minister reminded Sunday School pupils in 1883 that 'the Puritans have been a standing protest for over two hundred years against the arrogance, pride, immorality and presumption of those who advocated these very doubtful forms of amusement'.[88] But even outside Nonconformity the questionable propriety of plays and theatre audiences encouraged the respectable to keep away. 'No portion of the Theatre Royal is fit for a lady to sit in' a Birmingham journal declared in 1869, while the melodrama at the

Prince of Wales depicted a scene of violence and depravity not 'fitted for representation on the stage, however lifelike may be its portrayal'.[89] It was not until the late 1870s that the theatre began to lose its dubious reputation. Contributing factors to the shift in middle-class opinion were Bishop Fraser's speech criticising Puritan opposition to the stage at Manchester in 1877 and the first unexpurgated production of Shakespeare's *Romeo and Juliet*, performed in front of royalty in London in 1882, both of which were widely reported in the provincial press.[90] Yet by this time classical music was well established as the principal form of public art among the provincial middle class, free of the taints associated with drama.

As a consequence classical concerts represented the pinnacle of a loose but nonetheless definable hierarchy of cultural forms in the provincial city. From the late 1860s the Hallé concerts became the exemplar of public art in Manchester, the yardstick against which other musical and cultural institutions were judged and, inevitably, found wanting. Promenade concerts introduced by de Jong in 1871 were welcomed by local critics as evidence of an increased demand for music, but damned as inferior in quality compared to the Hallé. In Birmingham, reviews of the orchestral concerts organised by Harrison and Stockley were respectful, though lacking the encomiums reserved for festival performances. Orchestral series were differentiated in turn from improving popular concerts, such as those organised by the Birmingham councillor Jesse Collings in 1880, designed to 'educate the people to better understand music' and comprising the familiar mixture of ballads, marches and short extracts from concert-hall classics.[91] But the most vociferous criticism in all three cities was reserved for the 'singing saloons' and the music halls. In part, the critique was social, such institutions being condemned by virtue of the plebeian character of their audiences. In the 1860s the People's Music Hall was described as 'a nightly rendezvous of the lower orders and the working classes of Manchester' from which it inexorably followed that the 'entertainment made no appeal to either taste or intelligence'.[92] But as the legitimacy of popular entertainment was conceded from the 1870s, it was the moral and aesthetic shortcomings of the music hall that attracted most critical ire. 'That people require amusement no one could deny', a Birmingham critic commented in 1877, but the music of the halls was merely 'vulgar': 'a brawling voice, and a collection of the "the great Dissolving View" kind of songs constitute all the requirements of our modern music halls'.[93] By the later nineteenth century the music hall was represented as the social and cultural obverse of the concert hall, the former identified with brash vulgarity and commercialism, the latter with refinement, decorum and disinterestedness. 'Popularity invariably accompanies the lower styles of art', the Leeds municipal organist, William Spark, declared in 1892; the capacity to appreciate fine music, no less than other arts, ever divided the 'unlearned multitude' from the 'discerning few'.[94]

The constitution of classical music as the centrepiece of high culture in the later Victorian city, therefore, was not a simple function of the innate qualities of the music itself or of the social composition of concert audiences. It was the result of specific historical processes affecting the organisation of classical music, its construction as a social and cultural rite, and its relationship to a wider field of urban culture during the second half of the nineteenth century. In recent years historians have insisted that cultures were not the possession or the product of classes in any direct or simple sense. According to William Weber, terms such as 'high' and 'popular culture' say nothing about social class since each possessed a diverse, cross-class audience.[95] However, such arguments can be exaggerated. As the work of Pierre Bourdieu has consistently sought to demonstrate, there exists a powerful – and conventionally unrecognised – homology between cultural codes and practices on the one hand, and social hierarchies and unequal power relations on the other:

> The denial of lower, coarse, vulgar, venal, servile – in a word, natural – enjoyment, which constitutes the sacred sphere of culture, implies an affirmation of the superiority of those who can be satisfied with the sublimated, refined, disinterested, gratuitous, distinguished pleasures forever closed to the profane. That is why art and cultural consumption are predisposed, consciously and deliberately or not, to fulfil a social function of legitimating social differences.[96]

The Hallé concerts and the music festivals assembled the most powerful sections of the cities' populations at regular intervals to engage in a highly visible ritual performance. As a spectacle the concert hall embodied and represented the city's middle class *en masse* in a manner which no other cultural event or institution could match. What was envisioned in the concert hall was a public demonstration of collective refinement, decorum and self-discipline, a living symbol of the power of art and the art of power. At the same time, the development of classical music as the most prestigious public art form meant that it became an essential reference-point for judgements of cultural value. Classical music came to serve as a central resource for the elaboration not simply of a cultural hierarchy, but of the binary oppositions of 'high' and 'low', 'cultivated' and 'popular', 'sublime' and 'vulgar'. Ostensibly cultural and aesthetic in origin, they inevitably overlapped with moral and social categories. Spark's distinction between the 'unlearned multitude' and the 'select few' referred to musical taste, but its social connotations were obvious. In this sense, the homology between ideas of cultural and social hierarchies was mutually reinforcing, the binary opposition between 'high' and 'low' serving to invoke, once more, the fundamental distinction between mental and manual categories.

However, the heyday of the provincial concert hall was relatively short-lived. There are clear indications that after 1900 the most prominent musical institutions in each of the three cities were in decline. After Hallé's death in 1895 the concerts continued under the direction of Cowen and Richter, but by the early 1900s concert programmes were considered 'unprogressive' and there was a steady drift of musicians from Manchester to London.[97] In Leeds the status of the festival was waning by 1910 in the eyes of its chief chronicler, and there was criticism that the music hall was having a deleterious effect on concert programmes through its emphasis on 'variety in brevity'.[98] Most striking of all, the Birmingham festival was abandoned after 1912. 'Is it not clear that these old institutions are doomed, and that it is only a question of a sudden or lingering death?' a local journal presciently enquired.[99]

There were a number of reasons for this sea change in the fortunes of the main provincial musical institutions before and after the First World War. Firstly, the tradition of sacred choral music was seen as increasingly exhausted and irrelevant. This view was voiced most stridently in Birmingham, where performances of *Elijah* and *Messiah* in 1912 were derided by the city's leading Liberal newspaper, the *Daily Post*, as 'flogging a dead horse' and 'opera in holy orders'. 'The Festival is overdosing us with moral music', the paper complained; it had become emblematic of 'stuffy provincialism'.[100] At Leeds the *Mercury* noted the absence of oratorios in the 1913 Festival, while at Manchester a letter to the *Guardian* in 1905 complained of the 'shallow philosophy and mawkish sentiment' of the traditional oratorios, redolent of the 'smugness and self-sufficiency of the mid-Victorian age'.[101] Secondly, the existence of the festivals in Birmingham and Leeds was considered to have inhibited the development of a wider musical culture. Arthur Sullivan's jibe in the 1880s that music in Birmingham was akin to a boa constrictor 'that took an enormous gorge once in three years and fasted in the interim' was taken up by critics as evidence of the city's cultural deficiencies. As a local observer put it, 'the towns with the really rich musical life, such as Liverpool, Manchester and Glasgow, have no festivals and no need of them'.[102] In Leeds no full-time permanent orchestra was established till after 1945 and despite the existence of an amateur symphony orchestra and choral union from the later 1880s, the city's musical culture remained impoverished outside the festival.[103] Finally, and perhaps most significant, the social bases of the concert hall were beginning to crumble by the early twentieth century. 'In the past', a Birmingham correspondent noted in 1912, the festival depended 'upon well-to-do people in the town and neighbourhood to whom Festival week was one of the social delights of the year. Today the rich have many other toys to play with; some of them have fallen away from the festival, while others continue to support it partly for the sake of charity and partly from family tradition, but, as I can testify, not without some grumbling in private'. The Hallé, too, was seen as subject to a similar alteration in the social status of its audiences by the inter-war years: 'only here and there one of the old guard appeared with a satin or velvet cloak or a white shirt-front. Their social axis had changed too; and that is a reason for taking heart, since perhaps it means that a new and educated democracy is on the move to cultural freedom'.[104]

There were signs even before the First World War, therefore, and more conspicuously after it, that the ties linking the local middle class to the concert hall were beginning to loosen. The effects were registered not only in terms of audiences, but also in the organisation of classical music. Municipal intervention was evident in the foundation of the City of Birmingham Orchestra in 1920, while the Hallé joined with the BBC in the establishment of the 'Northern Proms' in 1930.[105] Shifts were also evident in a loosening of an older cultural hierarchy with the emergence of a distinct 'middlebrow' musical culture between the wars, identified especially with an expanding amateur operatic tradition.[106] By 1914 the heyday of a provincial high culture, with the concert hall at its centre, had passed. At its height in the last three decades of the nineteenth century classical music had been closely associated with the city as an important ingredient of civic pride. It is to the civic in its other manifestations that we shall now turn.

Notes

1   *Manchester Guardian*, 6 May 1857, p. 3.
2   Cited in M. Kennedy, *The Hallé Tradition: A Century of Music* (Manchester: Manchester University Press, 1960), p. 66.
3   J. Brewer, *The Pleasures of the Imagination: English Culture in the Eighteenth Century* (London: Harper Collins, 1997), p. 532; I. Kant, *Critique of Judgement*, trans. J. C. Meredith (London: Oxford University Press, 1952), p. 194; W. Weber, *Music and the Middle Class: The Social Structures of*

Concert Life in London, Paris and Vienna (London: Croom Helm, 1975), p. 16.

4 For eighteenth-century concert life see *inter alia* the entry under 'Concerts' in S. Sadie (ed.), *New Grove Dictionary of Music and Musicians*, vol. 3 (London: Macmillan, 1980), pp. 616–19; P. Borsay, *The English Urban Renaissance* (Oxford: Clarendon Press, 1991), ch. 5; Brewer, *Pleasures of the Imagination*, pp. 531–72 and 394–406.

5 G. Haddock, *Some Early Musical Recollections of G. Haddock* (London, 1906); W. Spark, *Musical Reminiscences* (London, 1892); J. F. Russell, *The Hallé Concerts* (Timperley, 1933); Kennedy, *Hallé Tradition*, ch. 1. For Birmingham see J. Money, *Experience and Identity: Birmingham and the West Midlands, 1760–1800* (Manchester: Manchester University Press, 1977), ch. 4; J. Sutcliffe Smith, *The Story of Music in Birmingham* (Birmingham, 1945).

6 For comments on popular concerts in the 1850s see D. Russell, *Popular Music in England, 1840–1914* (Manchester: Manchester University Press, 1987), pp. 27–30.

7 Cited in Kennedy, *Hallé Tradition*, p. 5; J. T. Bunce, *History of the Birmingham General Hospital and Musical Festivals* (Birmingham, 1873), p. 65.

8 D. Russell, 'Musicians in the English provincial city: Manchester, *c.* 1860–1914'. I am grateful to David Russell for early sight of this as yet unpublished paper.

9 R. J. Morris, 'Middle-class culture, 1700–1914' in D. Fraser (ed.), *History of Modern Leeds* (Manchester: Manchester University Press, 1980), p. 217. On aristocratic patronage see Bunce, *Birmingham General Hospital*, p. 68. For Birmingham concerts in the 1840s, *Birmingham Musical Examiner*, 1 September 1845–3 January 1846.

10 B. Scattergood, *A Short History of the Leeds Musical Soirées* (London, 1931); *Freelance*, 21 December 1867 and 5 December 1868; Money, *Experience and Identity*, pp. 85–6; 'Minutes of the Concert Hall General Committee, 1849–1865', Henry Watson Music Library, Manchester.

11 For examples of the mixed programmes in the various cities in the mid-nineteenth century see *Birmingham Musical Examiner*, 8 September 1845; Haddock, *Some Musical Reminiscences*, pp. 85–91; Kennedy, *Hallé Tradition*, ch. 3.

12 *Freelance*, 23 November 1867.

13 For an account of the Hallé and its cultural impact see S. Gunn, 'The sublime and the vulgar: the Hallé concerts and the constitution of "high culture" in Manchester, *c.* 1850–1880', *Journal of Victorian Culture*, 2, 2 (1997). A full description of the institution and development of the concerts can be found in Kennedy, *Hallé Tradition*.

14 M. Kennedy (ed.), *The Autobiography of Charles Hallé* (London: Oxford University Press, 1972), p. 138.

15 P. A. Scholes, *The Mirror of Music, 1844–1944* (London: Oxford University Press, 1947), p. 382.

16 *City Jackdaw*, 15 March 1878.

17 M. Musgrove, *The Musical Life of the Crystal Palace* (Cambridge: Cambridge University Press, 1995), ch. 7.

18 W. C. Stockley, *Fifty Years of Music in Birmingham* (Birmingham, 1913).

19 Sadie, *New Grove*, vol. 10, p. 601; W. Spark, *Musical Reminiscences*, p. 9; *Toby the Yorkshire Tyke*, 6 October 1883.

20 Bunce, *Birmingham General Hospital*, pp. 68–71; Money, *Experience and Identity*, p. 85.

21 Sutcliffe Smith, *Story of Music*, pp. 28–33; *Aris's Birmingham Gazette*, 31 August 1846.

22 By the 1870s the festival committees included the names of Mason, Beale, Kenrick and Chamberlain among others. Bunce, *Birmingham General Hospital*, pp. 63, 124–5; *Birmingham Daily Post*, 21 August 1873. For the names of presidents and vice-presidents, including representatives of the regional aristocracy, see *Birmingham Musical Festival Programmes, 1817–1914* (Birmingham, 1914).

23 Haddock, *Some Early Musical Recollections*, pp. 110–11.

24 F. Spark, *Memories of My Life* (Leeds, 1913), pp. 45–6.

25 For details of the conflict see F. Spark and J. Bennett, *History of the Leeds Musical Festivals* (Leeds, n.d.), pp. 39–57.

26 See Spark and Bennett, *Leeds Musical Festivals*, p. 92 for a list of committee members.

27 'Hallé's programmes, 1859–96', MSS, Henry Watson Music Library; *Guardian*, 9 March 1888.

28 See note 22 above.

29 Spark and Bennett, *Leeds Musical Festivals*, p. 228.

30 *City Jackdaw*, 15 March 1878; *Comus*, 13 December 1877.

31 *Birmingham Daily Post*, 31 August 1858; *Leeds Mercury*, 9 September 1858; Spark and Bennett, *Leeds Musical Festivals*, p. 370.

32 *Toby the Yorkshire Tyke*, 13 October 1883; *Freelance*, 19 January 1868.

33 G. Behrens, *Sir Charles Hallé and After* (Manchester, 1926), p. 2; Russell, *Hallé Concerts*, pp. 30–1.

34 Bunce, *Birmingham General Hospital*, p. 154; Spark and Bennett, *Leeds Musical Festivals*, pp. 188 and 193.

35 P. Bourdieu, *The Field of Cultural Production*, ed. R. Johnson (Cambridge: Polity Press, 1993), ch. 1.

36 'Hallé's programmes, 1863–4 season', Henry Watson Music Library; *Musical World*, 14 January 1860.

37 J. Benson, *The Working Class in Britain, 1850–1939* (London: Longman, 1994), p. 40; D. Russell, 'Provincial concerts in England, 1865–1914: a case-study of Bradford', *Journal of the Royal Musical Association*, 114 (1988), p. 47.

38 Bunce, *Birmingham General Hospital*, p. 75; *Aris's Birmingham Gazette*, 24 August 1846.

39 Spark and Bennett, *Leeds Musical Festivals*, pp. 31–2.

40 C. Ehrlich, *First Philharmonic: A History of the Royal Philharmonic Society* (Oxford: Clarendon Press, 1995), p. 112; Musgrave, *Musical Life*, p. 123; Spark and Bennett, *Leeds Musical Festivals*, pp. 204–5.

41 *Birmingham Musical Festival Programmes*, 1891; *Birmingham Daily Post*, 4 October 1900; Spark and Bennett, *Leeds Musical Festivals*, pp. 32, 88, 269.

42 The proportion of serial ticket holders increased from 38 per cent to 53 per cent between 1874 and 1886, estimated on the basis of figures in Spark and Bennett, *Leeds Musical Festivals*, p. 360; *Toby the Yorkshire Tyke*, 13 October 1883; *Leeds Mercury*, 10 October 1892.

43 Figures based on C. Hallé, 'Concert accounts, 1861–90', MS, Henry Watson Music Library.

44 *Freelance*, 5 January 1867; *Birmingham Daily Post*, 1 September 1858.

45 *Freelance*, 28 December 1872; *Leeds Mercury*, 11 September 1858; Spark, *Memories of My Life*, pp. 18–20.

46 *Freelance*, 9 November 1867; *Birmingham Musical Festival Programmes*, 20 August 1855; Spark and Bennett, *Leeds Musical Festivals*, p. 374.

47 *Birmingham Daily Post*, 26 August 1858; for an example of the lists at Leeds see *Leeds Mercury*, 9 September 1858 and 2 October 1913.

48 *Birmingham Daily Post*, 27 August 1873; *Freelance*, 5 January and 2 February 1867.

49 *Freelance*, 2 February 1867; *Momus*, 24 December 1879. For wider comment on music and the family see Weber, *Music and the Middle Class*, ch. 3; C. Ehrlich, *The Piano: A History* (London: Dent, 1976), pp. 92–4.

50 *Birmingham Musical Examiner*, 29 November 1845; *Birmingham Daily Post*, 1 September 1858 and 1 October 1900; T. Adorno, *Quasi Una Fantasia: Essays on Modern Music* (London: Verso, 1992), p. 69.

51 For comments see *Leeds Mercury*, 15 October 1874; Ehrlich, *First Philharmonic*, p. 161; K. Chorley, *Manchester Made Them* (London: Faber, 1950), p. 143.

52 *Leeds Mercury*, 6 and 7 October 1892.

53 Sadie, *New Grove*, vol. 2, p. 734; Spark and Bennett, *Leeds Musical Festivals*, p. 31.

54 E. J. Broadfield, *Sir Charles Hallé* (Manchester, 1886), p. 37.

55 M. Beckerman, 'The new conception of the "work of art"' in J. Peyser (ed.), *The Orchestra: Origins and Transformations* (New York: Charles Scribner and Sons, 1986), p. 347.

56 For an overview of these developments in a European context see Weber, *Music and the Middle Class*; Peyser, *The Orchestra*, esp. chapters by Beckerman and Weber; C. Dalhaus, *Nineteenth-Century Music* (Berkeley: University of California Press, 1989); P. Gay, *Pleasure Wars* (London: Harper Collins, 1998), ch. 2. For the United States, P. Dimaggio, 'Cultural entrepreneurship in nineteenth-century Boston: the creation of an organisational base for high culture in America', *Media, Culture and Society*, 4 (1982), pp. 33–50; L. Levine, *Highbrow/Lowbrow* (Cambridge, Mass.: Harvard University Press, 1988).

57 Kennedy, *Autobiography*, p. 125.

58 Russell, 'Musicians in the English provincial city', pp. 9–11; Kennedy, *Hallé Tradition*, p. 73; Stockley, *Fifty Years of Music*, pp. 27–9.

59 Sutcliffe Smith, *Story of Music*; Stockley, *Fifty Years of Music*, chs 1–4; Spark and Bennett, *Leeds Musical Festivals*; Bunce, *Birmingham General Hospital*, p. 121.

60 Bunce, *Birmingham General Hospital*, p. 154; Spark and Bennett, *Leeds Musical Festivals*, pp. 67, 124–6; Scholes, *Mirror of Music*, p. 110.

61 Hallé, 'Concert accounts' provide evidence of increased audiences when leading singers or instrumentalists were engaged to appear.

62 Bunce, *Birmingham General Hospital*, p. 114; *Freelance*, 5 January 1867.

63 Ehrlich, *First Philharmonic*, pp. 123–4.

64 For details of Mendelssohn's triumphs at Birmingham see Bunce, *Birmingham General Hospital*, pp. 95–112. On the conductor as 'personality' see R. Sennett, *The Fall of Public Man* (London: Faber and Faber, 1993), p. 211.

65 Cited in Spark and Bennett, *Leeds Musical Festivals*, p. 360.

66 Weber, 'The rise of the classical repertoire in nineteenth-century orchestral concerts' in Peyser, *The Orchestra*, pp. 361–8; Dalhaus, *Nineteenth-Century Music*, pp. 41–51; Ehrlich, *First Philharmonic*, pp. 44–7.

67 Kennedy, *Autobiography*, p. 138.

68 For Hallé's programmes see T. Batley, *Sir Charles Hallé's Concerts in England* (Manchester, 1896); Kennedy, *Hallé Tradition*, p. 53; Ehrlich, *First Philharmonic*, pp. 132–4.

69 Sadie, *New Grove*, pp. 734–45. For detailed lists of performances see *Birmingham Festival Programmes, 1817–1912*.

70 For Leeds programmes 1858–1892 see Spark and Bennett, *Leeds Musical Festivals*; *Birmingham Daily Post* and *Bradford Observer* cited in Spark and Bennett, *Leeds Musical Festivals*, p. 315.

71 *Leeds Mercury*, 14 October 1901; *Birmingham Daily Post*, 3 October 1900.

72 For a critical analysis of the construction of a classical canon centred on English composers, and the significance of the London-based Royal College of Music in this endeavour, see R. Stradling and M. Hughes, *The English Musical Renaissance, 1860–1940* (Cambridge: Cambridge University Press, 1993).

73 *Leeds Mercury*, 6 October 1892.

74 *Aris's Birmingham Gazette*, 24 August 1846; *Leeds Mercury*, 14 September 1858; *Birmingham Daily Post*, 1 September 1858.

75 *Freelance*, 16 November 1867.

76 J. H. Johnson, *Listening in Paris* (Berkeley: University of California Press, 1995), esp. ch. 13.

77 *Birmingham Musical Festival Programmes*, 1855, p. vii.

78 *Freelance*, 14 Sept. 1876; for accounts of the major oratorios see *Birmingham Musical Festival Programmes, 1846–1913*.

79 See, for example, the descriptions of concert behaviour in *Birmingham*

    Journal, 29 August 1846; *Freelance,* 14 November 1873; *Leeds Mercury,*
    10 October 1892.
80 *Leeds Mercury,* 14 September 1858.
81 Scholes, *Mirror of Music,* pp. 754–5; *Birmingham Musical Examiner,* 6
    December 1845; Sutcliffe Smith, *Story of Music,* p. 103.
82 D. Ayerst, *Guardian: Biography of a Newspaper* (London: Collins, 1971),
    pp. 179–81; N. Cardus, *Autobiography* (London: Collins, 1947), p. 51.
83 See, for example, the *Birmingham Musical Festival Programmes* which
    carried explanatory notes from 1852. From the 1880s the 'Book of Words'
    produced for the Leeds Festival carried 'analytical remarks' for each
    concert, Spark and Bennett, *Leeds Musical Festivals,* p. 194.
84 Dalhaus, *Nineteenth-Century Music,* p. 251; Ayerst, *Guardian,* p. 180.
85 *Leeds Mercury,* 6 October 1892; *Birmingham Daily Post,* 3 October 1900;
    Comus, 6 December 1877.
86 U. Finke, 'The Art Treasures exhibition' in J. H. G. Archer (ed.), *Art and
    Architecture in Victorian Manchester* (Manchester: Manchester University
    Press, 1985); C. Arscott, '"Without distinction of party": the Polytechnic
    exhibitions in Leeds, 1839–45' in J. Wolff and J. Seed (eds), *The Culture
    of Capital: Art, Power and the Nineteenth-Century Middle Class* (Manchester:
    Manchester University Press, 1988).
87 For examples see *Brum,* 4 November 1869; A. Darbyshire, *A Chronicle of
    the Brasenose Club,* vol. 1 (Manchester, 1892), pp. 32–3.
88 S. J. Reid, *Memoirs of Sir Wemyss Reid, 1842–1885* (London, 1905), p. 100;
    'East Parade Sunday School: Senior Scholar's Manuscript', vol. 1, no. 2
    (1883), Leeds City Archives.
89 *Brum,* 8 September and 18 November 1869.
90 For favourable comment in the Birmingham press see *Lion,* 8 February
    1877; *Owl,* 10 March 1882.
91 *Freelance,* 16 March 1872; *Lion,* 1 February 1877; Sutcliffe Smith, *Story
    of Music,* p. 60.
92 *Freelance,* 2 February 1867.
93 *Lion,* 4 and 18 January 1877.
94 W. Spark, *Musical Reminiscences,* p. 53.
95 Weber, *Music and the Middle Class,* p. 11. P. Joyce, *Visions of the People:
    Industrial England and the Question of Class 1840–1914* (Cambridge: Cam-
    bridge University Press, 1991) contains a forceful statement of this type
    of argument.
96 P. Bourdieu, *Distinction: A Social Critique of the Judgement of Taste* (London:
    Routledge, 1992), p. 7.
97 Scholes, *Mirror of Music,* p. 385; Russell, 'Musicians in the English prov-
    incial city'.
98 F. Spark, *Memories,* p. 48; *Leeds Mercury,* 1 October 1913.
99 *Birmingham Daily Post,* 7 October 1912.
100 *Birmingham Daily Post,* 2, 4 and 7 October 1912.
101 *Leeds Mercury,* 1 October 1913; *Manchester Guardian,* 4 October 1905.

102 Stockley, *Fifty Years of Music*, p. 57; *Birmingham Daily Post*, 7 October 1912.
103 Sadie, *New Grove*, vol. 10, p. 601.
104 *Birmingham Daily Post*, 7 October 1912; Chorley, *Manchester Made Them*, p. 144.
105 Sadie, *New Grove*, vol. 2, p. 733; *Listener*, 28 May 1930.
106 J. Lowerson, 'An outbreak of allodoxia? Operatic amateurs and middle-class musical taste between the wars' in A. Kidd and D. Nicholls (eds), *Gender, Civic Culture and Consumerism: Middle-Class Identity in Britain 1800–1940* (Manchester: Manchester University Press, 1999), pp. 198–211.

7

The rites of civic culture

The most spectacular organised manifestations of provincial culture in Victorian industrial cities were the public pageants that punctuated the urban year. Royal coronations and visits, the opening of public buildings, the unveiling of statues and monuments, and the funerals of civic worthies, were all occasions for lavish ceremonial display. 'Festivals of capitalism' and demonstrations of civic pride, they were theatrical events played out on the monumental stage-set of the Victorian city with its warehouses, exchanges and town halls.[1] The parades and processions that formed an essential part of these events represented the urban population to itself in a collective act of identification and celebration. As David Cannadine has observed, such spectacles did not so much serve as the expression of urban community, as its actualisation.[2] At the same time as representing community, however, the highly visible nature of ceremonial occasions offered special opportunity for the symbolic display of leadership and authority. On the civic stage authority could be embodied and performed through the choreographed spectacle, and projected to a still larger audience through extensive reports in the local press.

There is a close relationship between ritual and authority. Richard Sennett has defined authority as the 'emotional expression of power', ritual as 'emotional unity achieved through drama'.[3] The drama of civic ritual contained within it, simultaneously, the imaginary constitution of a united urban community and a symbolic claim to authority over that community on the part of a civic leadership. The purpose of this chapter is to examine the construction of civic ritual and middle-class authority and their interrelationship. It is concerned with the performativity of power: how authority was made visible, publicly enacted in symbolic ways, in the setting of the industrial city. This involves close analysis of the rituals themselves and of their changing forms and meanings in Birmingham, Leeds and Manchester between 1835 and 1914.

The construction of civic ritual

The efflorescence of civic ritual in provincial industrial cities from the mid-nineteenth century did not represent a simple continuation of earlier forms of urban pageantry and ceremonial. In old commercial and industrial centres like Norwich, Coventry and Ipswich civic ceremonies appear to have been in decline by the late eighteenth and early nineteenth centuries, together with the guild festivals with which they were intimately connected. In London, the Lord Mayor's Show, which had flourished in the 1730s, atrophied to the extent that it actively had to be revived in the 1880s.[4] Where such ceremonies did survive they were often exclusive to members of the corporation, their friends and relatives: the Colchester Oyster Feast in the early Victorian period, according to Cannadine, was 'not a public pageant, but a private party'.[5] In Manchester, Leeds and Birmingham there was a tradition of civic ceremonial, but it too showed signs of decay. The coronations of George IV, William IV and Victoria, for example, were marked with declining enthusiasm. At Birmingham, a public procession was arranged to mark Victoria's coronation in July 1838, enabling the pre-reform local authorities to parade for one last time: dragoons, beadles of the court leet, bailiffs and steward of the manor, Anglican clergy, together with 'inhabitants of the town and neighbourhood three abreast'. Yet as the *Birmingham Gazette* confessed, whether from 'the shortness of the notice, the previous engagements of many of the leading inhabitants of the town in the festivities of the day, or from some other cause, the attendance was by no means such as was expected'.[6]

One reason for the limited response to public and national events was the degree of inter-party strife at the period, the celebrations for Queen Victoria's coronation, for instance, being drawn into the larger struggle between Liberals and Tories over local government in Manchester and Leeds.[7] Moreover, urban Liberalism was slow to develop a repertoire of civic ritual after 1835. The creation of new municipal corporations in Manchester and Birmingham, and the reform of the old in Leeds, was not accompanied by an upsurge of public celebration, despite the importance of the event for Liberal elites and their sweeping victory at the first municipal elections in all three cities.[8] In Manchester, the first municipal elections in December 1838, after a long legal struggle over incorporation, passed 'without the slightest degree of excitement' according to the *Guardian*, while the first meeting of the council was given the barest mention in the local press.[9] Liberals were handicapped by inexperience in the etiquette of power as much as by hostility to ritual itself, exemplified by the confusion at the first meeting of Birmingham council as to the procedures appropriate for the election of the aldermen and mayor.[10] For all these reasons, civic authorities in the first half of the nineteenth century could not match the symbolic vitality of popular radicalism, the display of banners and emblems which transformed 'monster' demonstrations from Peterloo to Chartism into what James Epstein has termed 'highly stylised rituals of collective solidarity'.[11]

The events that did most to stimulate large-scale civic pageantry were the visits of Queen Victoria to the industrial cities in the 1850s. Paradoxically, it was the presence of the symbol of the nation and of the aristocratic hereditary principle that acted as the catalyst for the expression of provincial, bourgeois civic pride. It was not the first royal visit to these cities. Birmingham had played host to Prince Albert on three occasions between 1843 and 1855, while an estimated eighty thousand people lined the streets of Leeds in 1835 to watch Princess Victoria pass through the town on her way from Harewood to Went-worth House.[12] But the visits of Victoria to Manchester, Birmingham and Leeds in the 1850s were significant for a number of reasons. Not only were they the first official visits by the reigning monarch, but the corporations also used them specifically for the purposes of civic display. Briggs' account of the opening of the Leeds Town Hall by Queen Victoria in 1858 provides one well-documented example.[13] However, the prototypical event occurred seven years earlier with Victoria's visit to Manchester in 1851. From the outset the visit was conceived very differently by the two parties involved. For the royal party it formed a stage of the Queen's journey south from Balmoral to London; one day was to be spent visiting Liverpool, the next in a combined visit to Manchester and Salford. For the Corporation of Manchester, however, the event was seen as a civic as well as a royal occasion. It was elaborately planned not simply to welcome the sovereign, but to project the city itself, its regional role as the capital of the cotton industry and its national economic and political importance.

From start to finish, the event was designed as a mass pageant, enacted in front of vast crowds against the backdrop of the city specially embellished for the occasion. The leading parts in the ceremonial drama were taken by the Corporation and a largely unwitting monarch. Following the royal visit to Salford, the Manchester town council processed to the newly named Victoria Bridge in robes of scarlet and purple, the first time ceremonial dress had been worn. Italianate triumphal arches had been constructed to mark the passage through the city, on which were 'blazoned in high relief the arms of the incorporated borough'.[14] The royal party led by the carriages of the Mayor and High Sheriff then processed round the central streets, the warehouses festooned with flags and the streets crowded with spectators. At the Exchange, converted by the borough surveyor for the occasion, the Queen was seated on a throne surrounded by the town councillors and two thousand manufacturers, merchants and gentry invited from the city and region, deliberately evoking her coronation. Here she was presented with addresses from the Mayor and Corporation that carefully matched respect for the royal office with the promotion of Liberal causes: free trade, the advancement of commerce and industry, civil and religious freedom. In return, the Queen knighted the Mayor, John Potter.

As a spectacle, the royal visit worked at multiple levels. At one level it was conducted as a delicate series of reciprocal gestures between the monarchy and the representatives of bourgeois industrial society. Each of the events involved a mutual act of recognition; both parties were enhanced by the other's approbation. But concentration on the royal dimension can obscure the extent to which this was constructed as an urban occasion to which the community at large was witness. Press reports of the crowds noted not only their size and orderliness, but also their precise social composition: 'At different points in the course of the route a change might be perceived in the classes of society to which the individual components of the crowd belonged'. In Peter Street and Deansgate 'the middle-class character of the assemblage was pronounced', between Shudehill and Oldham Street there was a 'falling off in the appearance of the persons assembled'.[15] The procession was thus seen as delineating the social as well as the physical geography of the city, incorporating the diverse sections of the urban population within the event. It also had its commercial aspect, the triumphal arches and raised platforms being paid for by local firms in return for publicity, while commemorative medals embossed with both royal and civic insignia were struck for local consumption. Nor was the national significance of the event overlooked by the local press. The *Guardian* used the occasion to project Manchester as a 'community based upon the orderly, sober and peaceful industry of the middle classes' and to claim that 'social importance and political power have passed into the hands of those classes upon whose shoulders the burden of maintaining the national edifice has shifted'.[16]

Civic spectacles such as this did not meet with universal approval, even among the ranks of the propertied. While Tories were critical of the manner in which the monarchy was attached to the cause of municipal Liberalism, radical Liberals like Richard Cobden and John Bright were no less scathing of the civic 'junketing': 'a Mayor of Manchester importing the obsolete sensuality of the Cockney Corporation, which, like Smithfield, has outlived its time and ought equally to be the subject of sanitary reform'.[17] But the royal visit in 1851 was in many ways a prototype. The Leeds town council sought guidance on ceremonial practice from its Manchester counterpart prior to the Queen's opening of the Town Hall in 1858, and the preparations for the Birmingham visit were couched in the terms of civic rivalry, the council being 'confidently informed, upon the best authority, that Manchester never turned out anything so fine'.[18]

More generally, the royal visits to provincial cities in the 1850s served as the catalyst for the efflorescence of civic pageantry that reached its zenith in the 1870s. In Birmingham, Manchester and Leeds this was carried out under the aegis of urban Liberalism. Between the mid- and the late nineteenth century the councils in all three cities remained predominantly, and in some cases overwhelmingly, Liberal in composition; in Manchester there were only three Tory mayors between 1838 and 1870, despite the custom elsewhere of rotating the mayoralty between parties on an annual basis.[19] Liberalism was not the *sine qua non* for the growth of civic ritual, as the case of Liverpool and other Tory-dominated towns indicates, but it provided much of the ideological framework for ceremonial in Manchester, Birmingham and Leeds.[20]

The scope of civic ceremonial and pageantry developed in the mid-Victorian decades was substantial. It encompassed not only the most elaborate and highly publicised occasions, such as royal celebrations and the opening of town halls, but also a host of less noted events: the unveiling of memorials and statues, the inauguration of public buildings, annual festivals and rituals such as 'Mayor's Sunday', philanthopic treats and funerals of local worthies. The opening of the first Commission of the Assizes at Leeds in 1865 was used as the occasion for general civic celebration. It was held on a Saturday, since 'it was desired that, as a popular institution, it should be witnessed by as large a number of the citizens as possible'. The judges processed from the station to the Town Hall, where they were met by the robed members of the Corporation, watched by crowds whose size, it was estimated, had only been surpassed by those attending the Queen's visit in 1858. Even the reporter of the *Leeds Mercury* claimed some difficulty in accounting for 'the enthusiasm which was able to convert what is usually but an uninteresting and unmeaning formality into something like an attractive and even a brilliant ceremonial'.[21]

The number and variety of these spectacles between the 1850s and the 1870s is suggestive of the emergence of what can be termed a public processional culture in industrial towns and cities. Civic parades and pageantry were central features, but they were increasingly matched in scale from the 1860s by the great Liberal and Conservative party demonstrations, such as the Liberal reform meeting at Woodhouse Moor, Leeds in October 1866, which over 200,000 were said to have attended, and the mass Tory gatherings at Pomona Gardens, Manchester in the 1870s.[22] Equally significant in many industrial towns was the revival of older festive customs, such as the Whit Walks in Lancashire and the Bishop Blaize celebrations in the West Riding. They were indicative of the way in which popular traditions, often identified with guilds and trade societies, were incorporated into the new civic ritual from the 1850s.[23] Partly as a consequence, the trend was for civic parades and ceremonial to become more socially inclusive. On the one side, this extended to honorific roles accorded to figureheads of county society, such as Lord Calthorpe in Birmingham and Lord Derby in Lancashire. On the other, it incorporated urban voluntary associations and working-class trade societies under the mantle of local patriotism and civic pride.[24] As a processional culture burgeoned in the mid-Victorian decades, so the politics of civic display became at once more significant and more complex.

The meanings of the civic

There was no single overarching meaning to civic ceremonial and pageantry. Rather, civic ritual had multiple overlapping meanings, dependent on context and the position of the observer. First and foremost, it was intended to project the corporation itself as an elected public body representing the town. As the *Leeds Mercury* put it, following the 1835 Municipal Corporations Act corporations were 'divested of their character of juntos, and have obtained the character of public institutions, in the enlarged and legitimate sense of that term'.[25] Yet the transparency and accountability which the notion of the 'public' gave to municipal government were increasingly seen as a necessary but not sufficient condition of civic authority. 'The work of the town', the Birmingham Liberal J. T. Bunce wrote in 1882, 'should be done with such stateliness of manner as to dignify the corporate life'.[26] By this date, of course, Bunce was merely affirming what was already an established practice of municipal government. From the 1840s the General Purposes Committees of councils in Birmingham, Leeds and Manchester were charged with organising civic ceremonials and pageants whose aim was precisely to 'dignify the corporate life' and to enhance its symbolic authority. Particular attention was lavished on the mayoralty, the mayor serving as the central focus of almost every public ritual from 'mayoral Sunday', when the new mayor processed with the town council to church, to grand civic events. At the opening of Bradford Town Hall in 1873, the trades procession filed past the Mayor, the Tory brewer Matthew Thompson, 'who stood up in his carriage [and] saluted each of the trades'; the commencement of the mayoral part of the procession was the 'signal for vociferous cheering, renewed waving of handkerchiefs and cries from different quarters of "Bravo, Thompson" and other complimentary ejaculations'. Once the Town Hall had been reached, it was again the Mayor who was the focus of proceedings, the presentation of addresses and the ceremonial handing over of the Town Hall key.[27] As 'super-squire', in John Garrard's phrase, 'the mayor personified municipal government', his principal role being to represent the corporation within the city and beyond.[28]

As this suggests, civic ritual worked to merge the identity of the corporation with the city, so that the city, its trades and institutions, were the subject of simultaneous celebration. The addresses presented to royal visitors never failed to highlight the city's distinctiveness and importance, as with Birmingham in 1858: 'this ancient and enterprising town, the centre of so much of our manufacturing industry'.[29] The opening of the Manchester Town Hall in 1877 similarly brought forth paeans to the city, the region and their industries.

> We are here tonight standing in the centre of a district more wonderful in some respects than is to be traced out on the map in any other kingdom in the world. The population is extraordinary in its number, extraordinary for its interests and its industries, for the amount of its wealth, for the amount of its wages, and for the power which it exercises on other nations.[30]

Conversely, the city itself was identified with its most prominent institutions, the mayor and senior corporation members taking honoured guests on tours of buildings which collectively symbolised the city. In Manchester in 1881 the tour consisted of visits to the Athenaeum, Free Trade Hall, Owens College, the Royal Exchange and, finally, the Town Hall.[31] The extent to which representations merged the city and the corporation is further demonstrated by the numerous town histories published in the later nineteenth century, constructed largely through a chronicle of public events and municipal institutions. Significantly, these histories were increasingly used as civic gifts, such as the copy of the *Manchester Historical Record* presented to Queen Victoria by the Corporation at the opening of the Ship Canal in 1894.[32]

Patrick Joyce has suggested that 'the special significance of civic ritual seems to have lain in this notion of a corporate town identity'.[33] This was demonstrated sharply in relations with the outside world, notably the central state and the county. The royal visits of the 1850s were understood less as an act of subservience to the central state than of loyalty to the person of the monarch, who simultaneously recognised and consecrated the importance and independence of the industrial city. Thus the Birmingham press could congratulate the city in showing its 'reverence' for the Queen in 1858, while affirming its reputation as 'the most democratic town in England'.[34] The importance of the ideas of municipal autonomy and self-government were asserted particularly forcefully from the 1870s when local authorities increasingly sensed themselves to be under threat from the centralising tendencies of the Local Government Board. At a specially convened gathering at York in September 1873, in defence of municipal autonomy, the mayors of England and Wales in ceremonial dress paraded through the streets, characteristically combining politics with display.[35]

Relations with the county administrative hierarchy could also be edgy, taking symbolic form in struggles over custom and precedent. A particularly tetchy encounter took place during the mayoralty of the solicitor, Thomas Baker, in Manchester in 1881–82, between the Mayor and the High Sheriff of Lancashire over seating precedence at a dinner for the Assize judges. The matter was resolved in the Mayor's favour, but only after a threat to refuse all invitations from the Sheriff's office. In the 1890s further conflicts broke out in Manchester regarding the precedence of the Mayor and Corporation officers in civic processions over QCs and the High Sheriff. The assertion of the supremacy of the mayor within the borough over all persons except members of the royal family was persistently and successfully upheld in Manchester as elsewhere.[36] For these reasons, events such as the transfer of the Assizes to industrial cities and the appointment of members of the urban elite to county offices such as high sheriff were moments of urban triumph, celebrated in full civic style. On the appointment of Thomas Ashton, merchant-manufacturer of Hyde and Manchester, to the office of High Sheriff of Lancashire in 1883, twelve hundred 'gentlemen' of the city and district were invited to breakfast at his mansion in Didsbury. This was followed by a procession of two hundred carriages from Didsbury to Manchester to meet the arrival of the Assize judges.[37]

The affirmation of municipal autonomy and the tense relationships maintained with traditional sources of landed authority, whether in London or the county, point to the strong vein of Liberalism running through civic culture in Manchester, Birmingham and Leeds. If the 'non-political' character of municipal government was frequently asserted in these cities, it was on the basis of persistent Liberal predominance.[38] Addresses on civic occasions were steeped in the language and imagery of a bourgeois Liberalism that saw itself as the natural and authentic creed of the city, municipal government and industry. At the opening of the Birmingham Exchange in January 1865, with the Mayor, Corporation and local MPs in attendance, John Bright depicted the Exchange and the Town Hall as linked by absence of party spirit and commitment to the Liberal virtues of freedom, commerce and civilisation: 'for it is obvious to me that the power of the heretofore great authorities is waning, and that in every part of the world the power of the great industrial interests is waxing. [Hear, hear]'.[39] The iconography of civic building was also infused with Liberalism, most strikingly in the new Manchester Town Hall, opened in 1877, where representations of the struggle for civil and religious liberty were set alongside symbols of the progress of the cotton industry.[40] The matter of ceremonial dress was more contentious: at the Queen's visit to Manchester in 1851, four councillors refused to wear the new robes as a mark of their radicalism, including two future mayors, and the matter also invoked heated debate at Birmingham in 1858.[41] Yet, paradoxically, that the matter was an issue at all indicates the importance of symbol to urban Liberalism, and its effectiveness in creating a new symbolic language for civic ritual, despite opposition within its own ranks.

Ritual, order and authority

Civic ritual was thus a significant means by which relations with other, predominantly landed, groups were conducted. It could be a focus for rivalry over authority, as in debates on precedent, and a means of conciliation, as in the invitation to aristocratic representatives to participate in civic ceremonies. In Birmingham and Manchester Lord Calthorpe and Lord Egerton respectively were called on to undertake ceremonial tasks, notwithstanding the strong Liberal antipathy to landed intervention in urban affairs on both councils.[42] Ritual was also a register in which relationships between different groups within the city were played out, between the corporation, employers and major urban institutions on the one hand, and popular collectivities such as friendly and trade societies on the other. Historians of popular politics have pointed to the

significance of employer- and corporation-led manifestations of industrial and civic community in contributing to a more accommodative
political culture in the decades after 1850, marked by the integration of
popular radicalism within the organised ranks of both the Liberal and
Conservative parties.[43] Indeed, such ritual has been seen as part of the
closure and constriction of popular politics before 1867 as well as after
it, in contradiction of narratives centred on the increasing democratis-
ation of the polity after 1832.[44] However, as Robert Gray has argued,
what was involved in public ritual was always a matter of negotiation,
while the form and content of urban ritual itself underwent significant
changes in the second half of the nineteenth century.[45] In order to
examine the manner in which civic ritual was enacted, and the place of
authority and identity within it, it is necessary to look more closely at
the public processions that formed the centrepiece of ritual occasions.

Parades and processions of all kinds were staple elements of public
life in industrial cities throughout the nineteenth century. Processing
through the streets on festive and other occasions was part of the
experience of large sections of the urban population, including children
and workers. At one level, therefore, these events represented pure
pageantry, marching for the sake of marching without deliberate aim or
purpose other than the pleasure of participating in a traditional spectacle
of urban life. Yet such parades also embodied ideas of authority and
identity, above all on civic occasions. One fundamental aspect was their
gender-specific character. While women were actively involved in radical
demonstrations in the first half of the century, civic processions were
essentially all-male affairs, despite the symbolic importance of the Queen
on royal visits and the participation of young girls in events such as the
Whit Walks, usually under religious auspices.[46] Civic space was male
space, women's role in events being perceived as largely passive, as
spectators or organisers of private events. The tone of the *Leeds
Mercury*'s report of the celebration of Victoria's coronation in the town
in 1838 is characteristic: 'Neither in this account must we omit allusion
to the fairer part of our population. Numerous tea parties took place, at
which they showed their loyalty to be not less than those of the other
sex, who could exhibit their feelings in a more conspicuous manner'.[47]

Civic processions embodied authority and the principle of hierarchy
in highly visible ways, of which the exclusion of women was but one.
First and foremost, they assembled and presented the most powerful
institutions and individuals in the town in a single public space. 'The
grand procession' in Leeds marking the coronation of Queen Victoria in
1838 was composed of cavalry, yeomanry, mayor and councillors,

'gentlemen on horseback and on foot', together with representatives of the freemasons, the police, the fire brigade and temperance society, and accompanied by 'music, flags and banners'.[48] It was customary for the town's largest employers to be invited as 'gentlemen' where they were not council members, and named individually in the press reports, thus adding economic to political weight. The close alignment between civic and economic leadership continued throughout the nineteenth century. At the reception for the Assize judges in 1865 the Mayor and Corporation of Leeds were accompanied on the Town Hall steps by what were described as 'the leading public men' of the city, Crossley, Forster, Denison and Lupton, who were also major employers in the city and region.[49] Civic events thus gave urban authority the opportunity to display itself, not only to the large crowds who witnessed the spectacle, but also to those who read the voluminous reports in the columns of the local press.

The order of the procession itself symbolised degrees of authority and importance. The elevation of the office of the mayoralty, for example, was signalled in Birmingham by the tendency after mid-century to place the Mayor at the end, as the climax of the parade, rather than in its midst. In Manchester, on the other hand, the same principle dictated that the Mayor should head any procession.[50] Every procession had its own social logic, however. That this was clear to participants, at least, is indicated by the refusal of groups to co-operate if they were not assigned what was deemed an appropriate place in the rank order.[51] Such difficulties were exacerbated by the fact that the parade was a fluid entity whose composition changed over time. In Liberal-dominated Birmingham, Manchester and Leeds, units of the volunteers replaced the regular units of the army which had headed civic processions prior to municipal reform. From the 1860s in particular, wider groups of local associations and trade societies were involved on civic occasions, in step with the momentum for political reform. In Manchester and the cotton towns, representatives of artisan trades had been sporadically included in civic festivities in the early nineteenth century, as had groups of factory workers led by their employers.[52] But from the 1860s popular participation occurred on different terms, trade and friendly societies using such events to assert an independent social identity as well as to demonstrate local patriotism.

The entry of working-class groups into the civic arena was an inherently ambiguous enterprise, the significance of which was constructed in different, and sometimes conflicting, ways. The act of marching in orderly fashion through the city represented a public claim to social and political identity. Both the form and composition of processions signalled to contemporaries changes in the urban polity. Thus an editorial in the *Manchester Guardian* in 1874 commented on the significance of a trades demonstration in support of the striking agricultural labourers: 'The lengthy procession of Saturday, important enough in itself, was more important still in the representative character of the bodies of which it was composed. Nearly every group in the line belonged to some larger combination of workmen'. The demonstration spoke, in the *Guardian*'s words, of the 'newly-recognised brotherhood of labour'.[53] Where demonstrators marched was also significant: by processing around the central streets and major civic buildings, organised labour asserted its rights to public space and a political voice. As R. J. Morris and Richard Rodger have noted, in Glasgow by the turn of the century 'every labour and trades union leader knew that to hold a demonstration in George Square was to lay symbolic claim to power within the city'.[54]

The public processional culture that developed from the 1850s represented social order in the double sense of the term. By participating in parades social groups and institutions rendered themselves visible to the urban public and staked their claim to a place within the social body of the town. At the same time, the hierarchical ordering of civic processions framed such events and gave physical form to the expression of social authority. Within the civic procession itself, the sequential order in which groups and institutions were placed meant that they did not come face-to-face with one another. On major festive occasions social distinctions and identities could be maintained by holding civic and trades processions on separate days.[55] In the conception of the social order devised under the auspices of civic Liberalism, therefore, hierarchy and independence were held in mutual tension. Improvisatory, fluid and voluntaristic, the civic procession allowed for the representation of diverse social identities within a public pageant that also encompassed notions of hierarchy, stability and authority.[56]

The idea of parades as expressive of order extended more widely to popular celebration and demonstrations in the mid-Victorian period. The orderliness as well as the enthusiasm of the crowds for the royal visits in the 1850s was repeatedly noted by the local and national press in tones which mixed admiration and relief in equal measure. The disciplined character of crowd behaviour at public events continued to be a matter of congratulatory comment in the press for the rest of the century.[57] So too did accounts of popular processions. The extent to which middle-class attitudes to the sight of marching workers shifted between the two halves of the nineteenth century is striking, and extensively evinced in the reports of the local press. Whereas the quasi-military processions of workers in the Peterloo and Chartist periods were regularly seen as threatening, from the 1860s they were represented as evidence of the orderliness and loyalty of workers. A Manchester periodical in 1870 contrasted the violent events of the Paris Commune with the peaceable character of the several processions held in Manchester the previous Saturday: 'Probably not less than 40,000 people were gathered together in these localities, without taking into account the vast throng who lined the streets through which different processions passed. Flags were flying, bands playing, and all was harmony, rejoicing and peace'.[58]

In the second half of the nineteenth century, therefore, parades and processions were taken to be an index of civility. The bodily self-discipline of the marchers, the ordered disposition of the procession as a whole, and the ritualistic nature of events rendered them inherently respectable, a model of collective behaviour in public. They contrasted not only with earlier forms of popular protest, and with events abroad, but also with the disorderly character of the city streets and slums and the continuing fears of crime and violence which these aroused. The voluntarism of the parade and its public visibility served in this context as an ideal of the self-regulating urban community that policed itself through its own inherent codes of conduct. Order was maintained less by the overt assertion of authority than by the tacit rules that regulated the ritual itself.

However, as a wider population was incorporated within the processional culture, and as the forms that this took proliferated, so the opportunities for bourgeois display were reduced. By the 1870s not only did civic processions seek to include a vast range of urban bodies in events, they were also rivalled as public spectacles by the great demonstrations of the political parties and of organised labour. In Birmingham, the inauguration of the Assizes in August 1884 might have been expected to be the occasion of civic celebration, as had previously been the case at both Leeds and Manchester. In fact, it was poorly attended and went off with minimal ceremony. The event was overshadowed by the great Liberal demonstration at Bingley Hall in favour of franchise extension, addressed by Chamberlain, Bright and many city councillors, and involving an estimated one hundred thousand people in the procession.[59] Ironically, the very success of the processional culture initiated under civic auspices in the 1850s weakened specific aspects of civic display in the longer term.

Instead, the ritual that represented bourgeois authority and civic importance most publicly in the later nineteenth century was the 'centi-pedic funeral' of large employers and municipal dignitaries. There was nothing wholly new in lavish obsequies. When Sir Thomas Potter, Liberal manufacturer and first Mayor of Manchester, died in 1845, the corporations of Salford and Manchester and the representatives of a host of local institutions, together with ninety-eight carriages and a large contingent of 'gentlemen on foot', escorted the Gothic hearse while four hundred policemen lined the route through Manchester.[60] After 1850 the trend was for simpler, less extravagant funerals among the upper and middle classes. Yet this did not preclude a magisterial 'send-off'. Julian Litten has described the 1890s as the 'golden age of the Victorian funeral', culminating in the sober yet massive state funeral of Gladstone in 1898.[61] In the provincial and industrial centres, the decades after 1880 were notable both for the number and scale of funerals of local worthies, conducted in the public gaze with full civic pomp.

The funeral of Sir Edward Baines, owner of the *Leeds Mercury* in 1890, was characteristic. The cortege left the Baines mansion in Burley, on the edge of Leeds, to be joined by the carriages of the region's leading employer families, the Illingworths, Kitsons and Luptons, and wound its way through streets lined with spectators to East Parade chapel, seat of worship of the Baines family for over half a century. Mills were closed and the one hundred and sixty staff of the *Mercury* marched as a body to the chapel. After the funeral service, reserved for chief mourners and leading public figures, the procession, now half a mile in length headed northwards, the hearse led by the repre-sentatives of twenty-six public institutions and followed by the carriages of the city's civic and business elite. 'All the way there was evidence of mourning', the *Mercury* reported. 'Most of the shops were closed. Blinds were drawn at the Town Hall and Municipal Buildings'.[62] The Town Hall bell tolled and flags were hung at half-mast. The Mayor and town council met the cortege at Woodhouse cemetery, though Baines had never been a member. As a 'public man', however, he was given a civic burial.

Rites like this were regularly enacted on the death of urban notables in industrial towns and cities during the later nineteenth and early twentieth century. The public nature of funerals reflected the status of large employers, clergy and municipal councillors as public figures, closely identified with the city or locality. When the Congregationalist minister R. W. Dale died in Birmingham in 1895, 'the obsequies were such as befitted a public man'. Notwithstanding his role in national religious life, Dale was projected pre-eminently as a local figure: 'Birmingham was the scene for the beginning of his labours, Birmingham was the city of his adoption'. His funeral was a major civic event, attended by Joseph Chamberlain, the Mayor and Corporation of Birmingham, and representatives of the local and national bodies with which he had been associated. The procession was watched silently by thousands as it filed through the city to Key Hill cemetery, where Dale was interred close by Charles Vince, George Dawson and other 'co-workers, secular and spiritual', identified with the public life of the city.[63]

The highly-charged, symbolic nature of these occasions was registered in the routes adopted by the funeral procession, taking in locations specific to the life of the deceased – home, works, church or chapel – as well as the representative sites of civic monumentalism, the principal streets and squares, Exchange and town hall. As the *Birmingham Daily Post* observed of the funeral procession of Joseph Chamberlain in 1914: 'On his last journey he passed through the peace and charm of his Highbury home through the streets of the city he had so large a part in creating, to that eminent company company in the little Hockley cemetery who shared with him in bringing about the regeneration of Birmingham'.[64] It thus took in the leafy suburbs, the Unitarian chapel, the civic and commercial centre, and part of the West Birmingham constituency for which Chamberlain had been MP. In this manner, the life of the individual notable was figuratively aligned with the life of the city in an act that recreated the ideal of civic community while simultaneously highlighting symbolically the sources of bourgeois authority.

Not all such events, of course, were understood as representative of civic unity. In smaller industrial towns especially, the passing of a major employer was a momentous event, splitting the community in death as in life. Recalling the autocratic Ashton employer, Hugh Mason, W. H. Mills evoked in vivid terms the polarised emotions which Mason had inspired: 'either one belonged to that half of society which accounted him as little less than deity or to the other half which stoned his carriage windows, wrecked his lodge gates and even, as it was whispered, indulged their loathing of him in horrid rites, enacting his funeral while he was in normal health'. When Mason's death came in 1886, it left an indelible imprint on the minds of contemporaries. A generation later, Mills could 'still feel the hush which fell over the town during the last illness, and can hear those that were of the household of faith telling one another with voices of doom that "Mr Mason had gone"'.[65]

In the more anonymous environment of the large city, the deaths of employers and civic worthies do not appear to have given rise to such

torrid and divided feelings among a wide population. What were signalled in the funeral rites of public figures were both the death of the
patriarch and the continuity of patriarchal authority. They were in-
scribed in the public rites and in the published funeral addresses, which
sought to recreate a life devoted to the beneficent exercise of power and
to place the individual within a long line of patrimonial duty. The cotton
manufacturer and merchant of Manchester and Hyde, Thomas Ashton,
'lived and died like a patriarch'. At his funeral in 1898, the congregation
was reminded that 'his connection with them as workpeople had lasted
for very nearly fifty years, and now that his sons were becoming
associated with the business, they represented the third generation of
Ashtons, who employed, to a very large extent, the third and fourth
generations of workpeople'.[66] If a language of patriarchal continuity was
most closely identified with the passing of large employers, it was not
confined to them. The funeral rites of leading urban clergymen and
ministers similarly sought to embrace them within a tradition of religious piety and civic responsibility. In Manchester the evangelical Hugh
Stowell was depicted as representative of a long line of reforming
Anglican clergy stretching back to Cranmer, Bishop Fraser as the 'first
citizen of his diocese', full of 'civic virtues'.[67]

The processional culture of the mid- and late Victorian decades thus
offered rich resources for the display of civic pride and community, and
of authority, social order and identity. In differing ways the civic parade
and the 'centipedic funeral' symbolised a unity of leadership and authority in the industrial city more powerfully than any other events. On
these Olympian occasions, the pettiness of party politics and sectarian
strife were transcended in the collective expression of elemental themes:
authority, solidarity, mourning. In bourgeois funeral rites, especially,
civic virtues were sanctified, spiritual virtues magnified by the secular
glow of civic duty. Under the mantle of the civic, employers, ministers,
clergymen and municipal leaders shared modes of ritual expression
which had the capacity to transform evanescent authority into something
resembling the permanence of power.

The decline of civic ritual

The illusion of power embodied in mid-Victorian civic ritual was, of
course, transitory. While in many smaller industrial and market towns
the years between 1880 and 1914 represented the highpoint of civic
culture, in the industrial capitals there is evidence that enthusiasm was
waning in the same period.[68] The major civic projects of the late

nineteenth and early twentieth century were described no less minutely in the local press, but there were signs of weariness with the formulaic character of the ritual celebrations. At the opening of the Manchester Ship Canal by Queen Victoria in 1894, the *Guardian* reporter confessed to a certain civic *ennui*: 'One tired of the decorations, about which there was, after all, a considerable degree of sameness'. On the opening of City Square in Leeds in 1903, it was noted, 'the display of enthusiasm was not so great as it might have been'. Meanwhile, Birmingham's main municipal achievement, the Elan Valley Water scheme, was celebrated away from city, the Mayor and Corporation being transported by railway to the site in mid-Wales for the opening.[69] The sheer number and scale of public spectacles in the second half of the nineteenth century, it would seem, gradually satiated the appetite of observers for such events.

There were also other reasons for the appearance of decline. By the 1870s civic pageantry in the industrial city was forced to compete for public attention with other processional events, such as party demonstrations, and with the attractions of an increasingly commercialised popular culture, encompassing the music hall, the department store and professional sport. In short, it no longer occupied so unique a position in the repertoire of visual spectacle that the city had to offer. Indeed, John Garrard has argued that civic processions themselves were steadily infiltrated by a consumerist element, local firms using occasions such as the 1897 Golden Jubilee to display consumer ware, from kitchen ranges to umbrellas, on the processional floats.[70]

The decline in the appeal of civic ritual from the late nineteenth century can also be related to wider social and political shifts in these years. For Patrick Joyce the 'passing of the old order' among employers in the factory north around 1900 was the product of a series of inter-related changes. They included the advent of the limited liability company and the loosening of the bonds between the employer family, firm and workforce, together with the rise of socialism and more militant trade unionism, especially in the West Riding, which served to challenge employer versions of the 'community of interest' on which the old order had rested.[71] At the level of municipal politics, concomitant changes were occurring. From the mid-1870s there was a decline in the number of large proprietors on the councils of many town and cities, including Manchester. The increasing intervention of the Local Government Board and the growing number of interest groups in local affairs made municipal government itself considerably more complex and onerous than at an earlier period. In addition, Liberalism, which had provided much of the motive force behind mid-Victorian civic culture, was increasingly under challenge from Conservatives and economy-minded ratepayers in cities such as Leeds and Manchester from the 1880s.[72] The decline of civic culture can thus be attributed to a series of shifts in the constellation of urban authority between 1880 and 1914.

However, the evidence is ambiguous. Many of the tendencies noted above were slow to take effect, not having a decisive impact until after 1918.[73] Moreover, the extent and timing of change was registered differently in specific urban locales. At a political level, for example, the numbers of large businessmen on municipal councils in Leeds and Birmingham actually increased in the last decades of the century.[74] Many large employers had in any case never stood for election to the council or other public bodies, although they remained closely identified with civic life. More generally, the urban arena retained much its capacity to act as the chief focus of local interest into the early twentieth century. As Garrard has pointed out, judged by the number of local newspapers, and their 'sheer verbal footage', it was in the decades around 1900 that the local press reached its 'overblown zenith'.[75] Nor did all of civic ritual lose its appeal; an important part of the power of ritual resides precisely in its capacity to retain an aura or mystique independent of the personality of those immediately associated with it. Significantly, while there was a steady stream of criticism of the declining social status of town councillors from as early as the 1850s, the prestige of the mayoralty and corporation as institutions were little affected. It was precisely this symbolic prestige which made the mayoralty especially so prized a goal of the Labour party in northern towns and cities during the inter-war years, an 'embracing fixation' as one historian has recently put it.[76]

Overall, the balance of evidence suggests that while there was some waning of enthusiasm for civic events, especially in the large cities, and a loosening of the identification between the wealthiest sections of the middle class and municipal government, these trends were slow acting. Their impact on the prestige of civic office and institutions was only dimly apparent before the First World War, though it was to become all too evident after it. From this perspective the funeral of Joseph Chamberlain in Birmingham in July 1914 can be seen as valedictory moment for a whole civic culture. Commemorated in Birmingham less as a national statesman than as a local 'pioneer' who 'laid the foundations for Birmingham's civic greatness', Chamberlain's funeral was a testimony to the continuing power of provincial civic culture. Following his death in London, the body was conveyed back to Birmingham for burial. Birmingham itself was transformed into a 'city in mourning', in the words of the *Daily Post*: 'business was suspended so that all citizens might join in a last tribute to Birmingham's greatest citizen'. While the Mayor and Corporation headed the vast procession in which every significant institution in the city was represented, the crowds lining the streets were depicted as a silent chorus, a community united in memory of a common struggle enacted under Chamberlain's aegis:

> The bulk of those who gathered there, young and old, artisan and clerk, were people who felt that they had been intimately associated with the man who was being borne to his last resting-place. They were the rank-and-file who had ever responded to his call; they had fought for him in his battles, and they had cheered him in his triumphs. He was their member, and they, more than others, were his people.[77]

Yet if the funeral indicated the still powerful pulse of civic culture, it also registered its decline. Descriptions in the press pointed backwards to an already mythicised past associated with the highpoint of Liberalism and civic progress in the 1870s and 1880s. In this sense Chamberlain's funeral marked the passing of an era in Birmingham characterised by the primacy of the local and the identification of politics with the specific urban milieu. No civic leader in the provincial cities would henceforth receive a funeral of this scale and style; nor would civic ritual itself be imbued with so powerful a cultural and political resonance.

In reviewing the mixture of paternalism and deference which came to characterise social relations between industrial employers and workers in the mid- and later nineteenth century, Robert Gray has emphasised the extent to which these relations were increasingly ritualised and performative. The presentations of loyal addresses to employers and of 'treats' to workers were repeated in standardised forms across the industrial districts, 'episodes of ritual exchange' in which both the social leadership of employers and the independence of workers were maintained.[78] The pageantry and processions that characterised later Victorian and Edwardian civic culture were part of a wider repertoire of symbolic acts played out on the wider stage of the city. They enabled the personal authority of employers and 'public men' to be transmuted into larger, more formal and more permanent symbols of urban leadership. They incarnated the idea both of a social hierarchy and of the independence of organised social interests, thus representing the concept of urban community in physical form. Moreover, they contributed to the reorganisation of urban space and of bodies in space. Processions and demonstrations reaffirmed the symbolic centrality of certain streets, squares and buildings by virtue of their identification with the 'civic' as a source of power. As a ritual event, the parade itself embodied an idealised vision of urban order and sobriety set against the disorganisation of the city, its anonymous crowds, random streets and labyrinthine slums.

Such public rituals were integrally bound up with the historical moment of civic Liberalism. Liberalism provided the political creed that most strongly infused civic ritual, transcribing it into the familiar language of municipal pride and progress. It also shaped the larger vision of an urban social order, characterised by a specific admixture of voluntarism and hierarchy, independence and authority. Within this political culture, identity was intrinsically linked to visibility on public and ceremonial occasions. Participation in the rites of civic culture affirmed the rights of a group to recognition within the public life of the city. Those groups which were not represented in this way – women, the poor, minorities such as the Jews and the Irish – were effectively denied recognition as independent entities, and hence the right to public expression. The gradual decline of civic culture from the late nineteenth century was thus marked not only by the weakening of Liberalism and the withdrawal of sections of the middle class from active involvement in local politics, but also by the fragmentation of a politics of visual representation which had rested on systematic exclusion. Once the streets had been occupied by unemployed workers and by suffragettes, the claims of civic culture to represent urban community and social order were brought into question. The success of civic culture was partly its undoing in the longer term. By linking visibility, identity and power in explicit yet exclusive ways in the nineteenth century, it paved the way for the return of the repressed in the early twentieth.

Notes

1   C. Cunningham, *Victorian and Edwardian Town Halls* (London: Routledge, 1981), pp. 215–19.
2   D. Cannadine, 'The transformation of civic ritual in modern Britain: the Colchester Oyster Feast', *Past and Present,* 94 (1982), p. 129.
3   R. Sennett, *Authority* (London: Secker and Warburg, 1980), p. 4.
4   S. and B. Webb, *English Local Government: The Manor and the Borough* (London: Frank Cass, [1908] 1963), pp. 424, 441, 537, 538, 565, 583; P. Borsay, '"All the world's a stage": urban ritual and ceremony, 1660–1800' in P. Clark (ed.), *The Transformation of English Provincial Towns 1600–1800* (London: Hutchinson, 1984); D. Cannadine, 'The context, performance and meaning of ritual: the British monarchy and the "invention of tradition", *c.* 1820–1977' in E. J. Hobsbawm and T. Ranger, *The Invention of Tradition* (Cambridge: Cambridge University Press, 1984), p. 138.

5   Cannadine, 'Transformation of civic ritual', p. 113.

6   *Aris's Birmingham Gazette*, 2 July 1838.

7   For comments see *Manchester Guardian*, 30 June 1838; *Leeds Mercury*, 30 June 1838.

8   Whigs or Liberals won all 48 seats in Birmingham and Manchester in 1838 and all but 6 in Leeds in 1835 – see D. Fraser, *Urban Politics in Victorian England* (London: Macmillan, 1979), p. 124.

9   *Manchester Guardian*, 15 December 1838.

10 *Aris's Birmingham Gazette*, 31 December 1838.

11 J. Epstein, *Radical Expression: Political Language, Ritual and Symbol in England, 1790–1850* (Oxford: Oxford University Press, 1994), p. 89.

12 See A. Briggs, *The History of Birmingham: Borough and City, 1865–1938* (London: Oxford University Press, 1952), appendix E; *Aris's Birmingham Gazette*, 26 November 1855; J. Mayhall, *Annals of Yorkshire*, vol. 1 (Leeds, 1860).

13 A. Briggs, *Victorian Cities* (Harmondsworth: Penguin, 1968), ch. 4.

14 *Manchester Guardian*, 11 October 1851, p. 5. This account is drawn substantially from the description there.

15 *Manchester Guardian*, 11 October 1851, p. 7.

16 *Manchester Guardian*, 11 October 1851, p. 8.

17 Cobden cited in Fraser, *Urban Politics*, p. 204. See also the comments cited in N. McCord, 'Cobden and Bright in politics, 1846–57' in R. Robson (ed.), *Ideas and Institutions of Victorian Britain* (London: G. Bell, 1967), pp. 112–14.

18 Briggs, *Victorian Cities*, p. 171; *Birmingham Daily Post*, 16 June 1858, p. 4.

19 Fraser, *Urban Politics*, ch. 6; E. P. Hennock, *Fit and Proper Persons: Ideal and Reality in Nineteenth-Century Urban Government* (London: Edward Arnold, 1973); J. Garrard, 'The mayoralty since 1835', *Transactions of the Lancashire and Cheshire Antiquarian Society*, vol. 90 (1994), p. 42.

20 For Liverpool see B. D. White, *A History of the Corporation of Liverpool 1835–1914* (Liverpool: Liverpool University Press, 1951); P. J. Waller, *Democracy and Sectarianism: A Political and Social History of Liverpool, 1868–1939* (Liverpool: Liverpool University Press, 1981).

21 *Leeds Mercury*, 13 August 1865, p. 12.

22 For comments see P. Joyce, 'The constitution and the narrative structure of Victorian politics' in J. Vernon, *Re-reading the Constitution: New Narratives in the Political History of the Long Nineteenth Century* (Cambridge: Cambridge University Press, 1996), pp. 192–4; Joyce, *Work, Society and Politics: The Culture of the Factory in Later Victorian England* (Brighton: Harvester Press, 1980), pp. 280–2.

23 See, for example, the description of the procession in the celebrations of the opening of Bradford Town Hall in 1873 reported in the *Leeds Mercury*, 9 September 1873, p. 3.

24 For comments see P. Joyce, *Visions of the People: Industrial England and the Question of Class* (Cambridge: Cambridge University Press, 1991),

pp. 183–5. For a wider discussion of aristocratic involvement in civic ritual at the period see R. Trainor, 'Peers on an industrial frontier: the earls of Dartmouth and Dudley in the Black Country, *c.* 1810 to 1914' in D. Cannadine (ed.), *Patricians, Power and Politics in Nineteenth-Century Towns* (Leicester: Leicester University Press, 1982), pp. 103–13.

25   *Leeds Mercury*, 2 January 1836, p. 5.

26   Cited in Hennock, *Fit and Proper Persons*, pp. 321–2.

27   *Leeds Mercury*, 9 September 1873, p. 3. For a description of Thompson and his career see T. Koditschek, *Class Formation and Urban Industrial Society: Bradford 1750–1850* (Cambridge: Cambridge University Press, 1990), pp. 140–1.

28   Garrard, 'The mayoralty since 1835', p. 35.

29   *Birmingham Daily Post*, 16 June 1858, p. 6.

30   Speech of John Bright cited in W. E. A. Axon (ed.), *An Architectural and General Description of the Town Hall, Manchester to Which is Added a Report of the Inaugural Proceedings* (Manchester, 1878), p. 53.

31   *Manchester Examiner*, 14 December 1881.

32   *Manchester Guardian*, 22 May 1894, p. 7. For other examples of such histories see J. Mayhall, *Annals of Yorkshire*, vols 1–3 (Leeds, 1866–75); J. A. Langford, *Modern Birmingham and Its Institutions*, vols 1 and 2 (Birmingham, 1873); W. E. A. Axon, *The Annals of Manchester: A Chronological Record From the Earliest Times to the End of 1885* (Manchester, 1886).

33   Joyce, *Work, Society and Politics*, p. 278.

34   *Birmingham Daily Post*, 16 June, 1858, p. 6.

35   *Leeds Mercury*, 26 September 1873, p. 3.

36   T. Baker, 'Reminiscences of my own life', MS, Manchester Central Library Archives Department; 'The mayor's social status: a question of precedence', *Manchester Examiner*, 31 July and 1 August 1882; 'Precedence in public ceremonies' (1897), MSS, A257, Manchester Central Library Archives Department.

37   *Manchester Courier*, 16 April 1883; see also Ashton papers, Manchester Central Library Archives Department.

38   Fraser, *Urban Politics in Victorian England*, p. 151.

39   *Birmingham Daily Post*, 3 January 1865.

40   For a detailed description of the Manchester Town Hall see Axon, *Architectural and General Description of Town Hall, Manchester*; for comments see the chapters by Archer and J. Treuherz in J. H. G. Archer (ed.), *Art and Architecture in Victorian Manchester* (Manchester: Manchester University Press, 1985), and Joyce, *Visions of the People*, p. 182. Description of the interior and exterior of town halls more generally can be found in Cunningham, *Victorian and Edwardian Town Halls*.

41   *Manchester Guardian*, 11 October 1851, p. 7; Bunce, *History of the Corporation of Birmingham*, pp. 539–40.

42   Calthorpe presented the address to Prince Albert on the occasion of the

inauguration of the Birmingham and Midland Institute in 1855, for example, while Egerton performed the same task at the opening of the Manchester Ship Canal by Queen Victoria in 1894. See *Aris's Birmingham Gazette*, 26 November 1855; *Manchester Guardian*, 22 May 1894, p. 7.

43 See, for example, Joyce, *Work, Society and Politics*, esp. pp. 272–80; N. Kirk, *The Growth of Working Class Reformism in Mid-Victorian England* (London: Croom Helm, 1985), pp. 272–301; Joyce, *Visions of the People*, pp. 183–5; Epstein, *Radical Expression*, p. 165.

44 J. Vernon, *Politics and the People: A Study in English Political Culture, c. 1815–1867* (Cambridge: Cambridge University Press, 1993).

45 R. Gray, *The Factory Question and Industrial England 1830–1860* (Cambridge: Cambridge University Press, 1996), pp. 219–29.

46 Epstein, *Radical Expression*, pp. 86–9. For discussion of female participation in Whit Walks see W. H. Mills, *Grey Pastures*, ch. 4.

47 *Leeds Mercury*, 30 June 1838, p. 5.

48 *Leeds Mercury*, 30 June 1838, p. 5.

49 *Leeds Mercury*, 13 August 1865, p. 12.

50 In Birmingham, for instance, the order of the coronation procession in 1838 can be compared with that for the visit of Prince Albert in 1855. See *Aris's Birmingham Gazette*, 2 July 1838 and 26 November 1855. For Manchester see the letter from the town clerk W. H. Talbot of 16 January 1895 on processional order in 'Precedence in public ceremonies'.

51 As occurred with the freemasons at the coronation celebrations in Manchester in 1838. *Manchester Guardian*, 30 June 1838.

52 For descriptions of popular participation in Bolton and Salford see J. Garrard, *Leadership and Power in Victorian Industrial Towns, 1830–1880* (Manchester: Manchester University Press, 1982), pp. 27–8. For Manchester, *Manchester Guardian*, 30 June 1838.

53 *Manchester Guardian*, 22 June 1874, p. 5.

54 R. J. Morris and R. Rodger, 'An introduction to British urban history, 1820–1914' in Morris and Rodger (eds), *The Victorian City: A Reader in British Urban History 1820–1914* (Harlow: Longman, 1993), p. 9.

55 As occurred in the celebrations for the opening of the Manchester Town Hall in 1877. See Axon, *Architectural and General Description of the Town Hall, Manchester*.

56 This discussion draws on the illuminating analysis of Mary Ryan, 'The American parade: representations of the nineteenth-century social order' in L. Hunt (ed.), *The New Cultural History* (Berkeley: University of California Press, 1989), pp. 131–53.

57 See, for example, *Manchester Guardian*, 11 October 1851, p. 8; *Birmingham Daily Post*, 16 June 1858, p. 7; *Leeds Mercury*, 10 September 1873, p. 3 on the opening of Bradford Town Hall; *Birmingham Daily Post*, 19 March 1895, p. 6, on the funeral of R. W. Dale.

58 'Saturday in Manchester and elsewhere – a contrast', *Freelance*, 16 August 1870.

59 *Birmingham Daily Post*, 5 August 1884, p. 3.

60 *Manchester Guardian*, 29 March 1845, p. 9.

61 J. Litten, *The English Way of Death: The Common Funeral Since 1450* (Cambridge: Cambridge University Press, 1991), p. 170; see also P. Jalland, *Death in the Victorian Family* (Oxford: Oxford University Press, 1996), ch. 9.

62 *Leeds Mercury*, 7 March 1890, p. 8. This account is drawn substantially from the description given there.

63 *Birmingham Daily Post*, 19 March 1895, p. 4.

64 *Birmingham Daily Post*, 7 July 1914, p. 6.

65 W. H. Mills, *The Manchester Reform Club, 1871–1921* (Manchester, 1922), pp. 10 and 12. For Mason's obituary see *Manchester Guardian*, 3 February 1886.

66 *Manchester Guardian*, 22 January 1898; *Hyde Reporter*, 5 February 1898. See also the Ashton family papers in Manchester Central Library Archives Department.

67 J. B. Marsden, *Memoirs of the Life and Labour of the Rev. Hugh Stowell M.A.* (London, 1868), p. 453; T. Hughes, *James Fraser, Second Bishop of Manchester* (London, 1887), p. 362.

68 See Cannadine, 'Transformation of civic ritual' for the example of Colchester, and J. Garrard, 'Urban elites, 1850–1914: the rule and decline of a new squirearchy?', *Albion*, 27, 4 (1995), pp. 603–21, for Bolton and Rochdale.

69 *Manchester Guardian*, 22 May 1894, p. 7; *Leeds Mercury*, 17 September 1903, p. 8; *Birmingham Daily Post*, 21 July 1904, special supplement.

70 Garrard, 'Urban elites, 1850–1914', p. 606. The focus here is on Bolton although Garrard's point may have wider validity.

71 Joyce, *Work, Society and Politics*, epilogue.

72 For a wider discussion of these themes see Garrard, 'Urban elites 1850–1914'. For discussion of the political composition of the councils in Leeds and Manchester between 1880 and 1914 see T. Woodhouse, 'The working class' in D. Fraser (ed.), *History of Modern Leeds* (Manchester: Manchester University Press, 1980), pp. 362–3; A. Kidd, *Manchester* (Keele: Ryburn Press, 1993), pp. 148–9; I. Harford, *Manchester and its Ship Canal Movement: Class, Work and Politics in Late Victorian England* (Keele: Ryburn Press, 1994), pp. 152–3.

73 Joyce, *Visions of the People*, ch. 14.

74 Hennock, *Fit and Proper Persons*, pp. 35, 225.

75 Garrard, 'Urban elites, 1850–1914', p. 614.

76 Garrard, 'The mayoralty since 1835'.

77 *Birmingham Daily Post*, 7 July 1914.

78 Gray, *Factory Question and Industrial England*, pp. 225–9.

Epilogue

The decline of provincial bourgeois culture

During the nineteenth century a distinct industrial civilisation took shape in the regional capitals of England's manufacturing districts. It involved a physical and cultural transformation of an impressive scale and rapidity. In 1835 Alexis de Tocqueville was still able to remark on the rudimentary, unfinished state of Manchester. The scattered factories and workers' houses, he reported, were 'still without the amenities of a town. The soil has been taken away, scratched and torn up in a thousand places, but is not yet covered with the habitations of men ... The roads, which connect the still-disjointed limbs of a great city, show, like the rest, every sign of hurried and unfinished work'.[1] What de Tocqueville described was an embryonic landscape of primitive exploitation, human and environmental. But by the mid-Victorian period matters had changed significantly. The English industrial metropolises had come to be represented in a very different, though no less dramatic, manner. Birmingham, Manchester and Leeds were loudly acclaimed as the exemplars of the new urban, industrial civilisation. Thomas Wemyss Reid, the Newcastle-born editor of the *Leeds Mercury*, was characteristic in his encomium for the industrial capitals. 'Although they cannot boast of the historic glories of the great capitals of Europe', he asserted, the industrial cities 'are even now superior to many of them in wealth and population, and are laying broad and deep the foundations of a future destiny which may vie in interest and importance with of some of the most famous cities of the ancient world'.[2]

The growth of an urban bourgeois culture was a central component of this developing industrial civilisation. Its highpoint in Birmingham, Leeds and Manchester was attained in the decades between 1870 and 1900. Urban bourgeois culture was not a mere imitation of London-based or landed society as the proponents of 'gentlemanly capitalism' have argued. Nor was it reducible to a home-centred, suburban way of life or the manifestations of civic pride, as many historians have assumed.

While these last dimensions were important, they obscure the fuller picture of the public culture of the provincial middle class in the period, centred on the city itself. A public, bourgeois culture was inflected differently in the three industrial cities. Manchester was frequently to the forefront in terms of cultural innovation and significance, exemplified by the Art Treasures exhibition, the Hallé concerts and civic ceremonial. In Birmingham, bourgeois culture was identified more closely with rational exchange and civic improvement, evinced in the prominence of debating societies and the connection of much of cultural life with the milieu of municipal Liberalism. A coherent culture was slower to take shape in Leeds, and continued to be marked by patrician aspects, indicated by the longevity of the Philosophical and Literary Society and the dominance of a comparatively small group of old-established families in cultural initiatives, from the Conversation Club to the music festival.

Yet in all three cities a bourgeois culture with similar components was created from the 1840s onwards. It was based on the architectural and spatial reconstruction of the city centre as the embodiment of urban modernity and as the site on which new modes of social identity and symbolic representation were enacted. In the mid- and later Victorian decades the city centre was directly expressive of power, in its monumental proportions and moral inscriptions, as well as acting as the stage-set for the public rituals of bourgeois display. It was the focus of diverse forms of consumption and sociability associated with clubland, the department store, the art exhibition and the concert hall. This was a public culture not only because it was played out in the heart of the city, but also in the sense that it was depersonalised, accessible on the basis of cash payment, yet at the same time permeated by intricate codes of gender and class. If public space was first and foremost male space, women's presence or absence was charged with moral and social meanings which significantly affected how a context (the street, the club, the promenade) was viewed. Equally, acceptance within bourgeois culture was dependent on a high degree of social competence, of bodily demeanour and educated speech, acknowledged in terms such as 'standing', 'substance' and 'refinement'.

While bourgeois culture was not the possession of a class, in any direct sense, it was an important bearer of class in the nineteenth century. Culture provided the terms in which social and economic differences were frequently encoded. A direct correlation was maintained between the apex of wealth and influence on the one hand, and the possession of culture on the other, evident, for example, in the assumption of the Birmingham Liberal J. T. Bunce, that the 'large ratepayer' would be 'qualified by education and capacity' to 'give tone' to local government.[3] The moral authority of the Nonconformist minister derived from a particular conception of 'spiritual culture' which he was seen to personify, and which proclaimed the social importance of the chapel and its congregation as a whole. In the middle class leadership and culture were understood to be mutually constitutive. The analogy was given collective emphasis in the concert hall, where the association of classical music with 'high society' affirmed the correspondence between cultural and social hierarchy. Lower down the social scale, evidence of education and of a broad set of cultural references was important for those seen to be aspiring to middle-class status, notably clerks and shop workers, as well as providing a means by which social pretences could be uncovered. In each of these cases culture played a mediating role by transposing material inequalities and differences into a 'natural' dichotomy between the 'cultivated' few and the 'vulgar' many. As Pierre Bourdieu characteristically puts it, 'the bourgeoisie find naturally in culture as cultivated nature and culture that has become nature the only possible principle for the legitimation of their privilege'. Indeed, for Bourdieu culture became the historical successor to the aristocratic hereditary principle in the organisation of social identity and division during the nineteenth century.[4]

By the early 1900s, however, many of the forms that constituted provincial bourgeois culture were already showing signs of a decline that was to accelerate after the First World War. While older clubs and societies, like John Shaw's in Manchester and the Phil. and Lit. in Leeds, were more or less moribund by the 1880s, many of the bohemian and gentlemen's clubs of the later Victorian period themselves struggled after 1900. In Manchester the exclusive Bridgewater and Princes clubs were extinct by the first years of the twentieth century, and newer growths, such as the Manchester Arts Club, did not survive beyond 1939. In Birmingham and Leeds 'clubland' gradually disintegrated after 1918, with falling rolls, ageing memberships and increasingly outdated facilities.[5] The period after 1900 also witnessed the waning of a distinct musical culture, evidenced most spectacularly in the demise of the Birmingham Musical Festival in 1912, but also in the 'hard times' suffered by the Manchester Hallé during the 1920s and 1930s. At the same time there was a loosening of the boundaries between 'high' and 'low' cultures, epitomised by the growing acceptability of the music hall. In Leeds the influence of the music hall on the concert hall was credited with inspiring the shift from long oratorios to short, dramatic pieces in festival programmes before the First World War. Charting the extraordinary change in middle-class attitudes to the music hall in Birmingham, a journalist noted in 1912 that middle-class 'men and women go as readily to the first and second "houses" of the variety theatres as to the "legitimate" theatre'.[6] Partly as a result, the identification of 'high society' with 'high culture' was less axiomatic in 1914 than it had been in 1880. More generally, the bourgeois culture of the industrial cities was depicted from many quarters as vitiated and provincial by the early twentieth century. The failure of Manchester to develop a distinguished repertory theatre following the closure of Miss Horniman's Gaiety in 1920 led A. J. P. Taylor to wonder whether the Hallé 'exhausted the appetite of Manchester citizens for culture'. In similar vein, the leading members of the avant-garde Leeds Arts Club considered Leeds in the early 1900s a 'cultural wasteland'.[7] Such judgements were invested with their own particular viewpoints and prejudices, but collectively they point to the diminishing significance between 1900 and 1930 of a set of institutions which had done much to define the contours of provincial bourgeois culture in the mid- and later Victorian period.

With this went many of the characteristics of provincial culture, including the accent on public bourgeois display. It has been noted that civic processions were reported less enthusiastically and profusely in the industrial capitals from the 1880s, while the funerals of major civic figures thereafter were often conceived as testament to the passing of a heroic municipal era, rather than to its continuing resonance. The same period also saw the gradual disappearance of the regular, detailed reporting of promenades, 'street-types' and fashionable events. By the 1890s the local press had become more obviously commercialised, periodicals, for example, carrying greater numbers of articles which were thinly disguised advertisements for businesses as well as advertisements proper, and reflected a more commercial urban culture, with lengthy reports on music hall, sports and other types of popular entertainment.[8] It is, of course, impossible to tell whether bourgeois display actually declined from the late nineteenth century or whether it merely ceased to be reported in the press. But there is considerable circumstantial evidence to suggest the former. Two significant features of the years before 1914 were the diminished visibility of the trappings of display and the movement in bourgeois leisure from the public and the exterior to the secluded and the interior. The advent of the motor car among the wealthy, for example, could not match the opportunities for ostentatious display afforded by the full regalia of carriage, horses and liveried attendants. Equally, the forms of bourgeois culture that survived longest in the provincial cities were those that were most private and

sequestered, the freemasons and the house party as against the promenade and the procession. Part of the reason for this, it has been argued,
was that public space in the industrial cities was decreasingly the
monopoly of middle-class men from the late Victorian decades. The
entry of suffragettes, workers and other groups on to the urban stage
effectively challenged the equation of authority with visual appearance
that had marked the 'official' public culture of the city between the 1850s
and the 1880s. 'Men of wealth and influence' no longer had privileged
control of the visual and symbolic register of civic life. Other groups
knew how to work, and subvert, it for their own ends.

More fundamentally, the cities themselves ceased to be perceived as
centres of modernity, of new built forms and modes of experience. Little
or no architectural and spatial development of significance occurred in
the central areas of the cities in the decades after 1900. In Leeds the
idea of a distinct civic area was reinforced in the inter-war period by the
widening of the space in front of the Art Gallery and Municipal Buildings and the construction of a new Civic Hall to the rear of the old
Town Hall. Meanwhile, the Headrow was recreated as a new, widened
shopping street, complete with a monumental and lavishly furnished
branch of Lewis's department store.[9] But for all the rhetoric of scientific
town planning in the 1920s, these developments were essentially exten-
sions of trends in urban design which had been apparent in the industrial
cities from the later Victorian period. Where architectural modernism
was invoked it was often in connection with the public provision of
workers' housing, such as the Quarry Hill flats at Leeds, rather than
associated with bourgeois display.[10] By the inter-war years, in any case,
the industrial cities had ceased to be viewed as the locus of the 'modern'
to any significant extent. On the contrary, they formed an essential part
of the 'nineteenth-century Britain' which J. B. Priestley contrasted with
the authentic modernity of the newly built suburbia of bungalows and
light industries surrounding London.[11]

The decline of bourgeois culture in the industrial cities was
inextricably bound up with wider economic and political shifts in the
early twentieth century, though the effects were not always simple or
direct. Katherine Chorley spoke of Hallé audiences being hit by the
'economic blizzards' of the 1930s, and it was certainly the case that
economic recession and declining profits in key industries such as
textiles and engineering impacted deleteriously on many of the older
institutions of middle-class social and cultural life between the wars.[12]
In Manchester the membership of the Royal Exchange, which Douglas
Farnie considered a sensitive index of business activity in the city and

region, fell from an all-time high of 11,539 in 1920 to 4,669 in 1940, the lowest total since the days of the cotton famine in the early 1860s. In Leeds the depression had severe effects on large engineering firms, many of which collapsed in the 1920s and 1930s.[13] It is clear, however, that the inter-war depression hit smaller industrial towns harder than the industrial cities where economies were already more diversified and where decline in staple industries was offset by newer growths: the car industry around Birmingham, ready-made clothing in Leeds, electrical engineering in Manchester.[14] Moreover, many if not all of the institutions of provincial bourgeois culture were showing signs of decline before the worst effects of economic recession were registered, in the 1920s and early 1930s. There was therefore no direct relationship between the two. More important than the facts of recession in accounting for the weakening of bourgeois culture were changes in economic organisation, notably the coming of the limited liability company from the 1880s. While some major firms such as Cadburys in Birmingham and Mather and Platt at Manchester continued in family hands, the trend from the later nineteenth century, notably in textiles and engineering, was towards a model of 'impersonal capitalism' marked by limited liability, amalgamation and the fragmentation of patterns of industrial ownership. Together with the spread of directorships, the result was to loosen the ties that linked employers with the individual firm and the locale. Starting in the last decades of the nineteenth century, the patriarchal figure of the industrialist gave way to the more diffuse and anonymous figure of the businessman.[15]

Similar shifts were apparent in the domain of politics. At the municipal level, there was a significant decrease in the proportion of larger employers, manufacturers and merchants on the Manchester town council after 1875. In Birmingham and Leeds, by contrast, there was a substantial increase of large businessmen in the last decades of the nineteenth century, from less than 10 per cent to almost a quarter of the membership of the respective councils. From the early 1900s however, the experiences of the three cities began to converge, with the numbers of large employers diminishing and professionals emerging as the dominant grouping in each case by 1912.[16] In party political terms the same years saw a sharp movement to Conservatism. Between 1885 and 1900 Conservatives won 21 of the 30 parliamentary seats contested in Manchester, and in Leeds Conservatives outnumbered Liberals on the town council in all but four years between 1895 and 1914.[17] The political ramifications of these developments were complex, but they had two basic effects. They served to weaken the association between economic and political leadership and between the industrial cities and political Liberalism, both of which had appeared as defining features of the provincial middle class between 1840 and 1880. Furthermore, the impact of Labour may have been limited in electoral terms in the three cities before 1914, depending on Liberal abstention to gain parliamentary seats in Leeds and Manchester, but it too served to undermine forms of middle-class authority. As Patrick Joyce observed, 'Socialism may most effectively have worked not as a received body of ideology but as a force breaching the understandings of decades on which paternalism and deference had subsisted. It broke in on the employers' mastery of the situation'.[18]

The rapid decline of Nonconformity after 1900 removed a further prop in the constitution of provincial middle-class identity. By the post-war years the signs of the flight from chapel, as from church, were all too visible. From the mid-1880s the membership of the leading Congregationalist chapel in Leeds, East Parade, was in free-fall, and the chapel was demolished in 1900. At Bowdon Downs in the wealthy Manchester suburbs, ministers were faced with an ageing and dwindling congregation in the years after 1918. Attending a Sunday chapel in Birmingham in the early 1930s Priestley noted that although the form of the service remained unchanged from before the war the congregation was greatly reduced, consisting mainly of women and the elderly.[19] As a result, ministers of leading urban chapels did not exert the same influence over their congregations or denominations as they had done before 1914; they no longer served as models of 'spiritual culture' for broad sections of the urban middle classes.

In short, certain key markers in the political and cultural life of the provincial middle class had effectively dissolved by the 1920s. What this suggests is something approaching a seismic shift in the foundations of the middle class after 1900. Jurgen Kocka has suggested that in Germany and other West European states, the middle class disintegrated in the decades before and after the First World War and with it a distinctive bourgeois culture. This was a function, Kocka, argues, not of the weakness of the middle class but of its strength, and in particular of the 'built-in tendency to universalisation' in bourgeois culture. 'The middle class proved stronger than its opponents. It won. Its culture and principles have spread widely to all parts of the *classes supérieures*, and to a certain extent to the shrinking rural population, to the middle masses that used to be called "the lower middle class", and even to parts of the working class ... [But] in this victory the middle class lost much of its identity.'[20] Kocka's account is open to many objections, not least

its own seemingly universalist and determinist logic. But it does emphasise the scale of social and cultural changes in the middle class at this
period and their widescale historical significance.

In the English provincial cities these changes have been associated
with the exodus of the wealthiest and most visible segment of the urban
middle class, especially large manufacturing employers, and the cutting
of ties with the city itself. The characteristic mode in which this has
been interpreted is that of 'gentrification', the adoption and partial
absorption of this powerful segment of the urban middle class into the
gentry and an older rural landed order.[21] While the details of the
'gentrification' thesis have been extensively and effectively challenged,
the character and significance of the movement away from the local in
the late nineteenth and early twentieth century remain to be explained.[22]
For movement there certainly was. In Leeds the Marshalls, the great
flax-spinning employers, closed the family firm in the 1870s and
sold Headingley House a decade later, moving to the Lake District.
Headingley House was bought by the major clothing manufacturer,
Josiah Hepworth in 1888, before he himself moved to Torquay in 1900,
selling the house, in turn, to a syndicate. No less striking, by 1913 there
was only one member of the Baines family left in the city; as an
acquaintance remarked, 'he takes no part in the public life of Leeds, and
the once prominent name of Baines is now very rarely heard'.[23] In
Manchester also the outflow of established merchant and manufacturing
employers such as Barbour, McConnel and Murray, was apparent from
the late nineteenth century. For W. H. Mills, the social type of the
'Manchester man' had all but disappeared by the First World War,
leaving behind only the 'heavy four-square mansions' that were steadily
being transformed into nursing homes and charitable institutions.[24]

There were many reasons why this out-migration occurred: retire-
ment, declining profits in particular lines of industry, limited liability
and directorships which meant that families as a whole no longer
required to be involved directly in the running of firms. However, the
exodus was far from complete or total. In Birmingham many employer
dynasties, like the Chamberlains and the Kenricks, remained based in
the city in the inter-war years. Such outflow as occurred from the towns
and cities of the West Midlands after 1900 was predominantly to the
nearby countryside, where ironmasters and businessmen melded into
county society, forming a regionally-based 'upper middle class' that
straddled easily urban and rural domains. A similar configuration of
business and land has been discerned in Cheshire in the early twentieth
century.[25] More generally, families might be split, some branches staying

put while others migrated, evident in Manchester among major employer clans like the Birleys, Heywoods and Philips'. Anna-Maria Philips,
daughter of R. N. Philips, Manchester cotton magnate and Liberal MP
for Bury until the 1880s, lived at the the Park, Prestwich, till after the
Second World War, maintaining the family's radical faith to the end. At
the 1945 election she noted in her diary: 'I drove down to the polling
booth in the Ringley Road and voted for the Labour candidate, Tomlinson, as no Liberal was standing'. Yet from the 1870s the Philips family
were involved in an annual social round in which Manchester had been
merely a part. For long periods the family would stay at their 'gigantic
pile', Welcombe, near Stratford-on-Avon; from May to July they would
occupy the house in Berkeley Square, London, where large dinner parties
would be held twice weekly 'with footmen in black plush knee-breeches
and flesh-pink stockings, and pumps with gilt buttons'. Then there were
holidays by the sea before returning to the Park in August.[26]

The example of the Philips suggests that the changes occurring in
the provincial middle class in the late nineteenth and early twentieth
century did not so much involve a movement to a specific socio-spatial
location – the county or metropolitan 'high society' – than an increasing,
generalised mobility. Just as the capital of the wealthy was becoming
diversified in different types of property outside the family firm, so
wealthy urban clans were spreading geographically, as some branches
moved away and others moved between different residential locations.
By the early 1900s it was common for businessmen and employers in
Birmingham, Leeds and Manchester to have several addresses: a family
'home' in Bowdon, Edgbaston or Headingley, a town house in London,
a small estate in Scotland, perhaps, or a villa by the sea.[27] This shift was
often viewed locally with hostility as well as regret. 'Now, you do not
know our leading merchants, capitalists, etc. and our city is represented
for the most part by strangers who have no real touch with the
work-a-day community', the Ancoats councillor, Charles Rowley, commented in 1899. The middle classes were seen as divided between the
'best people', together with the 'selfish rich', who 'live apart', and the
'good folks' of 'municipal and philanthropic instinct' who retained close
connections to the city.[28] The division was phrased in characteristically
moral categories, but it hinged centrally on the new mobility of the
wealthy as against those sections of the middle classes whose outlook
and loyalties remained circumscribed by the local. The detachment of
the 'natural leaders', in the form of merchants and industrialists, was
seen to have cultural consequences. 'Their leisure interests and
recreations were elsewhere and the time they gave to civic duties

dwindled', wrote Katherine Chorley. 'The city was no longer the centre of their cultural lives.'[29] It was in fact in the sphere of urban bourgeois culture, of classical concerts, gentlemen's clubs and civic processions, rather than in municipal government, that middle-class withdrawal was most profoundly felt.

This account of the gradual withdrawal of important sections of the middle class from the industrial cities and the decline of a provincial bourgeois culture fits only in part with established interpretations of the inter-war middle classes. On the one side, the period has been viewed as witnessing the merger of industrial, commercial/financial and landed elites, fostered by a variety of factors including industrial amalgamations, the sale of landed estates, the formation of a new, more open plutocracy and the predominance of the Conservative party.[30] On the other side, the ranks of the 'middle classes' have been seen as swelled by the expansion of salaried and white-collar occupations, but also squeezed between Capital and Labour and defined negatively as 'not the idle rich' and, most vehemently, 'not the working class'.[31] Significantly, both 'upper' and 'middle' classes are heavily identified in recent historiography with the south of England, the former with London, the latter with the metropolitan suburbs and the Home Counties. Equally, the subordinate position of industrial interests within the newly 'unified' elites is held to have persisted into the inter-war years.[32] These lines of interpretation, however, can be reductive, and in some cases merely appear to reproduce the caricatured views of the middle classes of contemporaries such as Charles Masterman and George Orwell. More persuasive, not least because it is based on sensitive readings of a range of oral and provincial sources, is the account of Richard Trainor which argues for the creation of a national 'middle', or more precisely, 'upper middle class' between the wars. Trainor notes the widespread disenchantment after 1918 of a younger generation of the prosperous, provincial middle class with the civic and philanthropic high-mindedness of their parents. At the same time, such people did not automatically drift away form towns and cities like Leicester, Birmingham and Newcastle. Rather, what was striking about the more affluent sections of the provincial middle class was their mobility, the ease with which they moved between the provinces and the capital. This is exemplified by the figure of Michael Hope, interviewed for the Essex oral history project, 'who grew up in Birmingham as part of the Chamberlain/Kenrick clan and read *The Times* as well as the *Birmingham Post* in a businessman's home with very strong links to London'. A shared accent, education and Conservatism, Trainor argues, were all components in the creation of a new, national upper middle class in the 1920s and 1930s.[33]

If this national upper middle class was importantly defined by certain cultural attributes – accent, education, lifestyle – it was a culture that was simultaneously more concentrated and more fragmented than before 1914. The inter-war years were marked by the appearance of a distinct 'middlebrow' culture between 'high' and 'low', identified most strongly with music and literature: amateur operatics and 'light' orchestral music on the one hand, writers like Agatha Christie and Warwick Deeping on the other.[34] At the same time, cultural institutions and a diffuse high culture – national galleries, West End theatres and the literary intelligentsia, as well as the BBC and the national press – were increasingly centred on London. Thus the decline of provincial bourgeois culture was a product of both internal and external factors. It was the result of the break-up of an established urban middle class and of the diminishing appeal of cultural institutions based in the industrial city, many of which were to appear anachronistic by the First World War. Its fate was sealed in the inter-war period by the development of a mobile, national upper middle class and by the concentration of key national cultural institutions in London. At its height, the bourgeois culture of Birmingham, Leeds and Manchester was rooted in the identification of the middle class with the city, and in the display of wealth and power on the urban stage. Once this identification was broken, the distinctive bourgeois culture of the industrial cities became history.

Notes

1   A. de Tocqueville, *Journeys to England and Ireland,* ed. J. P. Mayer (New York: Anchor Books, 1968), p. 94.

2   T. Wemyss Reid, *A Memoir of John Deakin Heaton* (London, 1883), p. 84.

3   Cited in E. P. Hennock, *Fit and Proper Persons* (London: Edward Arnold, 1973), pp. 321–2.

4   P. Bourdieu, *The Field of Cultural Production* (Cambridge: Polity Press, 1993), p. 235.

5   F. S. Stancliffe, *John Shaw's 1738–1938* (Timperley: Sherrat and Hughes, 1938), pp. 340–68; R. J. Morris, 'Middle-class culture, 1700–1914' in D. Fraser (ed.), *History of Modern Leeds* (Manchester: Manchester University Press, 1980), pp. 219–20; *Manchester Evening News,* 5 April 1904; *Manchester Guardian,* 18 November 1925; A. Briggs, *History of Birmingham,* vol. 2 (London: Oxford University Press, 1952); T. Steele, *Alfred Orage and the Leeds Arts Club* (Aldershot: Scolar Press, 1990).

6   K. Chorley, *Manchester Made Them* (London: Faber and Faber, 1950),

p. 144; *Leeds Mercury*, 1 October 1913; *Birmingham Daily Post*, 11 September 1912.

7   A. J. P. Taylor, *English History 1914–1945* (Harmondsworth: Penguin, 1970), p. 393; Steele, *Leeds Arts Club*, p. 13.

8   This shift between the 1880s and the 1890s can be traced, for example, in the *Owl.*

9   *Leeds: The Industrial Capital of the North* (Leeds: Leeds City Council, 1948).

10 A. Ravetz, *Model Estate: Planned Housing at Quarry Hill, Leeds* (London: Croom Helm, 1974)

11 J. B. Priestley, *English Journey* (London: Heinemann, 1934), p. 401.

12 Chorley, *Manchester Made Them*, p. 144.

13 D. A. Farnie, 'An index of commercial activity: the membership of the Manchester Royal Exchange, 1809–1948', *Business History*, 21 (1979); W. G. Rimmer, 'Leeds between the wars', *Leeds Journal* (1958).

14 E. M. Sigsworth, *Montague Burton* (Manchester: Manchester University Press, 1990); J. Stevenson, *British Society 1914–45* (Harmondsworth: Penguin, 1986), pp. 110, 272; J. K. Walton, *Lancashire: A Social History, 1558–1939* (Manchester: Manchester University Press, 1987), pp. 332, 338.

15 A. G. Gardiner, *Life of George Cadbury* (London, 1926); P. Joyce, *Work, Society and Politics: The Culture of the Factory in Later Victorian England* (Brighton: Harvester, 1980), pp. 339–40; L. E. Mather (ed.), *The Right Hon. Sir William Mather, 1830–1920* (London, 1926); M. Savage and A. Miles, *The Remaking of the British Working Class, 1840–1940* (London: Routledge, 1994), pp. 48–9, 63–4.

16 Hennock, *Fit and Proper Persons*, pp. 34, 40–2, 267; A. J. Kidd, *Manchester* (Keele: Ryburn Press, 1993), p. 149.

17 Kidd, *Manchester*, p. 158; T. Woodhouse, 'The working class' in D. Fraser (ed.), *History of Modern Leeds* (Manchester: Manchester University Press, 1980), p. 363.

18 Joyce, *Work, Society and Politics*, p. 335.

19 C. Binfield, *So Down to Prayers* (London: Dent, 1977), pp. 95, 98, 245; Priestley, *English Journey*, p. 107.

20 J. Kocka, 'The middle classes in Europe', *Journal of Modern History*, 67 (1995), p. 803.

21 The classic statement of this argument is M. J. Wiener, *English Culture and the Decline of the Industrial Spirit* (Cambridge: Cambridge University Press, 1981).

22 A point made by W. D. Rubinstein in his essay 'Britain's elites in the inter-war period, 1918–1939' in A. Kidd and D. Nicholls (eds), *The Making of the British Middle Class? Studies of Regional and Cultural Diversity Since the Eighteenth Century* (Stroud: Sutton, 1998), p. 198. For a critical overview of the 'gentrification' debate see W. D. Rubinstein, *Capitalism, Culture and Decline in Britain, 1750–1990* (London: Routledge, 1993).

23 M. Beresford, 'The face of Leeds, 1780–1914' in Fraser, *History of Leeds*,

p. 104; F. R. Spark, *Memories of My Life* (Leeds: Spark and Son, 1913), p. 67.

24 S. Gunn, 'The Manchester middle class, 1850–80' (Ph.D. thesis, Manchester University, 1992), pp. 250–1; W. H. Mills, *Sir Charles W. Macara, Bart.* (Manchester, 1917), pp. 25–6.

25 R. H. Trainor, 'The gentrification of Victorian and Edwardian industrialists' in A. Beier, D. Cannadine and L. Rosenheim (eds), *The First Modern Society* (Cambridge: Cambridge University Press, 1989); J. M. Lee, *Social Leaders and Public Persons* (Oxford: Oxford University Press, 1963).

26 J. S. Leatherbarrow, *Victorian Period Piece* (London: Faber, 1954), pp. 25–9.

27 See, for example, the numerous directories of local businessmen and civic worthies produced in the 1890s and 1900s. H. H. Bassett, *Men of Note in Commerce and Finance* (London, 1901); 'Midland Captains of Industry', *Birmingham Gazette and Express*, 1907–9; W. B. Tracy and W. T. Pike, *Manchester and Salford at the Close of the Nineteenth Century: Contemporary Biographies* (Brighton, 1901); E. Walford, *County Families of the United Kingdom* (London, 1888).

28 C. Rowley, *Fifty Years of Ancoats* (Manchester, 1899), p. 11; Rowley, *Fifty Years of Work Without Wages* (London, 1911), p. 41.

29 Chorley, *Manchester Made Them*, pp. 138–9.

30 L. Davidoff, *The Best Circles* (London: Hutchinson, 1986), pp. 68–9; H. Perkin, *The Rise of Professional Society* (London: Routledge, 1989), pp. 78, 292–4; Rubinstein, 'Britain's elites', pp. 187–8.

31 B. Waites, *A Class Society at War* (Leamington Spa: Berg, 1987), pp. 49–53; R. McKibbin, *Classes and Cultures: England 1918–1951* (Oxford: Oxford University Press, 1998), chs 2–3.

32 This is unsurprising in accounts which stress the long-term primacy of the City of London and the service sector in Britain's economy, such as P. J. Cain and A. G. Hopkins, *British Imperialism: Innovation and Expansion 1688–1914* (Harlow: Longman, 1993), but it is also the case in the more neutral account of McKibbin, *Classes and Cultures*, in which the industrial cities are barely mentioned. See also W. D. Rubinstein, 'Britain's elites', p. 188.

33 R. Trainor, 'Neither metropolitan nor provincial: the inter-war middle class' in Kidd and Nicholls, *Making of the British Middle Class*, pp. 203–13.

34 A. Light, *Forever England: Femininity, Literature and Conservatism Between the Wars* (London: Routledge, 1991); J. Lowerson, 'An outbreak of allodoxia? Operatic amateurs and middle-class musical taste between the wars' in A. J. Kidd and D. Nicholls (eds), *Gender, Civic Culture and Consumerism: Middle Class Identity in Britain 1800–1940* (Manchester: Manchester University Press, 1999), pp. 198–212; McKibbin, *Classes and Cultures*, pp. 386–90, 477–88.

Index